IFP

JFK:
BREAKING
THE
NEWS

Hugh Aynesworth

JFK: BREAKING THE NEWS

Hugh Aynesworth
with Stephen G. Michaud

IFP
INTERNATIONAL FOCUS PRESS

Published by
International Focus Press
P.O. Box 1587
Richardson, Texas 75083
www.IFPINC.com

IFP provides additional educational information regarding the
content of this book at www.ifpinc.com. The companion
Public Television documentary, *JFK: Breaking the News,* is also
available from the publisher.

ISBN 0-9639103-6-1

Library of Congress Control Number: 2003112706

For quantity purchases, please contact
International Focus Press.

Printed in the United States of America
First Printing November 2003.

TABLE OF CONTENTS

LIST OF ILLUSTRATIONS/ARTIFACTS

CREDITS

ACKNOWLEDGEMENTS

Over the many months I spent preparing these recollections of the Kennedy assassination and my experiences in reporting that national catastrophe, many kind souls offered their time, advice, wisdom and shared their own memories of the assassination, as well as the long, long saga that has ensued.

This book is drawn from my memory, amplified by a vast personal archive of notes, clippings, photographs, wire service reports, recordings and memorabilia. But scores of friends, fellow reporters and editors, as well as former competitors and even a couple of historians helped me to flesh out the manuscript, and to weed out mistakes.

I must first credit my lovely wife, Paula, for her sage advice, her helpful suggestions toward improving my story, and also her love, which sustained me through this often-painful revisit to some emotionally-trying events and incidents.

To my long-time friend and editor, Stephen G. Michaud, I offer more than just praise. Without his guidance and superb organizational skills, this book could not have been done.

Even with a mountain of information and documentation to guide my recall, I found it a massive challenge to recreate events from as long ago as 1963, and then to place them in their proper context. Both Stephen and Paula, who were still school kids in 1963, offered me important guidance in this area.

I know my strengths; I'm a reporter, not a genius wordsmith. So I thank my lucky stars I found Paula LaRocque to edit, check, refine, and shape my story. Mrs. LaRocque, recently retired after 20 years at *The Dallas Morning News* as the paper's writing coach, is a pro's pro.

Speaking of professionals, many journalists whom I respect and admire offered their counsel and criticism and/or vetted certain parts of the manuscript.

These included Michael Ruby, Merrill McLaughlin, Bert Shipp, Robert Compton, Kent Biffle, James Ewell, Jim Featherston, John McMillan, Alex Burton, Murphy Martin, Eddie Barker, Bob Miller, Richard West, John Camp, Mike Cochran, David McHam, Jack Loftis, Howard Swindle, Tom Johnson, and Wes Pruden.

Given a tough design job along, with an almost unbelievably short amount of time to achieve it, the team at Focus2 delivered superbly. Thanks to Todd Hart, Chris Chapman, Duane King, Shane Bzdok, Shannon Watkins, and Aaron Guiles.

A special thanks goes to the incredibly talented team at KERA-TV, including the producers of the television documentary: Sylvia Komatsu, Rick Thompson, Krys Villasenor, Joe Belotti and many, many others.

Expert advice and photographic help came from the team of JFK experts at The Sixth Floor Museum at Dealey Plaza—thanks to director Jeff West, Ruth Ann Rugg, Megan Bryant, and Gary Mack.

I am proud that Shelly Katz, one of the top photojournalists of our time, offered to shoot the picture used on the book cover.

And thanks to Ramiro S. Salazar, director of the Dallas Public Library, and his fine staff, several of whom helped us immeasurably. And to Dave Perry, a special friend and JFK expert. Also to Dr. Robert Beavers, Robert Gemberling, William F. "Bill" Alexander, and Earl Ruby.

Last but not least, my publisher, Dan Korem of International Focus Press (IFP), labored long and hard to wrestle all the disparate elements of this book together in an amazingly short time.

A profiling expert, investigative journalist, and documentary producer, Dan is the author of several other books, including, *Suburban Gangs—The Affluent Rebels* and *The Art of Profiling— Reading People Right the First Time.* Dan provided us immeasurable support and useful input, particularly with the book's layout. And, Dan's wife, Sandy, who operates a leading catering company in Dallas, offered suggestions and delicacies during editing conferences, both vitally important, and deeply appreciated, contributions.

Hugh Aynesworth

FOREWORD

No one ever wanted to find the conspirators in the assassination of
John F. Kennedy more than Hugh Aynesworth. No one ever searched
with more diligence, more determination, or with more dogged
dedication to expose the plot and identify the plotters.

But Hugh, like every good reporter, learned early to follow
the facts. The good reporter loves the surprise of finding where the
facts lead, if not to a conspiracy to something more interesting and
more unexpected, to a tangled story of unlikely men and women
caught up in malice, misfeasance, and murder.

No one knows more about malice and murder than Hugh, who
has stalked politicians, movie stars, wayward preachers and priests
gone bad, mad men, crazed widows and serial killers, for more than
a half century. No one knows as much about this particular tale of
malice and murder in high places than Hugh, who through the
coincidences of a day fraught with coincidence and happenstance,
was the only person in Dallas present at the assassination of Kennedy,
the scene immediately following the slaying of Officer J. D. Tippit,
the capture of Lee Harvey Oswald, and the murder of Oswald by
Jack Ruby.

But was it coincidence? Or was it skill? Journalists will tell
you that good reporters are taught but great reporters are born, that
instinct is what gives great reporters the ability to sense where the
story goes next, the talent for being in the right place at the right
time when "news happens."

JFK: Breaking the News is, after four decades, the true story
of the Kennedy assassination. This, stripped of the speculations of

charlatans and the opportunism of greedy frauds, is what actually happened. But this is not only the true story of one of the pivotal events in the nation's history, but a fascinating education in how a great reporter does his work, following the trail through the grim underbelly of Dallas and New Orleans in a gritty search for the elusive fact.

Here is the familiar cast of characters if the reader has not seen them before: Lee Harvey Oswald, the abusive misfit with the mail-order rifle, determined to make a "name" for himself (and succeeding); his tiny, pouting wife Marina, a whining trophy from his years as a defector to the Soviet Union for whom Hugh became a sometime confidante; Marguerite Oswald, the assassin's mother who calculated what she could charge for an interview even as she was racing to Parkland Hospital to see her dying son; Jack Ruby, "the Dallas lowlife who searched for class as though he understood what it was," eager to become the avenging patriot; the bumbling cops, the stumbling FBI agents, the out-of-the-loop Secret Service; the conniving lawyers; and finally the horde of reporters from every corner of the globe and the rush of conspiracy theorists, from Jim Garrison and Oliver Stone to Bertrand Russell and Mark Lane, drawn to Dallas like an infestation of cockroaches to scraps of food left overnight on a pantry shelf. Hugh was the man who knew about all those pantry shelves, all those scraps of food.

Hugh, as a reporter on that damp, gray November day for *The Dallas Morning News,* was not assigned to the story. "The president's visit was the local news story of the week, of the year for that matter, and my paper...was deploying every available hand to cover the event—everyone except me," he writes. "...science and aviation was my beat—not government or politics." When he remarked, a bit wistfully, to a colleague that everybody but he and the copy boys and himself would be part of the newspaper's coverage of the president's visit, his colleague told him: "You may be the lucky one."

But lucky is, to paraphrase the old saying goes, as lucky does. When Hugh wandered down to Elm and Houston Streets to watch the passing presidential parade, he would step into the story that would occupy him for the next 40 years. "I was standing with my lawyer friends, maybe 10 feet from the curb," he writes. "I wondered what I was doing there....At 12:30, we heard the first loud pop!"

In this book, Hugh brings vividly to life the tumult of the next three days in America, when time seemed to stand still and the nation seemed to teeter on the brink of chaos: the public murder of the president; the stunned disbelief of the nation, with incredulity piled atop disbelief, when two days later the assassin was himself assassinated. The story grabbed Hugh by the throat and never let go. He scribbled his first notes on the back of his utility bill with a pencil he bought from a young boy for two quarters, and raced to the Texas Theater on a hunch, arriving in time to be present for the arrest of Lee Harvey Oswald, recalling with a reporter's talent for specificity that he was 10 feet behind the assassin who was "three rows from the back, five seats from the aisle." Two days later he stood a few feet from Oswald in the Dallas police station when Jack Ruby shot him, sealing the secrets taken to an assassin's grave in Fort Worth's Rose Hill Cemetery.

I first met Hugh Aynesworth when I was just out of high school and working as an apprentice sportswriter on the old *Arkansas Gazette* in Little Rock, and Hugh was hired as a sportswriter. We quickly became fast friends, prowling the city in the wee hours of the morning in search of after-hours beer and barbecue after helping put down the Final Edition. I first noticed that he had a way with the girls, and I took notes. I soon discovered what the editor had seen before me, that he had a way with everyone. Hugh had the gift of actually listening when people talked. People—coaches, quarterbacks, outfielders (and even the occasional homecoming queen)—told Hugh things, sometimes when for their own good they shouldn't have. Listening to people who talk too much for their own good is manna for a reporter. A good reporter never resorts to deception or tricks; listening is good enough. But it requires patience.

We both moved on to other newspapers and bigger things, but over the years we stayed in touch and occasionally worked on the same stories. Years later, after I had become the editor in chief of *The Washington Times*, I leaped at the opportunity to persuade Hugh to come to work for us. He became the icon of a generation of young reporters in our newsroom before we sent him back to Dallas as staff correspondent for the South and Southwest.

We were together as reporters in Dallas in November of '63, where I watched, with no little envy, as Hugh slowly made the Kennedy assassination *his* story. He became the man that celebrity journalists, opportunistic conspiracy buffs, literary con men and even law-enforcement officers called to check out their latest hot tips. Invariably, Hugh had already checked them out. He also had the gift of letting people down easy. Firmly, but easy.

In the years just after the assassination, and books about Dallas and the assassination became an industry, publishers went to him with attractive proposals. Many were merely propositions. One of the first was from a French publisher who offered him $75,000 to write "a conspiracy best-seller." Said the Frenchman: "Everyone in Europe agrees with your thinking." Hugh asked the logical next question: "And what is my thinking that everyone in Europe agrees with?"

The answer was that Lee Harvey Oswald was an agent-provocateur of the U.S. government, that the Warren Commission, assigned by Congress to investigate the assassination, was a tool of Lyndon B. Johnson, the vice president from Texas who made it to the White House with the death of JFK.

Hugh declined. He didn't hold the views the publisher thought he did. The publisher was incredulous: "But you don't make that kind of money at the newspaper."

Indeed, Hugh, who was making $9,500 a year, did not. "But they don't tell me what to write." The publisher from Paris learned what others after him would learn, that Hugh's native shrewdness, an inheritance from his origins in the hills of West Virginia, was accompanied by conviction and integrity as hard and as imperishable as the granite of those hills. "You can put lipstick on a sow," Hugh told the disbelieving (and no doubt puzzled) Frenchman, "but that doesn't make her a Homecoming queen."

Hugh decided years ago that Lee Harvey Oswald and Jack Ruby were, unlikely though it may have been, who they seemed to be, losers and lowlifes reaching for attention if not immortality in the only sordid and ignoble way they knew how. But 40 years on, Hugh is still the skeptical reporter, even of himself. "I am often asked why I do not believe there was a conspiracy," he writes in this gripping reporter's tale. "I usually say I don't know whether there was or was not a conspiracy. All I know is, there is no evidence of it."

Here is the search for that evidence, and a compelling story it is. This is the story, he says, that became his through "sheer coincidence and dumb luck." But as the reader learns, dumb luck had nothing to do with it. This is the story of a great reporter on the trail of the greatest story of his times.

Wesley Pruden
Editor in chief of *The Washington Times*

Secret Service agents scan the throngs along the motorcade route.

CHAPTER ONE

The Assassination: Witness to Murder

A damp, gray autumn sky hung over Dallas—weather to match
my mood.

Friday, November 22, 1963.

President John F. Kennedy was coming to town. There'd be a
motorcade, and then JFK would address a luncheon at the Dallas
Trade Mart.

The president's visit was the local news story of the week, or
even of the year for that matter, and my paper, *The Dallas Morning
News*, was deploying every available hand to cover the event—
everyone except me.

So what if science and aviation was my beat—not government
or politics. All my buddies at the paper had been talking about the
Kennedy visit for days. Now they'd all be part of a story big enough
to tell their children.

"Where you gonna be?" grinned photographer Joe Laird,
juggling several cameras. "Oh, Hugh's off today," columnist Larry
Grove answered for me. "He lucked out."

Grove, my best buddy on the paper, and I had just returned from
our first coffee break in the cafeteria, where I had told him I felt like
all the staff members except the copy boys were going to be with the
president at Love Field or at the Trade Mart luncheon.

"You may be the lucky one," Grove grinned. "I guess I'll get a
good column out of it, but..."

Grove and a handful of beat reporters especially assigned to
various aspects of the JFK visit soon took off for various staging areas.
Though the newsroom already was starting to thin out, the incessantly

ringing phones and the faster-than-usual pace of those "involved" only made me feel more excluded.

I guess I was somewhat spoiled. I had been covering all the U.S. manned spaceflight launches, the nation's underground nuclear testing program and various military stories, and I'd been to Cuba just days before the Cuban Missile Crisis in 1962. I was used to action—and there seemed none for me here today.

Senator Ralph Yarborough being interviewed by *Dallas Times Herald* reporter Bob Fenley.

Tired of answering the phones and running down reporters for editors—and vice versa—I drifted back down to the cafeteria, got another cup of java, and picked up the day's paper. I had at least three hours before I was scheduled to interview an aerospace scientist at Southern Methodist University.

The *News* that morning carried a Metro section interview by reporter Carl Freund with former Vice President Richard Nixon, who was in town under his lawyer's hat for meetings with Pepsi-Cola bottlers, whom Nixon's New York law firm represented.

A sidebar noted that Nixon's Baker Hotel suite was right down the hall from that of actress Joan Crawford, who had married into the company. We further informed our readers that Nixon would fly out of Love Field two hours before the man who barely edged him for the presidency in 1960 landed in Air Force One.

At a Baker Hotel press conference, Nixon predicted his old rival might drop Vice President Lyndon Johnson from the ticket in his 1964 re-election campaign if the Texan proved to be a political liability—as Nixon said he believed Johnson already was. As for his own prospects of running in '64, Nixon said, "I cannot conceive of circumstances under which that would happen."

Politics was in the air.

An Associated Press dispatch, quoting the *Houston Chronicle*, adroitly explained the major reason for Kennedy's Texas trip. Three years earlier, JFK-LBJ carried the state over Nixon and Henry Cabot Lodge by a razor-thin 46,000-vote margin, a critical electoral college triumph for which Lyndon Johnson deserved most of the credit.

Now the *Chronicle* reported a new statewide poll that showed Kennedy trailing Sen. Barry Goldwater of Arizona, his likely opponent in the 1964 election, by about 100,000 votes if the election were held that day. Although the most recent Gallup Poll showed the president pummeling the conservative Goldwater nationwide, 58 to 42 percent, Kennedy clearly needed to shore up his support in this important swing state.

A high-visibility, two-day, five-city tour of Texas accompanied by popular Democrats such as Gov. John Connally, Sen. Ralph Yarborough, and the vice president must have seemed just the thing to boost his standing.

Kennedy also knew that to have any chance at all against Goldwater in Texas he needed to forge at least some unity among the Lone Star State's fractious Democratic bickermeisters.

Liberal Ralph Yarborough, for example, detested centrists such as Connally and Johnson—and with some reason. The governor and the vice president were never seen doing the senator any favors. Just the opposite. On this trip they seemed determined to put Yarborough in his place.

Connally was scheduled to host a private reception for JFK at the governor's mansion in Austin that Friday night: Yarborough was absent from the guest list.

Yarborough's response to that snub: "I want everybody to join hands in harmony for the greatest welcome to the President and Mrs.

President Kennedy spoke in front of Fort Worth's Hotel Texas the morning of the assassination.

Kennedy in the history of Texas." Then: "Gov. Connally is so terribly uneducated governmentally, how could you expect anything else?"

On Thursday afternoon in Houston, Yarborough had defied Kennedy by refusing to ride in the same car with LBJ. He chose instead to be seen with Congressman Albert Thomas. In San Antonio that morning, Secret Service Agent Rufus Youngblood was gently nudging the senator toward Johnson's limo when Yarborough saw Congressman Henry Gonzalez, a political blood brother, and bolted toward him. "Can I ride with you, Henry?" he asked.

4

That evening, employees at Houston's Rice Hotel heard JFK and LBJ arguing over Yarborough in the presidential suite. Kennedy reportedly informed Johnson in strong terms that he felt Yarborough—who had much better poll numbers in Texas than Kennedy—was being mistreated, and the president was unhappy about that.

Years later, Yarborough told me that Maury Maverick, Jr., a liberal state Democratic committeeman, had complained to him that Maverick had been shut out of an airport greeting line for the Kennedys. He also warned Yarborough that the Johnson-Connally forces were out to embarrass him however possible.

"I already knew and could feel that," Yarborough said, "but they weren't going to find it any easy task." He added that JFK took him aside during a testimonial dinner for Rep. Thomas on Thursday night, and assured the senator, "I don't think you're going to have any more problems on this trip."

As it happened, Rep. Gonzalez also was nursing a peeve. He carped to the president aboard Air Force One on their way to Texas that Kennedy was spending only two hours in the Alamo City, while three hours had been allocated to Dallas, then a Democratic wasteland represented by the sulfurously right-wing Bruce Alger, the sole Republican in the Texas Congressional delegation. Alger was infamous for having once voted against free milk for kids.

Gonzalez had a point, but JFK was adamant about showing the Democratic flag in Texas' second-largest city, even though the president seemed unlikely to change many hearts or minds in Dallas County. Nixon had steamrolled him by 60,000 votes in Dallas. Goldwater promised to show even better in this black-earth redoubt of red-meat conservativism.

A number of well-known national Democrats, including U.N. Ambassador Adlai Stevenson, Gov. Connally, and Arkansas Sen. J. William Fulbright, advised the president to postpone or skip the Texas trip. Reason: Groups of virulently anti-

Vice President Lyndon B. Johnson is shielded from the morning rain.

Crowds gather in the rain in downtown Fort Worth.

Kennedy Texans, some extremely well-financed, planned to take advantage of the press coverage to make their sentiments better known to the world.

They feared that something really ugly might occur, especially in Dallas, where a long and vociferous list of Kennedy detractors was headed by E. M. "Ted" Dealey, former publisher of the *News*.

My boss.

The *News*, largest daily paper in Texas with a weekday circulation of 236,000, routinely excoriated Kennedy in its editorial columns, part of the paper's shrilly right-wing political slant that appalled and embarrassed many people in the newsroom, including me—as thoroughly apolitical as anyone on the staff.

In the autumn of 1961, Ted Dealey and a handful of other Texas media bigwigs were invited to the White House for a meeting with Kennedy. This was not a gathering of kindred souls. Yet a mood of strained decorum prevailed until Dealey produced prepared notes from which he addressed the president directly.

"You and your administration are weak sisters," said Dealey, who admonished the president that the United States needed "a man on horseback to lead the nation and many people in Texas and the

Southwest think that you are riding Caroline's tricycle."

Dealey's insults made front-page news across the country. Kennedy wasn't Dealey's only target. The *News* had so viciously attacked Fulbright during his 1962 re-election campaign that the chairman of the Senate Foreign Relations Committee now declined invitations from friends to even visit the city.

On Oct. 3, aboard Air Force One with JFK on their way to a dam dedication in Arkansas (and also later at the dedication luncheon), Fulbright told Kennedy that he was physically afraid to go to Dallas. He said he greatly feared the president's upcoming trip.

"Dallas is a very dangerous place," Fulbright said. "I wouldn't go there—and don't you go!"

In Dallas, U. S. Attorney Barefoot Sanders and U.S. District Judge Sarah T. Hughes sent word to the president's aides that they, too, thought the trip "inadvisable."

The day before Kennedy arrived, "Wanted For Treason" handbills started popping up around town. *News* reporters Ed Cocke and Harry McCormick brought examples to work on Thursday morning. The fliers depicted the president in full face and profile, as in a mug shot. "This man," they read, "is wanted for treasonous activities against the United States."

Among JFK's alleged crimes: "betraying the Constitution (which he swore to uphold)"; giving "support and encouragement to the Communist inspired racial riots"; and telling "fantastic LIES to the American people (including personal ones like his previous marraige [*sic*] and divorce)."

On Thursday afternoon, city editor Johnny King assigned me to track the pamphlets to their source and to discover, if possible, whether similar venom might be spewing forth the next day during the president's visit.

Harry McCormick, an old pro who'd once been kidnapped by Bonnie and Clyde's gang, suggested I look for leads in the paper's coverage of a "National Indignation Convention" (NIC) held in Dallas a few weeks earlier, where NIC delegates bitterly scorned Kennedy for allowing Yugoslavian pilots to train at Perrin Air Force Base in Sherman, about 75 miles north of Dallas.

McCormick's idea paid off. I located an NIC organizer who put me in touch with those who'd printed the "Wanted For Treason" posters.

"We're going to show Kennedy what we think of him," one of them said on the telephone. I reminded him that after UN Ambassador Adlai Stevenson's recent adversity in Dallas, the city council had passed a resolution making it a misdemeanor to curse or shout obscenities during a public event.

"Oh, we're not going to shout at him," the caller assured me. "In fact, we're going to have our mouths covered with tape so there's no possibility of such behavior. We're going to be law-abiding. We don't want to harm anyone. We just want Americans to wake up to what's happening in our country."

He closed, "Oh, by the way, you'll be able to recognize us easily. We're going to be wearing Uncle Sam suits."

Johnny King decided not to print what I'd learned. "No laws broken apparently," he said. "One might argue that they violated the laws of good taste [with the pamphlets], but I doubt anyone will care about that. Let's not make them heroes by writing about them."

God, I thought, it's going to be a zoo here tomorrow.

••••••••••••••••••••••••••••

Friday morning, as I browsed through the paper, I came to the most outrageous ad I'd ever seen in any Dallas paper. I had heard a woman in the library mention it with a "tsk tsk" an hour or so before, but had not stopped to examine it at the time.

It was a full-page, black-bordered page in the front section, paid for by a group that called itself "The American Fact-Finding Committee," its address a Dallas post office box number. We'd soon learn that Texas oil money was behind the ad. Donors included Nelson "Bunker" Hunt, son of oil billionaire H.L. Hunt. Another contributor was oilman H. M. ("Bum") Bright, who later was the majority owner of the Dallas Cowboys football team.

"Welcome Mr. Kennedy to Dallas," the "committee" announced in headline type, then proceeded to attack the president in a series of twelve questions—a sort of bill of particulars.

For example, Question No. 3 asked "Why have you approved the sale of wheat and corn to our enemies when you know the Communist soldiers 'travel on their stomachs' just as ours do? Communist soldiers are daily wounding and or killing American soldiers in South Viet Nam."

SECRET SERVICE HAS STEAK IN PROTECTION OF KENNEDY

President Kennedy will get a thick, juicy steak when he visits Dallas Friday. But some of the 2,000 guests at his Dallas Trade Mart luncheon may get thicker, juicier steaks.

It won't be the result of any Republican plot.

The Secret Service wants it that way.

A spokesman for the sponsoring organizations said Wednesday Secret Service agents vetoed a proposal that cooks select the choicest cut and broil it to the President's liking.

"They said they wanted the waiter to pick out a steak at random after they've all been broiled and carry it to the President," the spokesman related. "This was done, obviously, for security reasons. A would-be assassin couldn't be sure of poisoning the President's meal unless he put poison in every steak served at the luncheon."

THE MENU
Fresh Fruit Cup
Top Sirloin Club Steak (8 ounces)
Tossed Green Salad
French-Cut Green Beans Almondine
Rolls and Butter
Apple Pie
Coffee

The Kennedys and Connallys arriving at Dallas' Love Field (top left and above). *The Dallas Morning News* published the president's "secure" menu (left). A well-wisher presents a poster with Boston "accent" (right).

launched from surface ships only.

Mrs. Kennedy Coming to State With President

By JOHN MASHEK
Washington Bureau of The News

WASHINGTON—Mrs. John F. Kennedy will accompany the President on a political trip to Texas on Nov. 21-22, the White House announced Wednesday.

It will be the first political trip for the first lady since Kennedy was elected in 1960. And it is an indication the administration is pulling all stops in effort to snare Texas voters in next year's presidential election.

At the same time, the White House said the President would definitely make stops in Houston, Fort Worth, Dallas and Austin. A stop in San Antonio is still in the works. A detailed schedule of the trip will ished next week.

MRS. KENNEDY campaigning with her in the 1960 campaig she was then pregnai John F. Jr. She als to care little for stumping required wives.

Also, at the tim and death of the K child in August nounced Mrs. not take any functions until

It is believed nedy's first tr

She has nev any fund rai Washington office but w probably in

Mrs. Ke turned from Greece, Turkey and Moroc help recuperate from the loss of her son.

SOURCES HERE said Gov. John Connally and Vice-President Johnson suggested that Mrs. Kennedy

transit briefings, emphasized he did not want "to start a precedent of closed door sessions."

IN THE City-Dallas ing now

Tem Carle tion and George M. Und who said, "I too am weary of special transit committee meetings" seconded.

ansit committee member Mayor Cabell, chairman Golman.

y. Henry P. Kucera, nstairs to rule whethsessions are legal, his blessing.

INION is that you the right to sit down liscuss any matter ty attorney, regardt any other source ra stated.

onfine that to legal sked Cabell.

confine it to legal swered Kucera.

"I FILED A motion hearing. I pointed out

Pipeli

d a
d b
a ga
becau
woul

Na
To Nhu

SAIGON, (Thursday) President Ngo Dinh Die ised his army comma August that he would his brother Nhu and M but later reneged, acco a top member of Sou Nam's new ruling junta the broken promise le Nov. 1 coup in which D Nhu were slain.

Nhu was secret poli and his wife, now in Ca was a legislator and the First Lady for the president

We Welcome you with Vigah
J. F. K.
ss Roots Dem

Jack Kennedy insisted upon a stop in Dallas, despite multiple warnings it was unwise to visit Texas, period. Political, military, and racial issues inflamed his radical critics.

and Councilwoman Mrs. Blanche ... distraught, waits for word on her brother, Gov. Connally, at Parkland Hospital.

Blessing, came at... ing and several oth... members complain... ll and his special... mittee have not ke... ws completely inform... what started Wednes... on as an informal an...

Connally Wanted President To Call Off Trip to Texas

11-23

...EN DUCKWORTH ...has been waging a hard cam-... ...t Lake Pic-... strict, ...tears. ...Christ ...life I ...and I ...e. But ...and fa- ...out of ...he re- ...I can't ...l Com-...

midst of what had been the warm-est and friendliest reception that any President has received in Texas within my memory."

Daniel had attended the dinner Thursday night in Houston where the President spoke.

A "HOT LINE" was set up be-tween the governor's office and Dallas by the Department of Pub-lic Safety, so that there was con-stant communication about his condition.

Waiters had finished setting the tables for the banquet and rolls were already set out when news of the awful event was received.

the marquee out-...icipal Auditorium ...rning: ...ohnson Welcome ...oon, another word ...erneath:

...RVICE men await-...dent's arrival here ...from Western Un-...room that had been ...Commodore Perry Mr. Kennedy was to

papermen were ...credentials at ...when a Western ...d in and shouted: ...has been shot. ...n shot, and Lyn-...o.'' ...oped that the re ...was in error).

AT FORT WORTH

Heavy Protection Set for President

11-17

Incident-Free Day Urged for JFK Visit

By KENT BIFFLE

Dallas lead... against any d... cidents durin... nedy's visit... President ... and Vice-Pres... don Johnson... cade through... prior to a lu... the Trade M...

Robert B. ... the Dallas Ch... said, "The P... represents th... est office in,... will be welc... as the first ... friendliest to... been earned... people throug...

"THESE ... greet the Pr... States with t... that keep th...

normal, warm hospitality to the President of the United States on ... Saturday...

Monday in Judge Dallas Blanken-ship's courtroom on the fifth floor

thought he wa... Dave Smith, ... arrangements f...

n Union man w...djoining room a...ulletin from a t...A few seconds la...ion closed

...ent upstairs to ...men, who imm...hotel for Bergst...se to fly to Dall...

GOVERNOR OUTLINES ITINERARY

Kennedy to Make 5 Stops During 2-Day Texas Tour

By DAWSON DUNCAN
Austin Bureau of The News

AUSTIN, Texas — President Kennedy's Texas visit Nov. 21-22 will include five stops—in San Antonio, Houston, Fort

Reception plans, other details, Pages 4 and 5.

Worth, Dallas and Austin—Gov. John Connally announced Thurs-day.

The governor said the plans he outlined were "as firm as ... this time" imme-

Albert Thomas, veteran legisla-tor from Houston.

The governor said it had not been determined where Ken-nedy will spend the night of Thursday, Nov. 21. Alternate plans will be made for either Houston or Fort Worth, where he is to attend a breakfast at 8:45 a.m. Friday in Hotel Texas. Sponsors of the Fort Worth breakfast will be that city's Chamber of Commerce.

From Fort Worth the Presi-

dent will go to Dallas for a noon luncheon. Sponsors will be the Dallas Citizens Council and the Graduate Research Center.

Connally said the site is un-certain so far, because the Secret Service had not cleared the matter. Under consideration are the Trade Mart, with a seat-ing capacity of 1,800 but with security difficulties, and the Women's Building at the State Fair which is larger, Connally said.

Weather . . . Today's Index

Question No. 9: "Why have you ordered your brother Bobby, the Attorney General, to go soft on Communists, fellow travelers, and ultra-leftists in America, while permitting him to persecute loyal Americans who criticize you, your administration, and your leadership?"

The American Fact-Finding Committee referred to itself as "an unaffiliated and non-partisan group of citizens who wish truth." The only name attached to this anti-Kennedy screed was Bernard Weissman, identified as the committee's chairman.

Weissman, 26, a U.S. Army veteran from Mt. Vernon, N.Y., was an admirer of controversial U.S. Army Maj. Gen. Edwin A. Walker, under whom Weissman had served in Germany. Walker, a member of the John Birch Society, was fired in 1961 by Defense Secretary Robert McNamara for trying to indoctrinate troops under his command in his right-wing ideology. Walker, a native Texan, then moved to Dallas where he made a second career speaking out against communists real and imagined, as well as boosting other arch-conservative causes.

In September 1961, Walker had appeared in Oxford, Miss., to protest the enrollment of African-American James Meredith at Ole Miss. He was charged with seditious conspiracy, insurrection and rebellion and spent five days in jail for his trouble.

The next year Gen. Walker ran as a Democratic candidate for governor of Texas with the support of GOP Senators John Tower and Barry Goldwater and other prominent conservatives. Walker finished last in the race, but grabbed a significant ten percent of the vote.

In April of 1963, he barely escaped death when Lee Harvey Oswald just missed with a bullet meant for Walker as he sat at his desk in his Turtle Creek area residence, near downtown Dallas.

Bernard Weissman had left his job as a carpet salesman in Newark, N. J., (he'd previously sold encyclopedias and costume jewelry) to come to Dallas in early November 1963. He was lured south by a friend, Larry Schmidt, who had extravagant notions of uniting various of the extremely right-wing groups (including the Birchers, NIC, and the Young Americans for Freedom—YAF— of which Schmidt was local executive director) into a meta-organization to be called Conservatism USA, or CUSA, which Schmidt hoped to lead.

Dallas, Schmidt told Weissman, was "where the action is."

Together, Schmidt and Weissman conceived of the anti-Kennedy

WELCOME MR. KENNEDY

TO DALLAS...

...A CITY so disgraced by a recent Liberal smear attempt that its citizens have just elected two more Conservative Americans to public office.

...A CITY that is an economic "boom town," not because of Federal handouts, but through conservative economic and business practices.

...A CITY that will continue to grow and prosper despite efforts by you and your administration to penalize it for its non-conformity to "New Frontierism."

...A CITY that rejected your philosophy and policies in 1960 and will do so again in 1964—even more emphatically than before.

MR. KENNEDY, despite contentions on the part of your administration, the State Department, the Mayor of Dallas, the Dallas City Council, and members of your party, we free-thinking and America-thinking citizens of Dallas still have, through a Constitution largely ignored by you, the right to address our grievances, to question you, to dis-
agree with you, and to...
in asserting this constitu...
importance and interest...
These questions are:

WHY is Latin Ameri...
Department p...

WHY do you say w...
of your policy...
already murdered an...
Cubans are living in...

WHY have you...
soldiers "tra...
American soldiers...

WHY did you ha...
enemy, Khr...

WHY have you u...
other Com...
anti-Communist fre...

WHY did Camb...
leftist gov...

WHY has Gus H...
the party...

WHY have you...
Committe...

WHY have you...
travelers...
administration, an...

WHY are you...
just seize...

WHY has the F...
ing staun...

WHY have y...

MR. KENNEDY...
them NOW.

THE...

WANTED

FOR

TREASON

THIS MAN is wanted for treasonous activities against the United States:

1. Betraying the Constitution (which he swore to uphold): He is turning the sovereignty of the U.S. over to the communist controlled United Nations. He is betraying our friends (Cuba, Katanga, Portugal) and befriending our enemies (Russia, Yugoslavia, Poland).

2. He has been WRONG on innumerable issues affecting the security of the U.S. (United Nations-Berlin wall-Missle removal-Cuba-Wheat deals-Test Ban Treaty, etc.)

3. He has been lax in enforcing Communist Registration laws.

4. He has given support and encouragement to the Communist inspired racial riots.

5. He has illegally invaded a sovereign State with federal troops.

6. He has consistantly appointed Anti-Christians to Federal office: Upholds the Supreme Court in its Anti-Christian rulings. Aliens and known Communists abound in Federal offices.

7. He has been caught in fantastic LIES to the American people (including personal ones like his previous marraige and divorce).

The incendiary full-page advertisement that ran in *The Dallas Morning News* the day of the assassination and a "wanted" poster distributed on the streets of Dallas.

14

Flag-waving fans line the motorcade route.

ad. They designed and wrote the broadside, and then solicited donations to publish it.

Weissman in a later appearance before the Warren Commission said the ad was submitted only to the *News*, which charged $1,462 to run it, not to its rival, *The Dallas Times Herald*.

"They are a very liberal newspaper," he said of the *Times Herald*, "and we felt it would be a waste of time."

Thirty miles to the west in Fort Worth, where JFK and Jackie had spent the night in Suite 850 of the Hotel Texas, presidential aide Kenny O'Donnell pointed out the advertisement to the president early that morning. The president showed the ad to the First Lady, who blanched as she read it. "How can a newspaper do that?" she asked.

"Now we're entering nut country," Kennedy replied, according to O'Donnell.

Mrs. Kennedy recalled to author William Manchester that her husband had something else on his mind that morning—assassination. Speaking of their rainy, late-night arrival and reception in Fort Worth, Jack told her, "You know, last night would have been a hell of a night to assassinate a president. There was the rain and the night and we were all getting jostled. Suppose a man had a pistol in a briefcase."

Jackie recalled that the president pointed a finger at the wall of their suite and pretended to fire two shots.

Friday at about noon, the Kennedys would motor into downtown Dallas from Love Field in the back seat of a dark blue 1961 Lincoln Continental convertible. Gov. Connally and his wife, Nellie, would sit in jump seats directly in front of them. Secret Service agent William

R. Greer would be behind the wheel. Next to Greer in the front would sit Secret Service agent Roy H. Kellerman. He had been informed early that day by Kenny O'Donnell that if the rain let up in Dallas then the clear plastic bubbletop that fit over the presidential limousine in case of inclement weather was to be removed.

The second car in the motorcade would be filled with Secret Service agents.

LBJ and Lady Bird were to ride in the third car, along with the chagrinned Sen. Yarborough, who had no Henry Gonzalez equivalents with whom to hitch a ride in Dallas.

Wincing at the offensive *News* ad, I looked up to see an even less welcome sight. Dallas strip club owner Jack Ruby, 52, was waiting at the cafeteria cash register to pay for his eggs and toast. Ruby never traveled light. This morning he was burdened with an umbrella, scarf, heavy coat, newspapers, and a fistful of glossy photos of his strippers, pictures I suppose he hoped to finagle the *News'* night club columnist, Tony Zoppi, into running.

Also somewhere on his person there probably was a loaded handgun. Jack Ruby almost always carried a gun.

Ruby was a regular and noxious presence at the *News*—loud, pushy, always trying to hustle publicity for his seedy second-floor strip joint, the Carousel Club. I held my breath, hoping he wouldn't see me, and exhaled only after the unpleasant hustler with the big mouth stopped to talk briefly to two ad salesmen, then settled down, alone, at a table about 15 feet away.

I noticed that Ruby leered at our young cashier in her too-short skirt while waiting for his meal. Now I watched as he cut a peephole in his paper to keep up his surveillance as he pretended to read.

A television newsman from WFAA-TV across the street left his table and steered over to finish his coffee with us. He was an astronaut buff and always wanted to get the latest "scoop" from Cape Canaveral.

Leaving Love Field.

16

We chatted briefly about the President's visit and wondered aloud how the Democratic factions—Connally-LBJ vs. Yarborough—would make it through another few hours together. Even though I had dealt with the "Uncle Sam" guys the day before, it never crossed my mind to imagine there might be trouble—real trouble.

As I left the cafeteria I decided to walk over to Main Street and watch the motorcade ease by. After all, it wasn't every day a president came to town.

●●●●●●●●●●●●●●●●●●●●●●●●●●●●●●

It was a little before noon. The clouds had vanished and Dallas gleamed in the sun under a bright blue sky. It was almost like spring. The temperature was climbing toward the high 60s.

Agent Kellerman already had seen to it that the presidential bad-weather bubbletop was stored aboard an Air Force support transport for return to Washington.

From the *News* building on Young Street, it was a three-block walk to Market and Main, where Kennedy Memorial Plaza with its Philip Johnson monument to the slain president now stands. In 1963, the site was part of the Dallas courts complex, a bunch of nondescript businesses, mostly offices for lawyers and bail bondsmen.

Kennedy would pass by in just a few minutes.

Clearly, it was becoming a bigger occasion than I had imagined. The sidewalks were jammed three and four deep with Dallasites hoping to get a glimpse of their handsome, 46-year-old president and his lovely wife, just 34. An estimated 100,000 people turned out to watch the motorcade.

From Market I walked west on Main to Houston, the southeast corner of Dealey Plaza, where Kennedy's motorcade would turn right and proceed for a couple of hundred yards before turning sharply left down Elm, in front of a dreary brick warehouse, the Texas School Book Depository.

Until November 22nd, I was hardly aware the structure existed.

The crowds were as thick around the plaza as they'd been on Main, so when I saw a couple of familiar assistant district attorneys standing in front of the county jail near the corner of Houston and Elm, I walked over to join them.

A number of people on the street were tracking Kennedy's

Notice the Secret Service agent on a mini-stool at the back of the presidential limousine (below).

progress via their portable radios. I could hear the familiar voices of local news announcers describing the motorcade's move out of Love Field at 11:55 onto Mockingbird Lane, then Lemmon Avenue, Turtle Creek Boulevard and Cedar Springs Road in its serpentine route south toward downtown Dallas.

A "pilot car" driven by Deputy Police Chief George L. Lumpkin, full of cops and surrounded by a swarm of motorcycle officers, went out several blocks ahead of the parade to alert police along the way that the president was close behind.

Next came the lead car, an unmarked police sedan driven by Dallas Police Chief Jesse Curry. Riding with Curry that day was Dallas County Sheriff Bill Decker and U.S. Secret Service Agent-in-Charge Forrest Sorrels, as well as Secret Service Agent Winston G. Lawson.

Jacqueline Kennedy had been a sensation earlier that morning as JFK spoke to a packed breakfast at the Hotel Texas. Associated Press reporter Mike Cochran later said Mrs. Kennedy delayed her appearance by prearrangement—stopping momentarily in the hotel kitchen.

"Where's Jackie?" someone yelled good-naturedly to the president.

13

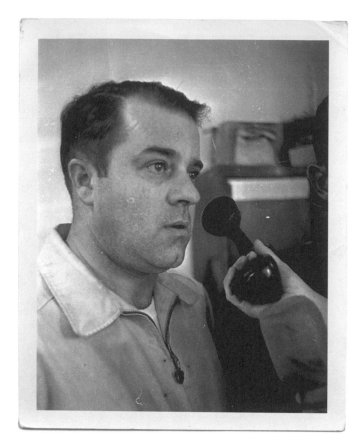

Dazed eyewitness to the assassination Charles Brehm.

"Mrs. Kennedy is organizing herself," JFK replied with a laugh.

"It takes her a bit longer but, of course, she looks better than we do when she does it."

When Jackie made her entrance a few moments later, clad in a bright pink suit and pillbox hat, she dazzled the already excited crowd. Even a few wolf whistles could be heard. Her husband, as astute in the ways of politics as any man ever to hold his job, discarded his notes and extemporized.

"Two years ago," he said, "I introduced myself in Paris by saying I was the man who accompanied Mrs. Kennedy to Paris. I am getting somewhat the same sensation as I travel around Texas."

When the laughter ebbed, Kennedy deftly delivered his punch line.

"Nobody wonders what Lyndon and I wear."

The presidential entourage boarded Air Force One at Carswell Air Force Base for the 13-minute flight east to Love Field where it was greeted by isolated boos and heckling in the otherwise adoring crowd. One demonstrator held up a sign that read "Help JFK Stamp Out Democracy."

But the general mood at Love Field and everywhere else— especially through downtown and in Dealey Plaza—was upbeat. Nobody shouted insults or threats or threw things. Frankly I was surprised given the venom I knew dwelt in many hearts in this city. But onlookers had good reason to mind their manners. Seven hundred state and local personnel, from Texas Rangers to Dallas firefighters, were deployed around the city to maintain the peace. Earlier that week, Chief Curry sternly announced on television that authorities would take "immediate action to block any improper conduct." Curry even encouraged citizens' arrests if necessary.

To a person, the spectators milling around me in front of the county jail building were enthusiastic, laughing, and calling to one another. I heard some people try to mimic Kennedy's famous Boston accent, saying "Hahvahd" and "Cuber" and laughing. Others waved little American flags.

We knew the motorcade was near when the police began, with minimal success, to shove people back onto the curb. The pilot car eased to the right around the corner from Main onto Houston and cheers and applause erupted.

"Well, Mr. President," Nellie Connally said to JFK, "You can't say Dallas doesn't love you!"

"No, you certainly can't," Kennedy answered with a smile.

I was standing with my lawyer friends, maybe ten feet from the curb.

As we watched the big blue Continental glide by—I vividly remember Gov. Connally's broad grin—a huge black woman nearby burst into shouts.

"She's got my dress on! She's got my dress on!"

Jackie's pink suit and hat weren't exactly the same shade, but it was close enough for the lady to realize a moment of glory.

At 12:30, we heard the first loud *pop*! At first I assumed a nearby police motorcycle had backfired.

Instead, it was an improbable loner, a confused and chronic malcontent firing his bolt-action Mannlicher-Carcano with its four-power scope down at the president from the sixth-floor window of the book depository, not 150 feet from where I stood.

Secret Service Agent Roy

Overcome by grief.

Kellerman in the front seat of the presidential limousine heard the *pop!*

Kellerman turned in his seat just as two more shots were fired and both Kennedy and Connally collapsed into their wives' laps.

"Step on it! We're hit!" Kellerman shouted at Agent Greer behind the wheel. It would be a three-mile drive to the emergency room at Parkland Hospital, the nearest available trauma unit.

As the Continental gained speed, Secret Service Agent Clint Hill leaped from the running board of the second car, and began sprinting toward the stricken president, as if to rescue him. Mrs. Kennedy turned, saw the agent reaching for the vehicle, and scrambled up onto the trunk. Their hands nearly touched as the agent fell back onto the street and the First Lady returned to her dying husband's side.

On the way to Parkland, Nellie Connally cradled the governor's head in her lap, whispering over and over to him, "Be still, it's going to be all right."

•••••••••••••••••••••••••••••••

Most agree that Lee Harvey Oswald squeezed off three shots from his $21.45 mail-order rifle that November 22nd. But whom he hit, and where, and how many other shooters might have been in Dealey Plaza that day has been endlessly debated. Thousands of books have been written and endless documentaries presented that claim more than Oswald were involved. (According to assassination researcher Dave Perry, the presence of 60 or more different gunmen has been posited at various times by various conspiracy theorists.)

What is known for sure is that President Kennedy took one slug to his upper back and another slug, the fatal bullet, blew a gaping crater in the back of his head. At impact, a geyser of blood, bone, and brain tissue shot into the air above Kennedy.

Gov. Connally was wounded, too, most probably (according to the Warren Commission), by one of the same bullets that hit the president. This is the controversial Single Bullet Theory, first propounded by Pennsylvania Sen. Arlen Specter, a Warren Commission counsel in 1964.

As Oswald's rapid rifle shots echoed across Dealey Plaza, the scene erupted into chaos. Terrified people ran in every direction, looking for cover, screaming, "Oh no! Oh no!" Some, frozen by fear, stood and wept on the sidewalks. Others tried to shield their children.

I had no idea who was shooting at whom, or why or where, except that it sounded very close.

When I turned to look around, I saw the large lady in pink, who was so overjoyed by Jackie's attire just seconds before, now doubled over and vomiting against a street lamp.

"The president's been shot!" someone yelled. Sirens blared. "I saw Lyndon get hit too," another man added.

That's when instinct kicked in. I was a reporter and I knew I had to start interviewing people—record the event. I remember three or four persons pointing toward the upper floors of the book depository. Police officers, sidearms drawn, approached the building. Others followed a motorcycle cop who ran his machine up the grassy area to the west of the book depository.

"My God, this is really happening!" I said to myself as I reached in my pockets for paper to start taking notes. The best I could do was a couple of utility payments I hadn't yet mailed, and a third piece of paper, a letter from Empire State Bank thanking me for opening an account.

Next I found I had nothing to write with. In the midst of the pandemonium, I spotted a scared little guy, embraced tightly by his dad—not yet crying, but aware things were more tense than he liked. He forced a half smile and I noted in his hands he gripped a fat jumbo pencil, like the ones kids used to use in early grade school. It had a little American flag on the eraser end.

"Hey, I'll give you fifty cents for that

Bob Jackson, Pulitzer Prize winner for his photograph of Ruby murdering Oswald. He saw a rifle protruding from the sixth floor window of the Texas School Book Depository and like most journalists, he heard three shots. Unfortunately, Jackson was out of film when the shots rang out.

Photojournalists trailing the president's limousine moments after the shots. Inset: This is the same shot as the one above without digital image enhancement—a relatively recent innovation in the brief history of photography.

pencil," I said, perhaps a little too eagerly. His father gave me a look of deep suspicion.

"Sure!" said the boy, grabbing my quarters as I clutched the ridiculous-looking pencil and plunged through the panicked crowd toward the book depository, grabbing witnesses and digging willy-nilly into the mass confusion.

Slain Officer 'Gave His All'

Policeman J. D. Tippit came home for lunch Friday at about 11:30 a.m. He hurried through his dinner and reported for duty.

Little more than an hour later he was the gunshot victim of a killer on an Oak Cliff street.

"He was always a man who gave everything he had," said a fellow policeman, Patrolman Bill Anglin, who lived just four doors down the street from the Tippit at 238 Glencairn.

Anglin had worked with Tippit on several occasions and had grown close since the two families each bought their new homes in the Southwest Oak Cliff area about two years ago.

Several other policemen lived in the general area.

Anglin was called from his duty spot shortly after it was learned that Tippit had been the victim of the bizarre Oak Cliff killing. Anglin rushed to the Tippit home and found that Mrs. Tippit, the 35-year-old officer's wife had long known the news.

"She was taking it real well, as well as could be expected under the circumstances," Anglin said. "Allen, the eldest of the Tippit children (13) was taking it

plenty hard. he and his dad were very close."

Mrs. Tippit was placed under heavy sedation in the late evening after several relatives and friends had converged on the Tippit residence.

The Dallas Police Association sent representatives to the Tippit home to present the widow with a check for $200.

The two other Tippit children, 10-year-old Brenda Kay and four-year-old Curtis Ray, didn't take the news of their daddy's death too hard, Anglin said. "They are still pretty young to realize what has happened," he said.

Anglin and Officer G. H. Harmon, another close friend of the slain policeman, told of the time Tippit was given a citation for bravery in 1956 when he helped disarm a man wanted for fleeing prosecution in another state.

Anglin said he had discussed the President's visit with Tippit about 10 a.m., when they last talked on the telephone. "That was pretty much on all our minds today (Friday)," he said.

Mrs. Tippit's parents and several brothers and sisters visited

J. D. Tippit . . . "He always gave everything he had."

her and tried to comfort her through the early evening. Some stayed all night. They, naturally enough, did not want to meet the press.

"One thing," Anglin said, "he didn't die in vain. Had he not stopped that guy the whole City of Dallas might have been wide open by nightfall."

Tippit, 39, had been a member of the police force nearly 12 years. His salary was $490 a month.

—HUGH ANYNESWORTH.

Among my first-day stories was this brief article about officer J. D. Tippit, the last bit of reporting on a very long day. (Nov. 23, 1963)

CHAPTER TWO

"I saw him real good"

From 8:15 to 9:00 on the morning of November 22nd, FBI Special Agent James Patrick "Joe" Hosty, Jr., and 40 or so other agents gathered in the Dallas office for their regular biweekly meeting with Special Agent In Charge (SAC) J. Gordon Shanklin. He told the group that if they picked up any indication of trouble for Kennedy's trip they were to immediately notify the Secret Service, and they were to put it in writing.

After the meeting, Hosty and two other agents met on unrelated matters, finishing up at 11:45, when Hosty headed out, hoping to get a glance at JFK in the motorcade.

"I noticed it was coming up Main Street," the 11-year veteran of the bureau told the Warren Commission a few weeks later. "That was the only thing I was interested in, where maybe I could watch it if I had a chance."

James Hosty did see President Kennedy glide by on Main Street, then the agent stepped across the street for a bite at a lunch counter called The Alamo Grill.

Minutes later, a waitress conveyed the dreadful news to him—the president had been shot.

Hosty was ordered to head at once for Parkland Hospital.

He found the presidential limousine pulled up to the Parkland emergency room. Gov. Connally, who'd suffered serious and perplexing wounds to his back, rib, chest, as well as inside and outside his right wrist, had been wheeled by gurney into Trauma Room No. 2, and then into surgery.

Kennedy, his head and shoulder covered by Clint Hill's suit jacket, was taken to Trauma Room No.1. A bouquet of yellow roses that Jackie had been given at Love Field rested incongruously on the gurney next to him. The First Lady, her pink suit thickly caked with the president's blood, was at his side. Doctors detected only the faintest signs of life in the president. At 1 p.m., Dr. Kemp Clark, the senior physician working on Kennedy, declared him dead. Two Catholic priests administered last rites.

By 1:30 a bronze coffin had arrived at Parkland from the Vernon B. Oneal funeral home, and soon thereafter Mr. Kennedy was on route back to Love Field, accompanied by his wife.

Dallas County Medical Examiner Earl Rose protested that according to Texas law the president's body must be autopsied in Texas. Federal agents effectively ignored Dr. Rose, whose role in the case nevertheless was not over. There were more deaths to come.

Parkland Hospital where Kennedy and Connally were taken.

In the immediate aftermath of the shooting, the sidewalk and street in front of the book depository were all mine for about two minutes. It took that long for the motorcade press corps to fan out from their vehicles as Agent Greer gunned the Continental toward Parkland Hospital. Chief Curry and the carload of Secret Service agents trailed behind. Dozens of other reporters immediately abandoned their original assignments around the city to converge on Dealey Plaza.

Spot news is not for the faint-hearted, particularly if the event is a presidential assassination. Every reporter in Dallas suddenly was chasing the biggest story of his or her life, so that the pressure of getting the story right that day was heightened by a good deal of shoving and elbowing to get it first.

There were the police to contend with, as well. Some intrepid reporters, including my *News* colleague Kent Biffle, TV reporter Tom Alyea, and radio reporter Pierce Allman ran inside the book depository in search of the shooter, only to find themselves trapped when officers sealed off the building. "The police were eager to lock that door behind us," Biffle recalled afterward, "and they did that, and so they were stuck with us. You know, what were they going to do—throw us out a window?"

Biffle ran for a phone, to check back with the City Desk.

"There was a phone in the office with buttons for two lines," he remembers. "I grabbed it and put it to my ear. A man was telling his broker to 'sell everything except Telephone.' I tried the other line. Another man was giving his broker similar instructions."

As he ran out of an office, two cops with riot guns threw down on the scared reporter. "I thought, oh my gosh." Later he witnessed and Alyea photographed the discovery of the Mannlicher-Carcano—which Oswald had stowed away between a mélange of boxes and crates.

Outside of the building, the police did their utmost not only to protect the general crime scene, but to insulate potentially valuable witnesses from the press.

Of the eight or so people I first tried to interview around the book depository, the most important was Howard Brennan, a 45-year-old steamfitter (he had his hardhat with him) who was stationed directly across the street opposite Lee Harvey Oswald. Brennan watched in awe as the shooter aimed and fired, then calmly aimed again and again.

The first police APB (all points bulletin) came at 12:45 and was based on Brennan's description of the shooter:

> *Attention all squads.*
> *Attention all squads.*
> *The suspect in the shooting at Elm and Houston is reported to be an unknown white male, approximately thirty, slender build, height five feet ten inches, weight 165 pounds, reported to be armed with what is thought to be a 30-caliber rifle.*

I saw Brennan talking to two officers and tried to poke my nose into their conversation. "I saw him up there," I heard him say as he pointed toward Oswald's sixth-floor perch, "in that window. No doubt he was the one. He wasn't even in much of a hurry."

One cop asked if Brennan could describe the shooter. "Of course," he answered. "I saw him real good."

Then Brennan noticed me and moved away, asking the officers as he did so to keep me and the other reporters away from him—a request they were glad to fulfill.

Brennan, I later learned, feared talking to the press lest he endanger himself or his family. Who knew what accomplices the assassin might have? In fact, it was for that reason that he hesitated to positively identify Oswald in the later police line-up.

Several witnesses spat out a few comments, some feared being quoted. One woman said she worked in the depository building "and I'll be damned if I am going to tell you what I believe."

Sometime during the early moments, I saw a man with a rifle in one of the windows of the depository and before I thought about what I was doing, I ducked to the pavement—tearing my trousers on a piece of lumber with a nail in it. I felt so foolish in seconds when a cop on the street said something to the man in the window and the Dallas cop leaned out casually.

I next caught sight of Paul Rosenfield, a talented feature writer for the *Times Herald* and a regular in our weekly poker game. Paul was standing with four or five other *Times Herald* staffers near the front of the book depository in what appeared to me to be an ad hoc editorial meeting. Hoping to spy a bit on the competition,

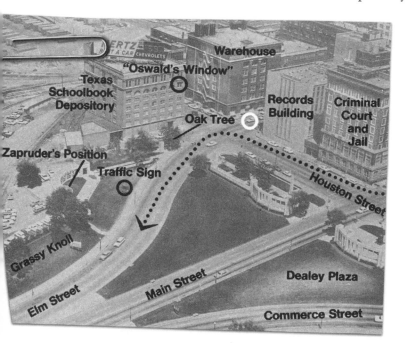

I was standing in the middle of Elm street (the white circle noted above), which was blocked off. It was here that the motorcade slowed down to make its left-hand turn from Houston Street onto Elm.

Note the photograph and the hand-painted arrow (using typewriter correction fluid) on the photographs used in *The Dallas Morning News*. (Nov. 26, 1963)

SECRET SERVICE AT SCENE

Onlookers lined the wreath-covered area on Elm Street Monday to watch Secret Service men check trajectory of bullets that killed President Ken nedy on Friday. Agent in street, lower arrow, stands at spot where the Presi dent was shot. Upper arrow marks window from where assassin fired.

—Dallas News Staff Photo

I cautiously sidled over. But Rosenfield spotted me and cocked a fist, threatening to punch me out. "Get out of here, Dallas News guy," he yelled.

And I did.

Just then I hooked up with a friendlier face, Jim Ewell, our daytime police reporter. As we stood there on the sidewalk, a cop whom Jim knew walked up. "They've probably got him trapped up there," he said, pointing toward the top of the building. "So damned many places to hide in there."

Reliable information was at a premium. We still didn't know for sure who, if anyone, besides Kennedy had been shot, or even if JFK was badly hurt. So, naturally, rumors sprouted like mushrooms. A story that LBJ had been hit began the moment Rufus Youngblood jumped on the vice president to act as his human shield. False news that a Secret Service agent had been killed persisted for days.

I made a point of hanging close to police motorcycles and their open radios. In such a crisis, I figured that police radios would be among the first news portals. Sure enough, the one we were standing near began to crackle. Then a male voice could be heard above the static.

"We've had a shooting out here," he said. "A police officer has been shot." The witness said the shooting had just occurred near the intersection of Tenth and Patton Streets to the south of us in Oak Cliff.

I felt strongly that this cop shooting had to be connected to the assassination, although I would have had trouble explaining why. I conferred with Ewell and we quickly decided that he'd stand by for possible developments at the book depository while I headed for Oak Cliff.

Ordinarily I would have taken off on my own. But my car was parked blocks away across a wild mass of terrified, confused humanity milling around the streets of Dallas. Time was a serious constraint. So I turned to Vic Robertson, a reporter for Channel 8 (owned by the Belo Corp., which also owns the *News*), and asked Vic if he'd heard what I just heard. He hadn't. But he and his cameraman, Ron Reiland, had a vehicle nearby, and therefore were the fastest way to Tenth and Patton. So I told them about the radio report from Oak Cliff.

"It can't be more than three or four miles from here," Vic said excitedly as I filled him in. "C'mon, we've got a car!"

With Reiland at the wheel of the WFAA station wagon, we

blasted out of Dealey Plaza, down the Houston Street Viaduct and over the broad brown Trinity River bottoms toward the scene of Officer J. D. Tippit's murder. We ran every red light: Vic and I yelled "Stop! Stop!" at cars at each intersection. We nearly crashed a couple of times, came close to hitting a pedestrian or two and blew right past one police officer who tried to stop us from approaching the crime scene.

Along the way, Vic pulled a few pages from his reporter's notebook for me to use; I'd filled up my utility bills.

The Tippit shooting occurred just before 1:15 in a scruffy working-class residential neighborhood of aging frame houses— within a mile of Lee Oswald's rooming house. The more I learned about the crime the clearer it became to me that it was impulsive, unplanned. The killer had reacted more than acted, and he made scant effort to cover his trail. Nine people or more saw the murder occur or watched as the shooter fled the scene. This was not a clever, experienced criminal.

The greatest challenge in reporting spot news is to gather as much *accurate* information as possible, without the luxury of time to assess how reliable this or that witness might be. The Tippit murder was a textbook case of such a challenge; we not only had to get it right, we had to get it fast.

Tippit shooting witness Helen Markham.

Officer Tippit in his '63 Ford police cruiser—DPD car No.10— probably heard the APB a half hour earlier, and was alert to anyone fitting the description. The Warren Commission would later conclude this was the reason the policeman stopped his car when he saw the suspect on the sidewalk.

"I saw this police car slowly cross and sorta ease up alongside the man," witness Helen Markham, 47, told me.

Markham was a waitress at the Eatwell Restaurant, a popular 24-hour eatery (Jack Ruby was a regular) in downtown Dallas. Dressed in her coat and scarf, she was walking to the bus stop at Patton and Jefferson about 1:12, headed for work, when she saw the man walking east on Tenth, away from her. Markham watched as Tippit stopped his vehicle and the man casually walked over to Car 10, leaned down, and spoke with the officer through the open passenger window.

Markham was shaken, very scared. When Vic Robertson fired a couple of quick questions at her I thought she'd break into tears. A man appeared with an empty Coca-Cola case and placed it on the pavement as a seat for her. The waitress gratefully accepted the favor, composed herself a bit, and went on.

"I thought it was just a friendly conversation, you know," she said. "But then all of a sudden the man stepped back a couple of steps and the officer opened his door and got out. I still thought they were friends. Then all of a sudden I heard three shots and the officer fell in the street."

"Did the shooter see you?" I asked.

"Oh, for sure, for sure!" Markham cried. "Strangest thing. He didn't run. He didn't seem scared or upset. He just fooled with his gun and stared at me. I put my hands over my eyes when I saw him looking at me. I was afraid he was fixin' to kill me, too. And then as I peeled my fingers away to look again, I saw him starting to jog away."

She said she waited until the killer was half a block away before she ran to officer Tippit's aid. Too scared to utter a sound in the killer's presence, Markham now began hollering as she knelt over the dying cop.

"I was screaming for someone to help me," she said. "I kept saying,

Scene of the Tippit shooting.

'Somebody has killed a policeman! He has killed him! Killed him! Oh God, help us!'"

J. D. Tippit tried to say something to her with his dying breath, Markham told me, but she couldn't understand his last words.

By now at least a half-dozen reporters had gathered around, each hurling question after question at the frightened woman. She told the group the most remarkable thing about Officer Tippit's slayer was his expression, which Markham described as "wild, glassy-eyed."

With that, several officers intervened to escort Helen Markham away from the press to a more detailed debriefing for the police.

It took a little digging to identify the civilian who'd broadcast the initial alert I'd heard over the police radio in Dealey Plaza.

Domingo Benavides, a 26-year-old auto mechanic employed at Dootch Motors on East Jefferson, just a block south of the crime scene, was driving his pick-up truck when Benavides noticed Officer Tippit standing by his patrol car. A second male stood near Tippit's right front fender, Benavides told me.

Seconds later, Benavides said he heard three shots and saw the policeman fall. He stopped his truck and watched the assailant run away. Benavides also noted where the shooter unloaded his handgun and tossed some shells into the bushes in a vacant lot.

"I thought he went behind that house there," the mechanic told me as we spoke together near the scene, easily identifiable by the pool of fresh blood staining the pavement. "So I waited a little bit. I was scared. He could have come back and started shooting again."

Benavides said he tried to help Tippit, but thought the officer was already dead. "He had this big clot of blood coming out of his head," he said, "and his eyes seemed to sink back into his face. I'd never seen anything like that."

He told me that he climbed into the patrol car, grabbed Tippit's mike and tried to broadcast the alarm, but failed to hook up to the dispatcher.

Benavides then left the scene, only to realize as he did so that he'd better go back and show the police where the spent shell casings were. He retrieved two of them, placed them in a cigarette pack and handed it to Officer J.M. Poe, saying nothing about witnessing the murder itself. Only after he returned to work and told his boss what he'd seen was Domingo Benavides finally persuaded to tell his full story to the police.

A later review of the police tapes showed that Benavides was correct—his hurried call had not been registered. The real author of the message turned out to be Thomas Bowley, a 35-year-old electric company employee who happened onto the Tippit murder scene on his way to pick up his wife en route to a vacation in San Antonio.

Bowley said he saw Officer Tippit lying on the street while Domingo Benavides struggled unsuccessfully with the patrol vehicle mike. So he stopped to help out. At about 1:18, or approximately three minutes after Tippit was shot, Tom Bowley broke into the police network with his news. This was the message that I had heard. For his trouble, dispatcher Murray Jackson admonished Bowley, "The citizen using the police radio will remain off the radio."

William "Bill" Whaley (left) the cab driver who unwittingly drove Oswald's "getaway" car, Whaley's cab. William W. Scoggins (right), the cab driver who was an eyewitness to Officer Tippit's murder.

I next spoke with Barbara Jeanette Davis, 22, a pretty young mother I'd noticed on the street with several cops, pointing out to them exactly where she had seen the shooter. Davis told me that she and her 16-year-old sister-in-law, Virginia Davis, heard loud shots coming from the street in front of her apartment at 400 East Tenth St.

Peering out the living room window to see what the ruckus was, both women saw a young man drop some spent shells and quickly walk away. As Barbara Jeannette spoke with me and a knot of other reporters, a Dallas police officer approached. "It'd be better, young lady, if you didn't talk to reporters anymore," he said. "We're going to want you to draw us a sketch of what you saw and we don't want you getting mixed up."

I could have told the cop he was way late. Mrs. Davis already had spoken to me and at least six other reporters, in detail.

A Dallas County deputy sheriff strode onto the scene, happy to share what he knew of the incident. He described the shooter almost exactly as Helen Markham and the Davis women had, then nodded his head at a taxi driver named William W. Scoggins. "You need to talk to Mr. Scoggins there," said the deputy. "I think he was the closest witness, the man who saw it all."

Not so. Scoggins hadn't been nearly as close to the actual shooting as Mrs. Markham, but he had seen enough to tell the pursuing police which way their suspect was headed. He even briefly took part in the chase.

A few minutes before the shooting, Scoggins, 48, parked his cab near the corner of Tenth and Patton, then walked a block over to the Gentleman's Club, a domino parlor and lunch spot on Jefferson, opposite Dootch Motors, where he watched the television coverage of the assassination as he waited for his take-out meal and Coke. Then he returned to his cab to eat lunch. He was still working on the Coke when he saw a lone male approach officer Tippit's cruiser, about 150 feet away. Scoggins couldn't see the guy's face as first, he told me, because the man was partially hidden behind some shrubs. But Scoggins saw J.D. Tippit leave his car and take a step or two. Then, as he recalled, four shots rang out.

"They were very fast," he told me. "Pow! pow! pow! pow! you know." Tippit grabbed his stomach and fell "like a ton of bricks."

William Scoggins jumped from his car and looked up to see the shooter walking directly toward him. "I sorta crouched alongside my cab, thinking I might be next," he said. "But he never looked at me. I heard him mumble, 'poor dumb cop' or 'poor damn cop.'"

A major mystery to the cab driver was the exceptional speed with which an ambulance crew appeared to treat officer Tippit; they were closing the ambulance door behind him as the first Dallas police officer arrived on the scene.

"It didn't seem like two minutes from when I called my dispatcher until they were here," he told me.

The explanation was simple: The Dudley M. Hughes Funeral Home ambulance was located only two blocks away on Jefferson, so the response time for driver J.C. Butler and attendant Eddie Kinsley on this occasion was practically instantaneous.

Used car salesman Ted Callaway, 40, confirmed Scoggins' version of events, except for the number of shots fired: Scoggins heard four, Callaway five. The car dealer, Domingo Benavides' boss at Dootch Motors, told me he was standing on the front porch of the dealership when he heard gunfire. Running out the side door onto Patton, Callaway watched as the killer walked past Scoggins and his cab and headed west.

"He was cutting across the street, gun in hand," Callaway told me. "I saw the cabbie, and it looked like he was hiding from the man. I didn't blame him. The shooter had a pistol in his right hand. I said, 'Hey man, what the hell are you doing? What the hell is going on?'"

The killer slowed his pace, as if confused. "He said something to me," Callaway recounted. "I couldn't understand what it was. Then he said something else, shrugged his shoulders and picked up speed going west on Jefferson off of Patton."

The car salesman walked over to the crime scene where he, Thomas Bowley, and another onlooker helped load J. D. Tippit on his stretcher into the ambulance.

Unsure if the police knew about the killing, Callaway got on Tippit's radio, too. "Ten-four," said the dispatcher, "We have the information. The citizen using the radio will remain off the radio now."

Ted Callaway, a Marine Corps veteran, then grabbed Officer Tippit's service revolver, turned to William Scoggins, and said, "Let's go get the sonuvabitch who's responsible for this!"

Domingo Benavides told me that Callaway and Scoggins invited him to join them. Callaway "kept yelling at the cab driver, 'He's running up Jefferson, let's go get him'," Benavides said. "The cab driver wasn't too convinced and when he suggested I come with them, I just grinned [as] they went off."

Together, the two men ran to Scoggins' cab. "I didn't think he'd ever get that damn cab turned around," Callaway later told the Warren Commission. "I said, 'C'mon fella, let's move! C'mon, let's go! We can get that s.o.b.' But he was a nervous wreck. He was driving this little stick shift checkered cab and he couldn't hardly shift gears.

"That's where I made my mistake. I should have gotten in the taxi cab on the driver's side because I used to drive a taxi after I got out of the war. But this guy was so nervous he couldn't drive, so we lost him."

A short while later the Callaway/Scoggins posse returned to Tenth and Patton where Ted Callaway gave Officer Tippit's sidearm to Officer Kenneth Croy.

At autopsy that afternoon at Parkland Hospital, J. D. Tippit, 39, was found to have suffered four bullet wounds, three to his chest and one to his right temple, which probably killed him instantly.

By now it was about 1:30, just an hour since the president was shot. Dr. Kemp Clark pronounced Kennedy dead at 1:00, but JFK's press aide, Malcolm Kilduff, wouldn't relay the devastating news to the rest of the world until 1:33, about the time that soon-to-be-president, Lyndon Johnson, Lady Bird, Jackie, and the rest boarded Air Force One to accompany JFK's body to Washington.

I knew nothing of this at that time. Tenth and Patton just then was a considerable psychic distance from the main story of the day. It was the epicenter of a massive manhunt for a particular kind of criminal, the cop killer, for whom brother officers typically reserve a special vengeance. I don't know how many members of the Dallas Police Department believed, as I did, that if they caught Officer Tippit's slayer they also would have in custody the president's assassin, but I do remember how angry and determined they were. There was lot of muttering about what they should do with this criminal when they caught him.

Police cruisers, carloads of reporters, and a steady stream of the curious kept rolling into the vicinity.

Another scratchy bulletin from the police radio sent me scrambling again. "He's in the library," Officer Charles T. Walker said over the mike. "What's the location?" asked the dispatcher. "Marsalis and Jefferson, in the library. I'm going around the back. Get some on the back."

Under less dire circumstances, this episode would have been good for a laugh. As it happened, Officer Walker observed a young white male, more or less matching the latest description of the fugitive, sprinting across the lawn of the Jefferson Branch Library. Walker reasonably assumed the police should talk to this individual.

The runner turned out to be 19-year-old Adrian D. Hamby, a college student who worked part time at the library, two blocks from the intersection of Tenth and Patton. When Hamby reported for work on the 22nd at about 1:20, a pair of plainclothes policemen stepped up to accost him. "Sir," said one of the cops, "what are you doing in this area?"

Hamby replied that he worked at the library. "Well, listen," said the officer, "someone just shot and killed a police officer in the vicinity and we think the suspect is loose. Do us a favor, go into the library,

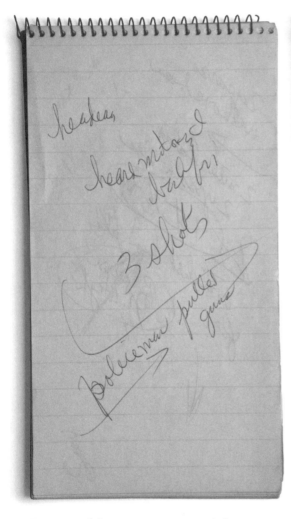

First notes of the assassination recorded
on utility bills, transferred to my notebook.

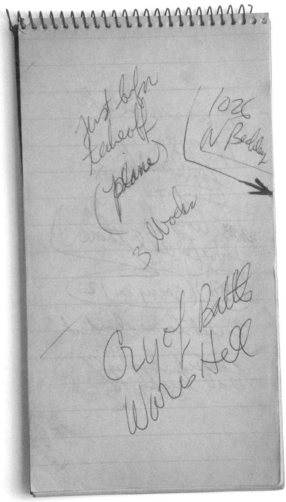

"Cry of Battle" and "War is Hell" were
movies playing at the Texas Theater. 1026
N. Beckley is Oswald's rooming house.

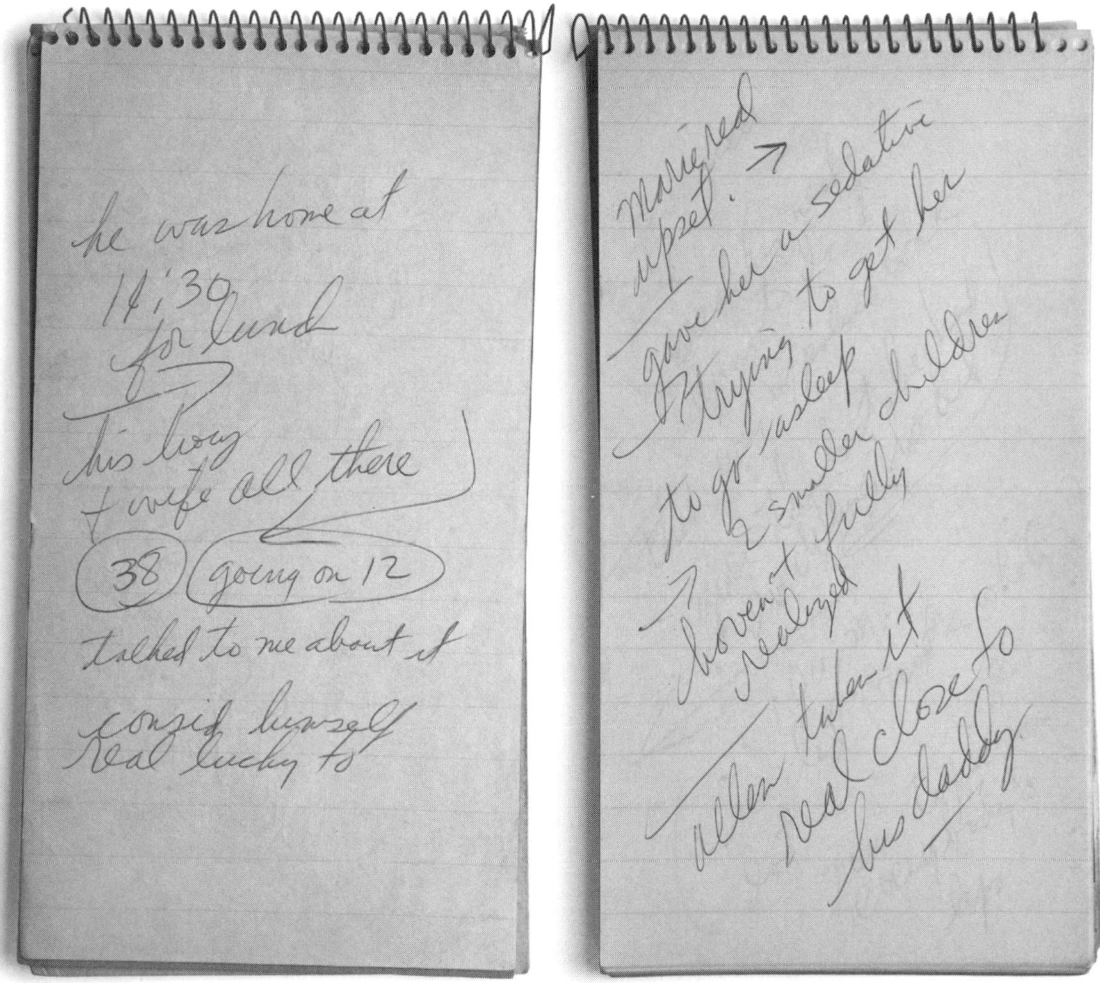

he was home at
11:30
for lund

his boy
& wife all there
(38) going on 12

talked to me about it

consid himself
real lucky to

married
upset. →
gave her a sedative
trying to get her
to go asleep
2 smaller children
haven't fully
realized

Allen taken it
real close to
his daddy

Recorded at the Tippit family home
the night of the assassination.

get ahold of management, tell them to lock the doors and not let anyone inside until we secure the area."

Adrian Hamby was eager to do as he was told. He took off at a run, which attracted Officer Walker's attention to the library, and within moments the building was surrounded by police.

Walker led a police phalanx, firearms drawn, to a basement entrance where Hamby awaited them. "There was about 20 or 30 police officers out there with rifles, pistols—you name it—and they were pointing it at me and told me to come out with my hands up," Hamby later told Dale K. Myers, author of *With Malice: Lee Harvey Oswald and the Murder of Officer J.D. Tippit*. "I got scared and closed the door."

The officers took Hamby's panicked reaction for guilty knowledge. "They told me that if I didn't come out they would fire," he remembered. "You talk about being scared. I thought I was doomed."

As Hamby and the rest of the group inside filed through the door, their hands above their heads, Officer Walker, a DPD accident investigator, recognized the figure he'd seen running across the lawn, and the police moved forcefully to seize him.

"They immediately grabbed me and pushed me up against the wall—my legs spread apart—and frisked me," he told Myers. "I was so scared. I just came apart and I started crying and screaming, 'I work here! I work here! I don't understand! I work here!'"

An unnamed Secret Service agent finally stepped forward to vouch for Hamby, explaining to the assembled police that he'd already ascertained the subject was telling the truth.

A disappointed Officer Calvin B. Owens contacted the dispatcher. "It was the wrong man," Owens explained into his mike.

"Ten-four," came the reply. "Disregard all the information on the suspect arrested. It was the wrong man."

By this time, I was running out of people to interview—and had the feeling that some who had drifted into the area were not, as they claimed, really witnesses, but just excitement chasers who loved to be interviewed. My hunch was confirmed when a teen-ager was being interviewed by a TV guy and his buddy suddenly snapped, "C'mon Jack, you weren't even here. You were with me. I'm gonna tell your family."

Meanwhile, thanks to a report that came over a radio in an

unmarked police vehicle, I heard that a "possible suspect" was hightailing it into an old furniture storage house on Jefferson. As I arrived, I heard someone say, "He's in there. I know he's in there."

I recognized Assistant District Attorney Bill Alexander as he and five or six policemen headed into one of the houses. So I followed them. Inside it was dim and dusty. Part of the group split off to search the upstairs.

For the first time this busy, busy afternoon, I was suddenly afraid. Oh, when the shots rang out in Dealey Plaza, I was unnerved like everybody else, but after a few seconds there was nothing but confusion and chaos, no glaring danger.

But now, as I crept inside that old house, I had a feeling a showdown was near. Frankly I stayed pretty close to the front door as the others poked around the piles of used furniture, yelling things like, "Come out of there you sonuvabitch! We got you now!"

Suddenly, one of the upstairs searchers came crashing through the rickety ceiling. "Oooh," I shouted, as I looked up to see legs dangling down, dust swirling and a couple cops close to me, guns drawn, hitting a firing stance.

Within seconds the man—half in, half out of the ceiling—said, "Damn!" and called to another cop, as nervous laughter rose from several areas of the old room. I recall looking around the dirty old house and thinking: "Every damn guy in here has a gun! What am I doing here?"

And I scrambled out to the street. Actually this turned out to be a smart move. The suspect was nowhere nearby. Within seconds I heard on an FBI car radio that a suspect had just run into the Texas Theater, about six or seven blocks up Jefferson Ave. I didn't see any newsmen close by and I was hesitant to ask a carload of cops to ride with them, so I took off at a run.

As I sped west on Jefferson, I noticed my stomach hurt quite a bit. I realized I was just hungry. I hadn't eaten breakfast, because my wife had been suffering morning sickness with our first pregnancy and I had just skipped breakfast and then had coffee at the *News*.

I plunged on—thinking I didn't have a choice. Not right now anyway.

•••••••••••••••••••••••••••••••

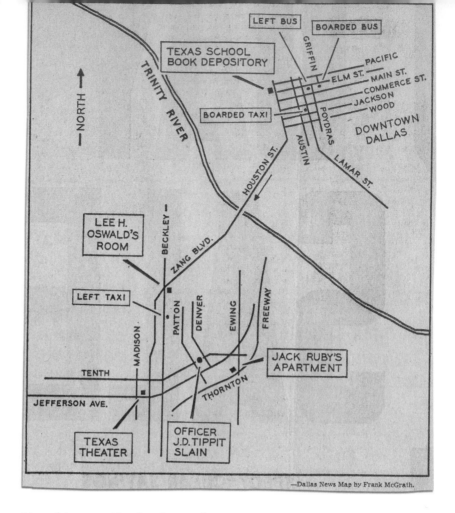

LEFT BUS   BOARDED BUS

TEXAS SCHOOL BOOK DEPOSITORY

GRIFFIN

ELM ST.   PACIFIC
MAIN ST.
COMMERCE ST.
JACKSON
WOOD

POYDRAS

DOWNTOWN DALLAS

BOARDED TAXI

AUSTIN

LAMAR ST.

HOUSTON ST.

NORTH

TRINITY RIVER

LEE H. OSWALD'S ROOM

BECKLEY

ZANG BLVD.

LEFT TAXI

MADISON

PATTON

DENVER

EWING

FREEWAY

JACK RUBY'S APARTMENT

TENTH

THORNTON

JEFFERSON AVE.

TEXAS THEATER

OFFICER J.D. TIPPIT SLAIN

—Dallas News Map by Frank McGrath.

Map of the critical locales of November 22, 1963. The distance from Elm Street to Oswald's room is about two miles. (*The Dallas Morning News*, Nov. 28, 1963)

Oswald did a fair job of making himself scarce from the time he left the Tippit crime scene, about 1:16, until about 1:36, when 22-year-old Johnny C. Brewer, manager of the Hardy's Shoe Store at 213 West Jefferson, saw a man he later identified as Oswald step into the shoe store's recessed foyer.

Brewer was listening to radio reports from Dealey Plaza. "We knew the president had been hit," he later told me, "and there was this rumor a Secret Service man had been killed, also. The radio reporters were just going wild."

Outside his shop, police cars whipped up and down the avenue, tires squealing, sirens wailing. When Oswald ducked into the front of the store, "I thought it was funny," Brewer remembered. "He looked scared. His shirt was out of his pants and his hair messed up. Seemed like a man who had been running. He just stared at me a moment or so."

A squad car pulled an abrupt U-turn out on Jefferson and sped away east. Brewer watched as Oswald glanced over his shoulder toward the street, then, without saying a word, headed west, to his right. The Texas Theater was six doors away.

The store manager went back to his work for a half a minute or so, then heard yet another squad car whiz past, headed west this time. Curious, Brewer walked out the front door and glanced right to see Oswald about 50 yards away, still walking west as he neared the Texas Theater. In front of the theater stood ticket clerk Julia E. Postal, drawn from her box office by the commotion. Brewer noticed Postal and he also noticed that with her back turned to the theater entrance, she couldn't have seen the young man with the tousled hair duck inside without paying.

The situation looked suspicious, so Brewer approached Postal. "I asked her if that man in the brown shirt had bought a ticket to get in," he said.

"No, by golly," replied Postal, who was listening to the assassination news on a small transistor radio.

Brewer stepped into the lobby where he found 22-year-old Warren ("Butch") Burroughs behind the concession stand. "I grabbed Butch Burroughs and asked him which way the man had gone," Brewer told me. "He said he didn't see anyone enter; he was busy behind the counter. He asked me why I wanted to know about this man. I told him the man was just very suspicious, the way he acted and all."

Back on the pavement, Brewer and Postal drew up a plan. She would watch the front door while the two men checked the two other exits. Brewer and Burroughs also looked for their suspect upstairs and down, but couldn't find him. (They'd later learn that they passed within a few feet of the seated suspect.)

Postal declared that she was going to call the police, and asked Brewer and Burroughs to stand by the two exits until officers arrived. "I don't know if this is the man they wanted," she remembered saying to Brewer, "but he's running from them for some reason."

Butch Burroughs meanwhile was getting caught up in the excitement. "I thought about getting him myself," the concessionaire told me, "but Johnny stopped me. Told me I didn't have a gun and I might need one."

Postal told me that when she described Oswald, the officer on the phone said, "Well that fits the description, no doubt about that."

A dispatcher relayed the call to Officer Bill Anglin, J. D. Tippit's best friend on the force, who at the moment was working his buddy's murder scene. "Have information that a suspect just went in the Texas Theater on West Jefferson."

"Ten-four," Anglin answered. The first squad car arrived in front of the theater ninety seconds later, at 1:47. I wasn't far behind.

I raced beneath a theater marquee that said:

Cry of Battle
Van Heflin
War Is Hell

Julia Postal was at her ticket counter. "Oh my God! I just heard the president is dead!" she said. This was the first I'd heard of it. She'd later tell me she recognized J.D. Tippit as a former part-time security guard at the theater.

On the way inside I ran into my *News* colleague, Jim Ewell, who'd hitched a ride to Oak Cliff with the police. Jim decided that he'd head up to the balcony while I took the first floor of the auditorium, where I saw four or five policemen standing on the stage, reconnoitering the nearly empty seats. I counted no more than a dozen patrons in the movie house.

The film was still running, and the house lights were up part way, which created an eerie confusion, like being half way into a dream. From my vantage it was impossible to sort out the action, except that there was a voice coming from behind the stage, directing the officers' attention to the man in the brown shirt, Lee Harvey Oswald.

"As the lights went up," Brewer told me, "I looked out from behind the curtains and saw the man. I showed the officers which one he was. Then he got up and walked to his right to the aisle, stopped a moment, then turned around and walked back and sat down."

I didn't see the suspect get up and move toward the aisle as Brewer had but I probably missed that when I moved from the first entry door to the second—closer to where most patrons sat. As I eased the door open, just a few feet behind and to the right of Oswald, I saw two officers walking up the aisles from the screen. The lights had been turned up a shade brighter, but the movie was still running.

Coming up the left aisle was C. T. Walker, 31, who'd recently led the assault on the Jefferson Branch Library. On the right was Officer Maurice ("Nick") McDonald, 35, an eight-year veteran of the force. He was the first to reach Oswald, who was sitting three rows from the back, five seats in from the aisle.

McDonald moved deliberately. Stopping a few rows in front of Oswald, he had two male movie-goers stand as he searched them for weapons. It seemed to me that McDonald was taking forever, but the officer was just being careful. When I later spoke with him about that moment, Nick McDonald recalled, "I looked over my shoulder and he [Oswald] sat there quiet, just looking at me."

When he reached the suspect's row, the policeman turned suddenly and said, "Get on your feet."

"Well it's all over now," he heard Oswald reply.

Except it wasn't. Not quite.

Oswald stood up, raised his hands in an apparent gesture of surrender, then socked McDonald in the face with his left fist. With his right hand, he pulled a .38 Smith & Wesson from his belt.

At that point the poorly-lit scene exploded into a blur. A motorcycle officer named Thomas Hutson, 35, jumped Oswald from behind, as Nick McDonald recovered with a fist of his own into Oswald's face or head. A plainclothes cop, Sgt. Gerald Hill, 34, grabbed an arm and he and another cop finally got handcuffs on Oswald. McDonald later told me that he got his hand on the pistol's firing mechanism to prevent Oswald from firing, which, he said, obviously saved his life.

Another cop grabbed Oswald's .38 pistol and stuck it in his belt.

Just then a couple seated near the melee abruptly jumped up and fled toward the exit, brushing past me as they ran. The woman screamed until they were outside the theater.

Officers pray for their fallen president and fellow officer.

I remember Oswald crying out, "I protest this police brutality! I protest this police brutality!" There was quite a tussle. The cops knocked him around a lot, and he had a forehead cut and black eye to show for it.

By the time Oswald was subdued, five or possibly six cops had been there hands-on. As they marched him out the theater door, a crowd of several hundred people was gathered outside. I have no idea how they came together so quickly; it was only 1:50 when the police put Oswald in Sgt. Hill's unmarked squad car—as it happened, the car Jim Ewell had ridden in from Dealey Plaza—for the ride to city hall.

The people were in an ugly mood. "Get him! Kill him!" they chanted.

Closed for business: Dallasite carries
final edition through quiet city streets.

Books for Everyone
On Your Gift List!
Reviewed in the
CHRISTMAS
BOOK SECTION
Coming Sunday

87th Year—No. 292

THE DALLAS TIMES HERALD

CONTINUOUSLY PUBLISHED FOR 87 YEARS · THE TIMES 1876 · THE HERALD 1886 · CONSOLIDATED 1888

DALLAS, TEXAS, FRIDAY EVENING, NOVEMBER 22, 1963

Telephones— Classified, Rl2,4144 / Other Depts., Rl.4455

3 Parts

FINAL
EDITION

Price Five

PRESIDENT DEAD

Connally Also Hit By Sniper

By GEORGE CARTER

President Kennedy died of assassin's bullets in Dallas Friday afternoon.

The President and Gov. John Connally were ambushed as they drove in the President's open convertible in a downtown motorcade.

Two priests announced shortly before 1:30 that the President was dead.

Bullets apparently came from a high-powered rifle in a building at Houston and Elm.

A man was arrested and taken to the sheriff's office.

The President immediately clutched his chest and slumped into the arms of his wife.

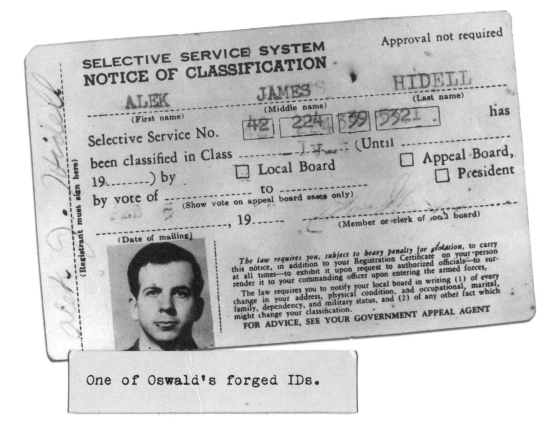

SELECTIVE SERVICE SYSTEM
NOTICE OF CLASSIFICATION

ALEK   JAMES   HIDELL
(First name)   (Middle name)   (Last name)

Selective Service No.   42 224 39 5321   has

been classified in Class _____ IV ____ (Until _____
19_____) by _____   ☐ Local Board   ☐ Appeal Board,
                                                ☐ President
by vote of _____ to _____
              (Show vote on appeal board cases only)
_____ , 19_____   _____
(Date of mailing)   (Member or clerk of local board)

The law requires you, subject to heavy penalty for violation, to carry
this notice, in addition to your Registration Certificate on your person
at all times—to exhibit it upon request to authorized officials—to surrender it to your commanding officer upon entering the armed forces.

The law requires you to notify your local board in writing (1) of every
change in your address, physical condition, and occupational, marital,
family, dependency, and military status, and (2) of any other fact which
might change your classification.

FOR ADVICE, SEE YOUR GOVERNMENT APPEAL AGENT

(Registrant must sign here)

One of Oswald's forged IDs.

CHAPTER THREE

Cover-up: "What the hell do you think Hoover's going to do?"

I know of just one reporter to whom the name Lee Harvey Oswald meant anything before November 22nd: Kent Biffle. Still inside the book depository at 2 p.m. when the suspect's name was first made public, Kent received a memory jolt. Biffle remembered that in 1959, when he was a reporter for the old *Fort Worth Press*, he'd written several stories about some turncoat ex-Marine from Fort Worth named Lee Harvey Oswald.

He recalled the *Press* had tried to connect Oswald's bizarre 52-year-old mother, Marguerite, via telephone to her son in Moscow from the paper's newsroom, but Lee had hung up on her.

FBI agent James Hosty in the bureau's Dallas office, who had a far fresher recollection of the suspect, was dumbstruck at the news of Oswald's arrest. Agent Hosty was supposed to be keeping an eye on Lee Harvey Oswald and his young wife, Marina. Hosty had known for weeks that Oswald was working in the book depository, along the path of Kennedy's motorcade.

"I had no reason prior to that to believe he was capable or potentially an assassin of the president of the United States," Hosty would insist to the Warren Commission.

Later I would help find evidence that contradicted Hosty's assertion.

Lee Harvey Oswald was what law enforcement today calls "a person of interest." In 1959, following a brief and bumpy career in the Marine Corps that included a court martial for fighting and an "undesirable" discharge, he defected at age 19 to the Soviet Union, unsuccessfully attempting to renounce his U.S. citizenship in the process.

But life in the workers' paradise didn't pan out. In May of 1962,

James Hosty, Special Agent in the FBI field office (top) and his Special Agent in Charge (SAC), Gordon Shanklin.

Oswald returned to the United States with his wife, formerly Marina Nikolayevna Prusakova, and their 3-month-old daughter, June Lee. The family lived for a time in the Dallas-Fort Worth area, then moved to New Orleans in the spring of 1963.

The FBI kept an eye on Oswald, as it would any returned defector with a Russian-born spouse. The bureau noted in his file, for example, that Oswald was arrested in New Orleans in August of 1963 after getting into a scuffle while handing out "Fair Play for Cuba" fliers.

On Oct. 3, the FBI office in New Orleans informed Dallas that the Oswalds had left Louisiana, presumably headed back for Texas. Marina and her daughter were seen driving away with a woman in a station wagon with Texas tags. James Hosty was told to find them. It was a routine assignment—"no particular note of urgency," Hosty later said—until New Orleans also reported that in September Oswald had traveled to Mexico City and visited the Soviet embassy there.

"Did this increase your effort to find him?" a Warren Commission lawyer would ask. "Very much so, yes," Hosty answered. "I became curious then."

Thanks to another tip from the New Orleans office, on Oct. 29 Hosty tracked the Oswalds to suburban Irving, eight miles west of Dallas, where Marina and her daughters, little June Lee, and Rachel, born Oct. 20, were living with a close friend, Mrs. Ruth Paine at 2515 Fifth St. It was Mrs. Paine, 31, who'd driven Marina to Dallas from New Orleans.

Hosty visited Ruth Paine on Nov. 1. She explained how she'd recently helped Oswald, an unskilled high school dropout, land a $1.25-per-hour, part-time job filling orders at the Texas School Book Depository on a corner of Dealey Plaza in Dallas.

(Depository superintendent Roy Truly later told me that he filled two similar openings the day he hired Oswald; one at the Dealey Plaza warehouse, and one at another facility in Dallas. Oswald just as easily could have been assigned to the second location.)

Mrs. Paine also told Hosty that Oswald was staying at a rooming house in Oak Cliff. She said she was aware there had been considerable discord between the Oswalds, and that Lee had been physically violent toward Marina. According to Hosty's notes of his conversation with Mrs. Paine, she "didn't want [Oswald] at her home; that she was willing to take in Marina Oswald and her two children but she didn't have room for him and she didn't want him at the house. She was willing to let him visit his wife and family but didn't want him residing there."

Hosty visited the Paine household one more time, on Nov. 5, but did not speak with Marina. Nor did he ever attempt to interview her unstable husband.

The next he heard of Lee Harvey Oswald was his arrest in the Texas Theater, a suspect in both the Kennedy and the Tippit shootings. Under orders from SAC Gordon Shanklin, the agent grabbed his Oswald files and hustled over to City Hall (and police station), where the suspect would be brought for questioning.

As I reported in the *News* five months later, under the two-column headline "FBI Knew Oswald Capable of Act, Reports Indicate," Hosty arrived at City Hall about 2:05 and rode up in an elevator with Lt. Jack Revill, head of the DPD Criminal Intelligence Squad, and Officer V. J. "Jackie" Bryan. According to Revill's written account of the episode, typed up 45 minutes later and delivered to Chief Curry that afternoon, in the basement Hosty "stated that the Federal Bureau of Investigation was aware of the Subject [Oswald] and that they had information that this Subject was capable of committing the assassination of President Kennedy."

Hosty denied making the statement to Revill. Over the years he has refused my interview requests.

A few months after the assassination, I asked Gordon Shanklin why the bureau didn't at least tell the Dallas police about Oswald, and where he worked. I observed that the cops surely would have wanted to babysit such a character.

"We didn't want him to lose his job," Shanklin explained.

"Well, Mr. Kennedy lost his," I said quickly, appalled at what I'd just heard.

Though Shanklin never deliberately—to my knowledge anyway—caused me any difficulty, I was told by some of his agents that I was not his favorite person.

A few years later—as I sought to expose a famous Texas law enforcement official as a perjurer and thief—I asked Shanklin and J. Edgar Hoover to verify certain facts to which they had access, thinking the bureau would be pleased to clean up a case involving one of their own. Shanklin referred me to Hoover, who sent me a courteous letter of refusal. The official in question later—through my efforts—was indicted and convicted.

••••••••••••••••••••••••••••••

Newsgathering in 1963 was primitive work by today's standards. Our physical tools in the field were paper and pen, and precious little else. We had no mobile voice communication. Reporters used pay phones. There were no computers. No satellites. No PDAs. No Internet. No e-mail. No FedEx. No fax machines. Photocopying was even pretty new.

The third-floor newsroom at the *News* was antediluvian. The big room was outfitted with maybe two dozen battered gray metal desks, arranged in rows. (Mine was in front.) Normally, a reporter sat at each desk, and was equipped with a clunky manual typewriter and a telephone. I recall a single communal file cabinet standing at the end of each row of desks. There were no barriers between us and no privacy.

One other thing: There were very few female reporters, none as far as I can remember, assigned specifically to the Kennedy story, though I recall Vivian Castleberry at the *Times Herald* came through with a fine interview of Judge Sarah T. Hughes after she had sworn in President Johnson.

To write a story in those days, a reporter had to laminate two sheets of 8-by-11 newsprint around a piece of carbon paper, roll this sandwich into an ancient old Underwood and start banging away.

There was no "Delete" button, of course. No spell check. No "Google" or other on-line database to query from your desk. When your piece was completed, you impaled the original on a big spindle at the city desk and deposited the copy in a tray for the Associated Press guy to pick up.

On a typical day, a reporter hung around until the piece was edited and sent to the copy desk and beyond, which to most reporters was terra incognita. Few of us had more than a rudimentary idea of how a newspaper actually was assembled, printed, and distributed.

November 22, 1963, was not a typical day, of course.

Not only was the newsroom swarming with our reporters coming and going, people taking telephoned notes from the field, editors barking assignments and

Opposite: When working on a developing story in the early 1960s, a reporter's handwritten notes were often expanded in the newsroom with typed written notes, like these shown of the author's interview with Ruth Paine. The story was then typed on a typewriter in multiple copies using carbon paper. One copy was then impaled on a spindle on the city desk and another placed in the Associated Press bin.

THE DALLAS TIMES HERALD

BODY STYLE	SECTION	EDITION	DAY
HEAD STYLE	HEADING OR GUIDE LINE		

By BOB DUDNEY

and HUGH AYNESWORTH

Staff Writers

Lee Harvey Oswald appeared to

for someone to stop him in 1963--months an

Nov. 22 assassination of President John F.

The two entities capable of st

assassin, the FBI and Oswald's wife, Marin

the warning signs and so did nothing.

The FBI ignored a direct Oswal

personally delivered ▉ to FBI offices h

assassination. Though the letter appare

president by name, it did not even result

on Oswald by the FBI.

MORE

D C. 13 telephone with ruth paine.....

Mrs. Ruth Paine.....says she hasn't seen Marina in days (this is Dec. 13) and doesn't expect to.....suggest seeing Malliatoff on Mingbird for letter to Marina on book subject.."She is capable of making her own decisions, but not in English...the SS has a tutor with her now. tons of mail there, some of it not pressing....contact SS at 505 N. Ervay...she charges $5 for 90 minute session....Malliatoff was interpreter for police that Friday.....teaches three classes at SMU.... Ruth Paine at BL31628....Irving....About time: "Yes we're not doing al- right...we've even gotten a Christmas tree up...we're not going to lose our Christmas like we did our Thanksgiving.....2 children.....

Jesse Curry, Dallas chief of police, fielding reporters' questions.

working copy, but we were also inundated with our brothers (and a couple of sisters) from the national media. As many as a hundred of them descended on us like locusts, and soon were about as welcome.

Under deadline pressure, those reporters needed desks and typewriters, telephones and text transmission facilities to get their stories filed. Under the circumstances, the editorial management of the *News* and the *Times Herald* were happy to accommodate our out-of-town colleagues.

But the visiting press quickly abused local hospitality. Some tried to usurp our desks when we needed them to get our own work done. Al Altwegg, business editor at the *News*, nearly started a fistfight with a White House correspondent from *The New York Times* who commandeered Al's desk and wouldn't give it up.

Then there was the assault on our reference department. This spacious facility, filled with desks and chairs, offered access to practically any periodical imaginable, plus the invaluable local news clip files, arranged by name and subject in envelopes, with which a reporter quickly could find background information on everything from Police Chief Curry's recent pronouncements to the history of Dealey Plaza.

By that evening the room looked like Genghis Khan and the golden horde had stormed through it. Files were strewn everywhere. Some clip envelopes had been stolen.

By Saturday morning, access to the reference department was strictly limited to *News* staffers. Guards were posted to enforce the prohibition.

Over at City Hall, Chief Curry was stirring up a storm of his own. After returning from Love Field, where he was on hand at

2:38 p.m. to witness Judge Sarah Hughes swear in Lyndon Johnson as the 36th president, Curry read Lt. Revill's report on his basement conversation with FBI Agent Hosty with considerable interest.

"If we had known a defector or extremist was anywhere in the city, much less on the parade route, we would have been sitting in his lap," Curry was later quoted by the Associated Press.

Up on DPD's third-floor office complex, "I was stopped going down the hall," the chief told me, "and the press wanted to know all about what evidence we had and why a Russian defector had been ignored along the motorcade route. I told them that there was a rifle and a pistol belonging to Oswald. And I guess I stepped a bit too far at that point. I said, 'The FBI knew all about this man, knew he was capable of killing the president' and so forth."

Within the hour FBI Director J. Edgar Hoover dispatched Gordon Shanklin to Curry's office with a message. The bespectacled Shanklin apologized for being there, Curry told me, but nonetheless insisted that the chief retract his statement.

Curry trusted that Lt. Revill's report was accurate, but "at that point," he explained, "I didn't see what all the shouting was about. I knew the truth would come out soon. But when Shanklin told me the bureau had not had Oswald under surveillance, I agreed, and did soften that statement a few minutes later."

Shanklin hadn't been entirely truthful with Curry.

While Oswald wasn't kept under surveillance, the FBI had been very interested in locating him, particularly after they learned in October that he'd visited the Soviet embassy in Mexico City.

But Curry kept his word. As the chief returned to Capt. Will Fritz's office in Homicide and Robbery a few minutes later, he told the big crowd of reporters, "I do not know if and when the bureau interviewed him (Oswald)."

My story of the Revill memo and Hosty's remarks must have stung sharply over at the *Times Herald*, for the paper promptly published a poorly-considered response that caused embarrassment even to some of its own reporters.

The afternoon my story ran, the *Times Herald* bannered its front-page with "FBI Denies Statement on Oswald," and quoted Hoover directly. Of Revill's recollection, the director was quoted, "That is absolutely false. The agent made no such statement and the FBI had no such knowledge."

It was a great second-day knock-down of my original story, except for one problem—the Hoover quote was a fabrication. My source for this information was the article's putative writer, George Carter. Angry and deeply embarrassed, George called me to say that not only was his name put on the story without his knowledge, but that the Hoover interview had never occurred. The director would not talk to the *Times Herald*, Carter told me, so the newspaper blithely spliced his name to another official's words or, even worse (he said he wasn't sure), made up the quotes altogether.

When the investigation was concluded, it was easy to discover that my original story was correct.

The controversy over Agent Hosty's remark to Lt. Revill wasn't the only negative fallout for the bureau in the aftermath of the Kennedy assassination. There were other FBI shenanigans going on as well—a cover-up, if you will, that I helped to illuminate a dozen years later.

In 1975, I was working at the erstwhile competition, the *Times Herald*, when my publisher Tom Johnson walked into my office with eyes as big as saucers.

"I've got the biggest story you ever heard of," he said. "It's about Oswald."

Tom said he'd learned from a highly reliable source the previous night that just a few days before the assassination an irate Oswald visited the local FBI office and left a threatening note for Hosty. As Johnson heard the story, Oswald threatened to kill Hosty or to blow up the FBI offices.

Johnson had given his word not to reveal his source, and I was frankly dubious about the story. By 1975, I'd run down dozens of equally tantalizing, but invariably false, self-aggrandizing tales spun by people allegedly "in a position to know."

Nevertheless, I was assigned—with my investigative partner Bob Dudney—to check it out. Since I knew the event Johnson had attended, I scanned the guest list for possible leads. Sure enough, two FBI agents had been at the dinner as well. One, I knew, was an information sieve. The other wouldn't share such a secret with his mother on her death bed.

With the help of the tenacious Dudney, I dug through every source we could think of and discovered, by golly, Johnson was right.

On Aug. 31, under a page one headline that read "Oswald Threat

Dozen knew of Oswald FBI visit

By BOB DUDNEY

November 22, 1963

Captain W.P. Gannaway
Special Service Bureau

                    SUBJECT: Lee Harvey Oswald
                               605 Elsbeth Street

Sir:

On November 22, 1963, at approximately 2:50PM, the undersigned officer
met Special Agent James Hosty of the Federal Bureau of Investigation in
the basement of the City Hall.

At that time Special Agent Hosty related to this officer that the Subject
was a member of the Communist Party, and that he was residing in Dallas.

The Subject was arrested for the murder of Officer J.D. Tippit and is a
prime suspect in the assassination of President Kennedy.

The information regarding the Subject's affiliation with the Communist
Party is the first information this officer has received from the Federal
Bureau of Investigation regarding same.

Agent Hosty further stated that the Federal Bureau of Investigation was
aware of the Subject and that they had information that this Subject
was capable of committing the assassination of President Kennedy.

                    Respectfully submitted,

                    Jack Revill, Lieutenant
                    Criminal Intelligence Section

INDEXED
DATE 4-27-6
INITIALS S

INT 2965-

Lt. Jack Revill's memo the day of the assassination and a 1975 article
reporting that many in the FBI office knew of Oswald's visit—reported
by Bob Dudney, my investigative partner at *The Dallas Times Herald*.

I reported in the April 24, 1964, *Dallas News* that a Dallas police detective had reported the FBI knew Oswald was a potential threat to the president. Hours later, the *Times Herald* published a bogus knock down. Hoover never spoke to the paper.

FBI knew Oswald Capable of Act, Reports Indicate

APR 24 1964

By HUGH AYNESWORTH
© The Dallas Morning News, 1964

A source close to the Warren Commission told The Dallas News Thursday that the commission has testimony from Dallas police that an FBI agent told them moments after the arrest and identification of Lee Harvey Oswald on Nov. 22, that "we knew he was capable of assassinating the president, but we didn't dream he would do it."

In a memorandum to superiors on Nov. 22, Lt. Jack Revill, head of the Dallas police criminal intelligence squad, reported that FBI special agent James (Joe) Hosty had acknowledged awareness of Oswald in the basement of the City Hall at 2:05 p.m. Nov. 22. His remark was made as five officers brought Oswald in from Oak Cliff, Revill reported.

LT. REVILL appeared before Warren Commission investigators here several weeks ago. Police Chief Jesse Curry testified before the commission in Washington Wednesday. Neither would comment on their appearance or their testimony.

Chief Curry was reported to have been questioned about the incident and was said to have given the commission a photostatic copy of Lt. Revill's 5-paragraph memo. He also was said to have given the commission the name of a second Dallas police officer who supported Revill's statement and filled in other parts of the conversation between Revill and Hosty.

The second officer, V. J. (Jackie) Bryan, a member of the criminal intelligence squad,

also declined comment.

CHIEF CURRY had Lt. Revill's report in hand within hours of President Kennedy's death, even before all the facts and circumstances concerning Oswald were known.

Gordon Shanklin, special agent in charge of the Dallas FBI office, would make no comment.

The commission Thursday had not talked to agent Hosty, but The News' source said he anticipated that the agent would be called to testify.

CURRY WILL not show the report to reporters, nor will he comment on it or any other phase of the assassination. "That's for the Warren Commission to talk about," the chief said.

Revill's memo is still in Chief Curry's possession.

In addition to mentioning that Hosty said the FBI knew Oswald was capable of such an act, the memo said Hosty told Revill other facts about the one-time Russia resident and admitted Marxist.

DALLAS POLICE officers watched several known extremists prior to the Kennedy visit and even sent representatives as far as 75 miles to interview others thought to be planning demonstrations.

Curry privately has told friends, "If we had known that a defector or a Communist was anywhere in this town, let alone on the parade route, we would have been sitting on his lap, you can bet on that." But he has refused public comment.

59

THE DALLAS TIMES HERALD

FINAL EDITION

Today's Markets
Latest Available Quotations
From New York Stock Exchange
See Pages 19 and 20-A

CONTINUOUSLY PUBLISHED FOR 86 YEARS   THE TIMES 1876   THE HERALD 1886   CONSOLIDATED 1888

88th Year—No. 115 ★★   DALLAS, TEXAS, FRIDAY EVENING, APRIL 24, 1964   3 Parts   Price Five Cents

FBI Denies Statement on Oswald

Dallas Military Offices To Be Combined

McNamara Cites Other Changes

Three Dallas military offices with some 500 employes will be combined into a single agency in one of 63 money-saving changes in military offices and installations announced Friday by Defense Secretary Robert McNamara.

The three Dallas offices handle contract management of military materiel for the Army, Air Force and Navy.

The consolidation of these offices at 25 cities is expected to bring an annual saving of $18.6 million and reduction of 1,800 employes when the changes are completed.

The offices are responsible for materiel inspection, industrial security, property accountability and disposal and payment of contracts.

The reductions and changes announced Friday, added to others carried out since 1961, will result in an eventual operational saving of $18 million and elimination of 81,000 personnel positions, a spokesman said.

It will also release about 700,000 acres of real estate for non-defense use.

A spokesman for the offices said some it is not yet known how much personnel reduction will result from the Dallas consolidation, but he said several affilates should take care of the reductions over the two-year period of amalgamation.

Secretary McNamara Thursday announced closings of military bases, depots and arsenals, and consolidation of military offices would bring an estimated annual saving of $18 million.

Total permanent reduction of 51 Negro prisoners in affected by the changes.

2 PRISONERS IN SOLITARY AFTER RIOT

By JERRY RICHMOND
Staff Writer

Two Negro prisoners were placed in solitary confinement at the Dallas County jail Friday for touching off a violent, screaming riot in two top floor cell blocks.

The rebellion raged for some three hours Thursday night as some 50 prisoners in the jail's seventh floor smashed windows, ripped out plumbing fixtures and burned mattresses.

Sheriff Bill Decker, who used water hoses and police dogs to crush the riot, said he would fire assault charges against the two men in solitary for injuring a jail privileges for the other prisoners who defied the offers of law enforcement until he displayed the Sheriff said.

The riot, built on the complaints of Negro prisoners about jail conditions, erupted shortly around 8 p.m. Thursday. After leaving hours ended for Negro prisoners on the seventh floor.

BEGAN FIGHTING

Deputy Sheriff Ray Hamers, Penn, which will be the making the rounds with fresh jail in June.

DALLAS OFFICES

The Dallas offices to be consolidated are the Air Force's Dallas Contract Management District.

Two other prisoners raided the command by Lt. Charles Fred Moore old Inter, who was Burley, the office of the Inspector, part of a minor slander on his Naval Material, commanded three and lockdown. The pair by Capt. Burton D. Wood, and the three off the attackers and Army's Dallas Branch office, moved keep in prisoners in two, Louis Procurement District, cell blocks began yelling and Marine branch offices.

Currently the Air Force offices is in the Merchandise Mart, the Navy office at 708 Jackson and Maritime, their most are going the Army office at 312 Commerce had been enough street. The regional offices presently placed because they...

Izvestia Declares Russ Back Cuba

MOSCOW (AP)—Izvestia, the put up with it, and will side with government paper, on Cuba. It has declared this backed today the Soviet Union and comforts this non-will side with Cuba if the non-The dispute, which flared up invasion about U.S. economics in Havana and Washington this major flights made it a tit-to-tat, which pose back to the measures goes ...

Grim President engulfed by enthusiastic crowd.

POVERTY TOUR OPENS

Happy Students Mob LBJ

SOUTH BEND, Ind. (AP)—ments and had difficulty steering it President and Mrs. Johnson were through because most of the shouting endured in an all-engulfing crowd youngsters did not recognize of which children as the partly arrested mob actively swept the presof South Bend today by a dense of party away from the president his side—poverty tour.

Neither the President nor the first lady was injured in the wild crush, however, but grim expressions set on the chief executive's face and his aides...

THE WEATHER

Dallas and Vicinity Considerable cloudiness and warm Friday night and Saturday. Widely scattered afternoon and evening showers and thunderstorms Low temperature Friday night upper 60s. High Saturday near 82. Wind mostly southerly 10-20 m.p.h.

TEXAS MEDICS CONVENE

Fluoridated Water Given Good Report at Meeting

By BILL BURER
Staff Writer

HOUSTON — Fluoridation emerged here Friday as a key issue facing the Texas Medical Association while one of the country's top nutritionists advanced that fluoridated water probably has more benefits than prevention of tooth decay.

WHERE TO FIND

	Part	Page
Amusements	A	20-21
Billy Graham	A	4
Bridge	A	4
Business		
Comic strips	A	16
Classified	B	5-9
Comics	A	12-13
Cross Country	A	6
Crossword Puzzle	A	16
Editorials	A	2
Horoscope		4
Jumble	A	4
Markets	A	19-20
Radio-TV		7
Sports		
Women's Features	A	17

TODAY'S CHUCKLE

The rich may get free wine, but it certainly seems like it to their poor relations.

Capability To Kill Claimed Unknown

By GEORGE CARTER, Staff Writer

Capability To Kill Claimed Unknown

By GEORGE CARTER, Staff Writer
Copyright, 1964, The Dallas Times Herald

FBI Director J. Edgar Hoover briskly denied Friday that the agency knew Lee Harvey Oswald was "capable" of killing President Kennedy prior to the Nov. 22 assassination in Dallas.

Mr. Hoover told The Dallas Times Herald by telephone that the published report was "absolutely false."

A memorandum written by a Dallas police officer

60

THE DALLAS TIMES HERALD

Oswald threat revealed

Note to FBI destroyed; Kennedy not named

By TOM JOHNSON
Staff Writer
© 1975, the Dallas Times Herald

Lee Harvey Oswald personally carried a "threatening" letter to the Federal Bureau of Investigation offices here several days prior to the assassination of President John F. Kennedy, The Dallas Times Herald has learned.

The letter was reportedly destroyed by FBI personnel shortly after the assassination and its existence kept secret from the Warren Commission investigating the death of Kennedy, also, according to sources within the FBI.

The FBI has launched a full internal inquiry into the Oswald visit and possible criminal violations in

connection with destruction of the note and failure to report its existence.

In response to inquiries by The Times Herald, FBI Director Clarence M. Kelley said in Washington that investigation "tends to substantiate that Lee Harvey Oswald visited the Dallas FBI office several days prior to the assassination of President Kennedy."

FBI statement,
Page 18-A.

He did confirm that Oswald's visit was recorded in a statement given by Dallas Times Herald director Nov. 9, 1975, reached with Kelley in Washington. FBI headquarters. The Times Herald has learned that FBI personnel destroyed the note and failed to disclose its presence to the Warren Commission that had nearly

Kelley said Saturday that "inquiries are continuing to determine the full circumstances of the FBI matter."

Kelley and Attorney General Edward Levi is being kept informed on the progress of the investigation.

The note apparently was destroyed the morning after the assassination.

The incident was first brought to the attention of FBI superiors by a former FBI employe, the Dallas source said.

The note apparently was assigned to the FBI office in an effort to cover up the public at the time of the assassination and the visit.

times had been no immediate comment on the visit and note. However, the note is no being borne was made available to her by the investigation, Another imperative and the note is no in question in

Oswald, who on Nov. 1, 1963, was 24
Oct. before the assassination, handed
the note to the receptionist at the
FBI office, the Times Herald learned.

The FBI gave the Oswald's visit was recorded in a statement given by Dallas

"Prior to the current FBI inquiries."

See OSWALD on Page 18

Times Herald query
prompted FBI probe

The FBI internal investigation into the Oswald visit and handling of a note of a July visit been kept from the Times Herald until recently.

Only a few high level officials knew of the note's existence. The Times Herald had uncovered Oswald visit to the Dallas FBI offices prior to the assassination, as well as information on a "threatening" note that Oswald left in a threatening manner.

Because the newspaper has received hundreds of uncorroborated reports over the years, the Times Herald did not report the information until it could be verified.

See OSWALD on Page 13

The first story revealing the existence of
Oswald's threatening note. (Aug. 31, 1975)

Revealed," we published a package of stories that for the first time publicly revealed the note's existence, explained how it possibly was kept secret even from FBI headquarters, and that it had been deliberately destroyed by Agent Hosty shortly after the assassination.

"I am worried it will further damage the FBI," a confidential source inside the bureau told us. "It was a bureaucratic screwup. Nobody did the followup on it, and the letter was destroyed. They didn't want anyone to know that Oswald had come by the offices, that he had left a threat, that we had failed to put him under surveillance."

This is how it occurred. Ten days before the assassination, after learning from Marina that an FBI agent twice had been out to the Paine house on Fifth Street, Oswald went to the Dallas FBI office in search of Hosty. Informed that the agent was not in, Oswald handed receptionist Nannie Lee Fenner an unsealed envelope, asked her to give it to Hosty, and departed.

As Hosty later recalled in his memoir, *Assignment Oswald*, "It said, in effect, 'If you want to talk to me, you should talk to me to my face. Stop harassing my wife, and stop trying to ask her about me. You have no right to harass her."

According to Hosty, the note was unsigned.

Others who read it say otherwise. Not only did Oswald sign it, they told us, but in it he directly threatened to blow up the FBI office. The note did not mention President Kennedy.

Fenner read the note and showed it to Kyle Clark, assistant special agent in charge (ASAC), who also read it and instructed the receptionist to place it in Hosty's mail box. Hosty reports that he filed away the note after reading it, and thought no more of the matter at the time.

Our *Times Herald* stories caused quite a stir, leading to an internal

61

FBI investigation and congressional hearings in October. That month, the FBI's Deputy Associate Director James B. Adams told a House Judiciary subcommittee that Hosty remembered destroying the note, but claimed he did so under orders from his SAC, Gordon Shanklin, who had twice directly denied to Dudney and me that he knew anything about the note.

In Hosty's version of events, Shanklin confronted him with the letter on the night of Nov. 22. "What the hell is this?" he recalled the SAC saying. "It's no big deal," Hosty replied. "Just your typical guff."

Shanklin was apoplectic. "What do you mean, 'typical guff'? This note was written by Oswald, the probable assassin of the president, and Oswald brought the note into this office just ten days ago! What the hell do you think Hoover's going to do if he finds out about this note?"

Still, according to Hosty, when Shanklin calmed down, he ordered the agent to compose a memo that explained the circumstances of the letter. Two days later, following Oswald's murder by Jack Ruby, Hosty was summoned once more into the SAC's office.

James B. Adams, FBI deputy associate director.

Shanklin, a chain smoker, put a lit cigarette in his ashtray and stood up behind his desk to speak. "Jim," Hosty remembers him saying, "Now that Oswald is dead, there clearly isn't going to be a trial."

Hosty watched as Shanklin reached into his desk drawer, produced the Oswald note together with the agent's Friday night memo, handed them both to Hosty and said, "Here, take these. I don't want to ever see them again." Hosty says he began tearing up the papers there in the SAC's office.

"No! Not here!" said Shanklin. "I told you I don't want to see them again. Now get them out of here."

So, James Hosty left the SAC's office, and remembers walking down to the men's room, which was empty. He headed for the first stall, where he tore the papers into little shreds and flushed them down the toilet.

"Down the drain, I thought. Literally. I hoped the cliché didn't turn out to be prophetic."

J. Edgar Hoover, who died in 1972, probably did find out about the Oswald letter, according to his former No. 3 man at the bureau,

William C. Sullivan, whom we reached at his New Hampshire retirement home in 1975.

Sullivan pointed out to us that Hosty was suspended for 30 days and then given a disciplinary transfer to the Kansas City office after the Warren Commission finished its work in the autumn of 1964. Hoover, Sullivan explained, "was responsible for the transfer. Somebody must have discussed something with him, or Hosty wouldn't have been transferred."

Gordon Shanklin, now deceased, retired in 1975, insisting to the end that he knew nothing about the Oswald visit or letter, even though Bob Dudney's later review of the Justice Department's assassination files revealed that a dozen or more employees of the Dallas FBI office knew of the assassin's visit.

In September 2003, the newly-built FBI offices in Dallas were officially named the J. Gordon Shanklin Building.

At February 1964 news conference, I scratch my head and try to sort it all out.

Aynesworth visits Oak Cliff street where Oswald shot Tippit.

A return visit in 1964 to the Texas Theater, as well as to the scene of Officer Tippit's murder.

CHAPTER FOUR

"They're like a pack of wild dogs"

At some juncture in the newsroom that Friday afternoon I came up with several possible Oak Cliff addresses for Lee Harvey Oswald, plus a couple of other names to check out, along with an alias, Alek Hidell. I can't recall how I got this information—it's possible that Jim Ewell or Harry McCormick or some other reporter gave it to me—but the original source was the wallet Oswald carried that day.

I headed out in my '61 Ford Fairlane, little realizing how strange and convoluted a journey I was embarked upon. For the great majority of reporters in Dallas that day, the Kennedy assassination would be an intense but brief brush with history, something to tell the grandkids about. That certainly would have been my expectation, had anyone asked.

But for reasons I cannot fully explain the story grabbed me and wouldn't let go. Part of the reason was sheer coincidence and dumb luck; I was at the right places at the right times. But as the saga unfolded, I picked up threads that were impossible to put down.

As other reporters returned to their routines, almost by default I became the guy at the *News* who looked into new leads, as well as the bogus assertions of the countless nuts and fakes irresistibly drawn to the Kennedy assassination. I met a lot of very unusual people and heard a number of bizarre stories. In time I also grew weary of it all.

On Day One, though, I was energized. At 32, I had been a professional newspaperman since my mid-teens, working at papers in West Virginia, Arkansas, Kansas, and Texas, as well as United Press International in Denver, Colo. So far in my career, I'd covered everything from high school sports to tornadoes, statewide political races, rapes, murders, and space travel, but clearly nothing so cataclysmic as a presidential assassination.

The first address on my list was an apartment building. There was no sign that Oswald had ever lived there. I asked around the neighborhood. "Do you know Alek Hidell or Lee Harvey Oswald?"

Nothing.

So I moved on to address No. 2, a little house where I could hear music and voices from within. I knocked on the door and waited, and waited and knocked again. No answer. So I knocked once more and a very large Spanish-speaking male opened the door with a scowl. He was completely nude, as was the female I saw behind him dashing toward a bathroom.

"Do you know Lee Harvey Oswald?" I asked, possibly the most pointless question of my entire career. I might as well have tried to sell him a set of encyclopedias. "No, no, no," the man said in a way that strongly discouraged further discourse.

"Well, thank you," I answered, backing steadily away. "I'm sure I can find somebody, uh…"

The third address, a rooming house at 1026 North Beckley, was the charm. Earlene Roberts, 58, the housekeeper, greeted me at the door. Peering from behind thick eyeglasses, Mrs. Roberts told me that I was the first reporter on the scene, that the police and federal agents had just left after thoroughly searching the place.

She said she knew Mr. Oswald as Mr. Lee, a quiet loner who'd rented a room for $8 a week since Oct. 14. She even offered to give me the rooming house register, a loose-leaf notebook in which Oswald had printed the name O.H. Lee. Like a fool, I declined.

Mr. Lee had suddenly appeared about one o'clock that afternoon. "He came in running like the dickens," she said, and didn't respond when she asked him his hurry. "[He] just ran in his room, got a short tan coat and ran back out."

Inside, Mrs. Roberts showed me the spare, eight-by-eleven, first-floor room Lee Harvey Oswald had

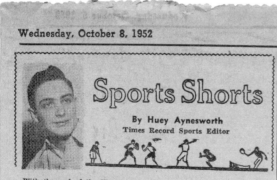

An early incarnation of "Huey," the sports editor at the *Fort Smith Times Record*, in Fort Smith, Arkansas.

Wednesday, October 8, 1952

Sports Shorts

By Huey Aynesworth
Times Record Sports Editor

With the end of the World Series yesterday, baseball is supposed to step out of the way and let ole Mr. Pigskin take over, at least until the winter baseball meetings in late December . . .

But we'd like to stretch baseball out for at least another day by looking back some six or seven months ago and jotting down some of the remarks made by the major league managers a short time before the season began . . .

At Miami, Chuck Dressen, refused to be too concerned about the loss of big Don Newcombe to

Mays to the army . . .

Eddie Stanky, taking over as Card manager, said, "I'll have no alibies." . . . And the scrappy little guy needed none as the Birds, picked by most for fifth place, stalked right up into third place, only 8½ games behind the champion Bums . . .

"My Phils will hustle this season," said Eddie Sawyer . . . And hustle they did, only it started after Steve O'Neill replaced Sawyer as manager . . . The Phils finished fourth, one game back of the Redbirds . . .

Casey Stengel said he was

occupied over the past several weeks. There wasn't much to see; no personal items, nothing on the walls, just some cheap furniture, a torn-up bed, and a banana peel discarded in the waste basket.

Mr. Lee was very neat and clean, she said, ate a lot of fruit and made himself coffee and sandwiches in his tiny room. He also kept early hours.

"He was always in bed by 9:30 or 10 p.m.," said Mrs. A.C. Johnson, Oswald's landlady, who walked in with her husband as I was speaking to the housekeeper. Mr. Johnson recollected that Mr. Lee liked to listen to the radio.

"He was always was very quiet and polite," Mrs. Roberts added, but kept to himself, rarely mixed with the other roomers, and never received visitors.

He did use the telephone quite a lot, Mr. Johnson said, and frequently called a prefix in the Dallas suburb of Irving. (I never figured out how he knew that; it was not a long distance call.) Oswald always spoke "in that foreign language" on the phone.

On my second return to the newsroom, Harry McCormick called the city desk from city hall to report that the cops were questioning someone who apparently knew Oswald. Harry's call was forwarded to my desk about 7 p.m.

"I don't know what role he plays," McCormick told me. "But I looked through Capt. [Will] Fritz's office window and he's sitting in there wearing some kind of uniform. He doesn't look angry or scared, seems to be laughing and chatting amiably."

Thanks to Harry's tip, we sent a photographer down to get a picture of the mystery witness. I was planning to go snoop around Capt. Fritz's office, too, when Johnny King came by my desk. The city editor wanted to know if I'd written up everything I'd reported in Oak Cliff that day.

When I said I had, he indicated my next assignment would be to find H.L. Hunt and Gen. Walker. "Find out where they were today and what they're saying," King began, then changed his mind.

"Oh wait a minute," he said. "We haven't anything from the Tippit family. We don't know hardly anything about them. Run on out there and see what you can come up with. I'll handle the Hunt angle."

This was not a plum assignment. Although cop killings are always big news whenever they occur, they tend to put the fallen officer's fellow cops in an angry, even belligerent, mood. Reporters often bear

Oswald defiant at the Dallas police headquarters. (Nov. 23, 1963)

the brunt of this hostility.

In those days, most city editors had just the reporter for such stories, some crusty old veteran totally indifferent to what the dead policeman's colleagues and family thought or felt. He'd go the victim's house, write down the hot quotes, even steal a picture if need be.

Not me.

"Oh my God!" said McCormick when I told him by phone where I was headed instead of City Hall. "They're making you do that?"

Then he considered his own situation. Harry was a dogged police reporter, but he was no bulldog. Past the age of 60 by then, and a dapper dresser, he did not revel in the bedlam that was engulfing City Hall.

Looking out the window of the Burglary and Theft Bureau, he said he saw at least 80 wild-eyed reporters battling for position on the third-floor corridor, clamoring for comment from the police, witnesses, and even Lee Harvey Oswald himself, then being held in a high-security cell on the fifth floor. "They're like a pack of wild dogs," McCormick said.

When I arrived at the Tippit house there were cars, pick-ups, and police cruisers lined up in each direction. I was not about to approach Tippit's shocked and grieving wife, Marie, or any other member of the family for comment. But I couldn't go back to the newsroom with nothing, so I gleaned what comment I could from the gathered police officers, including Bill Anglin, who was kind enough to talk to me for a few minutes.

I returned for a third time to the *News*, typed up my notes and finally headed home. It was about ten o'clock. What a strange day, I thought as I drove along.

It was about to get a bit stranger.

As I approached my apartment I found an odd, bedraggled little man sitting on my doorstep. He was wearing an overcoat despite the mildness of the evening.

My wife whispered to me that she hadn't known what to do with him. "He almost cried when I told him he couldn't wait for you," she explained. "So I said, 'Sit down here and you'll see him when he arrives.' I told him you might be late."

He introduced himself as Rodney Stalls, and told me that until recently he'd worked as an engineer at one of the many electronics and

Oswald was questioned in a room shielded by blinds in the Homicide and Robbery Bureau. Detective Jim Leavelle, seated at the desk in a light colored hat and suit, accompanied Oswald when he was shot by Jack Ruby. (Nov. 22, 1963)

aeronautical companies in and near Dallas. I couldn't imagine what Mr. Stalls wanted with me at that hour, until he began to spin a conspiracy theory of the day's shootings, the first of hundreds I'd eventually hear.

I moved him away from my door and over to the stairwell.

"It's the Russians and H. L. Hunt," he began. "I've been getting messages about it for weeks now."

New to such thinking, I made the mistake of trying to reason with my visitor. The Russians very possibly were mixed up in the assassination, I agreed, but not in league with H. L. Hunt, who feared and hated Commies as intensely as anyone I'd ever encountered.

"Listen!" Stalls interrupted me. "I know what I'm talking about." His voice began to rise; his tone turned urgent. "It was Hunt who caused me to get fired, because I knew what the Russians were planning, and tried to convince my bosses."

Stalls clearly was troubled. But was he a complete nut? I knew I'd better make sure, so I asked if he had any evidence. Immediately he produced from beneath his heavy coat a fat sheaf of yellowed and well-thumbed pages, and handed them to me. I spent half an hour plowing through the mess.

There was no mention of Oswald, Dallas, Kennedy, or assassination anywhere in them, just a lot of gibberish. So now I needed an exit strategy.

"May I copy these?" I asked, "and discuss them with my editor?"

"Absolutely not," he answered. "If you don't trust me with all that I have shown you, then I must look for an honest reporter, one who will listen."

This is what I hoped he'd say. Stalls explained that I wasn't his first choice in any event. That person was Bob Fenley at the *Times Herald*. He said he'd tried to reach Fenley at the paper, but "obviously they got to him. He's not even in the phone book anymore. Do you know him? I saw his name on a story yesterday, but they wouldn't give me his home number at the *Times Herald*. I'll bet he would listen to me."

"Of course I know Bob," I said as a realization dawned inwardly. "He and I cover science and aerospace together." I'd wondered how Stalls connected me to the assassination; my first day stories hadn't even yet appeared. Of course he hadn't. He'd sought out Bob and me because we covered stories of professional interest to him.

Stalls hauled out an envelope with the name Bob *Finley* written on it. This accounted for his trouble with the phone book. He'd misspelled Bob's name.

Then an insidious idea occurred to me. "I'm sure Bob would be pleased to talk to you," I said, and informed Mr. Stalls that I'd seen Fenley just that day, that he looked very well indeed, and I was certain "nobody has gotten to him." To help him along even further, I corrected his spelling.

My wife at last rescued me with a call to dinner, a blessing because I had no desire to hurt or further upset this zany soul. Stalls quickly rolled his papers under his arm and pleasantly made his exit.

I never saw him again, and of course was afraid to mention Stalls to Fenley. About three years later, however, at a Dallas Press Club committee meeting, I asked Bob if he remembered talking to an ex-engineer about H. L. Hunt and the Kennedy assassination.

"Oh that," he laughed. "I knew you sent him to me. He told me that you were too inexperienced to handle it, and that you'd recommended that he approach me. Thanks. And by the way, how do you know I haven't sent some weirdos to you, too?"

He didn't have to, of course. There were plenty to go around.

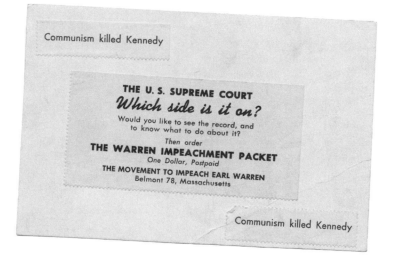

One of many bizarre solicitations sent to me in 1963.

The exclusive "Escape Route" story that I broke with Larry Grove six days after the assassination. (*The Dallas Morning News*, Nov. 28, 1963)

TRAFFIC HELD UP BUS
Oswald Planned to Ride by Scer

NOV 2 8 1963 21-1

By HUGH AYNESWORTH
and LARRY GROVE
© The Dallas Morning News, 1963

Lee Harvey Oswald planned to ride a Dallas Transit bus past the scene of his infamous crime just 20 minutes after he assassinated President John F. Kennedy.

But traffic was congested on streets around the Texas School Book Depository. He caught a bus—seven blocks east of the building he used for his ambush—and rode it less than a block. Impatient with the delay, he scampered to the Greyhound Bus Station and took a taxi.

"Take me to 500 North Beckley," he ordered.

For the past two days, we have retraced Oswald's escape route. We have pieced it together, for the first time here, from actual interviews with the men and women whose testimony has been relayed to officials. Sometimes, as the careful reader will note, the information apparently was garbled in its transmission to reporters.

A POLICE OFFICER detained Oswald temporarily in the lunchroom of the School Book Depository building. But the detention was short. The building superintendent, R. S. Truly, identified Oswald as an employe, and the assassin was allowed to leave the building.

Less than 10 minutes after he had fired the fatal shots, the 24-year-old killer was walking into a crowd that was surging, unnoticing, toward him. He worked his way a lone block north to Pacific Street, turned right, and hurried east on Pacific for six blocks.

APPARENTLY, he had found enough daring to rejoin the crowd.

He turned right one block and made his way back to Elm, near the old Blue Front Restaurant, where he tapped on the door of a Marsalis bus.

"It couldn't have been later than 12:40 p.m.," said 45-year-old C. J. (Mac) McWatters, a cigar-smoking bus driver of 2523 Blyth Drive.

"I was driving down Elm and had reached Old Griffin. The run originated in Lakewood, and I was on schedule at the checkpoint on St. Paul Street—12:36 p.m. There weren't more than five or six passengers . . .

"Then this young man knocked on the door of the bus—there is no regular bus stop at Elm at Griffin—and I let him in.
"He took the third chair back, seniority of the entire taxi sys-

—Dallas News Staff Photo.
Bill Whaley . . . "if you can call a nickel a tip, I guess he tipped me."

THERE WAS no reaction from Oswald when the working man told the driver "The President has been shot—that's why traffic is blocked . . ."

The bus driver said "A lady behind me had been giving me a hard time — she wanted to catch a train at the depot. She wanted off so she could make it."

And Lee Harvey Oswald, also, wanted off.

"Give me a transfer," he said.

THE TRANSFER that he got was punched with McWatters' own mark. Each driver has a different kind of punchmark. FBI agents, about midnight, 10 hours later, would trace that transfer to McWatters' bus and learn the intriguing story of Oswald's first moments after the shooting.

The time is now approximately 12:42 to 12:45 p.m. Oswald hurries south across Elm to Lamar Street, then two blocks south to the Greyhound Bus Terminal on the corner of Lamar and Commerce.

"CAN I TAKE this cab?" he shouts to the driver, 58-year-old William Wayne "Chief" Whaley. Whaley — top man in

away from the scene of his crime.

The driver, a resident of Lewisville, tried to make conversation with Oswald.

"What the hell you think happened out there?" he recalled asking Oswald as an opener.

Oswald hasn't answered him yet.

"I just thought to myself here's a guy who wants to be left alone," Whaley said. "So I left him alone."

The cab went across the Houston Street viaduct and turned left on Beckley, not far across the bridge.

WHEN THE CAB made that turn it was almost directly in front of the mottled brown rooming house where Oswald roomed for $8-a-week at 1026 North Beckley. The taxi hurtled on for five more blocks and Oswald snapped, "This is fine, right here."

"I pulled over to the curb and he got out, didn't say anything else," Whaley said.

The fare was 95c. Oswald wasn't too gracious. He handed Whaley a dollar bill and got out.

DID HE LEAVE a tip? Whaley was asked.

"Well, if you can call that nickel a tip, I guess he did," the burly cabbie replied.

Whaley's logbook shows that he had gone to the Greyhound Bus Station with a passenger he had picked up at Methodist Hospital about 15 minutes before he picked up Oswald.

Why did he take a zig-zag route to Oak Cliff?

"I miss two stoplights that way."

TSE LOGBOOK shows he had 13 calls that day, 8 pickups—and 29 passengers in all. The notation that recalls the ride with the assassin is marked "12:30 to 12:45."

"That's understandable," Whaley said, "I always mark 'em down in 15 minutes intervals."

The next we know of Oswald's whereabouts is only minutes later.

Mrs. Earlene Roberts, housekeeper at the 17-room boarding house where Oswald had spent most of his nights except weekends in a 5x12-foot bedroom cubicle, was watching television.

"A FRIEND HAD called and said the President had been shot," said Mrs. Roberts. "I said 'You're pulling my leg,' but I turned the set on. She

—Dallas News Staff Photo.
C. J. McWatters . . . he didn't know Oswald was his passenger until the FBI traced a yellow transfer slip to him 12 hours after the President's death.

Still in Mrs. Roberts' possession is the black covered loose-leaf notebook that she uses as a registry for her tenants. In Oswald's hand, the name O. H. LEE is printed boldly.

That is the name he used when he moved in last Oct. 14—the day before he started work as a $50-a-week employe at the book depository. "I asked him for next-of-kin in case something happened. He said, 'It's not important, forget it.' So I forgot it . . .

"NO, HE NEVER was out much that I noticed. He was gone on weekends. Never got any mail that I recall—I put the mail out, all that comes in. Never made much noise. He never spoke any English on the telephone, some foreign language . . .

"His alarm clock always went off at 7 in the morning.

"Yes, I did remember seeing a Humble filling station map of Dallas, all folded up, and I never disturbed anything that was his. Just dusted around it . . ."

THE MAP IS among the evi-

tween Denver and Streets on East 10th—th of Beckley, and, oddly almost in a direct line way between his own r the 223 S. Ewing apar the man who would late assassin, Jack Ruby.

Three witnesses say was ordered to stop, m the block, by Dallas po cer J. D. Tippit.

Tippit was cruising Car 10, in front of 404 when he signaled the ure to halt.

AS TIPPIT JUMPED his patrol car to check the who fitted the all-points bu he had received just minute fore, Oswald fired three into the heroic police vete

The three witnesses tol lice Oswald ran off—cha his course—toward the bu portion of Oak Cliff. C came up with other repo "a racing maniac."

Oswald was reported in a furniture store that occup tall, weather-beaten frame building at 413 E. J son. About the same time, tators at a service stat i ther west up the street saw run into a vacant lot, whe lice say the killer discarde newly acquired jacket and pistol shells.

THEN FOLLOWED a in and out of alleyways Jefferson - Beckley - C land-Zang area.

About 1:45 p.m., Julie cashier at the Texas Thea 231 W. Jefferson saw a ing stranger rush past into the theater.

To this day, she can't whether or not h ebou ticket.

"I was so upset listen the radio about the Pr and all," she said.

FIVE MINUTES or elapsed before Johnny manager of a shoe store doors away, ran to Mrs and said he thought he h "somebody running from lice" duck into the thea

The cashier imm called police—who had j en masse to a false alarm Dallas Library branch ferson, further to the e police sirens wailed aga

Oddly enough, it was library that McWatters driver who, unknowing Oswald as a passenger had his second brush w His bus pulled up at th section as a swarm of police cars zeroed in o

CHAPTER FIVE

Escape: How Oswald Got Away — For a While

November 22, 1963

In the early hours after Oswald's arrest, a question foremost in many people's minds was how he'd pulled off such an audacious crime, especially how had the killer slipped out of the book depository so quickly, then made his way back to Oak Cliff? He seemed like a phantom.

Friday afternoon in the newsroom, Larry Grove kept asking me what I knew about Oswald's escape. At the time, the answer was nothing. But I agreed with Larry that we needed to nail that down.

We quickly learned that Oswald normally spent Monday through Thursday nights at 1026 North Beckley. On Fridays, his book depository co-worker, Buell Wesley Frazier, drove him out to Mrs. Paine's house in Irving for the weekend. Frazier, who lived very near Ruth Paine, then drove Oswald back into Dallas on Monday mornings to make an 8:30 start at the depository.

The evening before the assassination, Oswald varied his routine. He rode out to Irving with Frazier, played for a while with June Lee, ate an early dinner with Marina and Mrs. Paine, and turned in at nine.

When he arose the next morning—Marina was still asleep—Oswald slipped off his wedding ring and placed it on the dresser next to his wallet, which contained $170. When he was arrested several hours later, he had $13.87 in cash on him.

As Buell Frazier was finishing his breakfast that morning, his sister Linnie Mae Randle saw Oswald walking toward Buell's car carrying what she described as a "heavy brown bag," which he placed on the rear seat.

As he walked with Oswald from his back door to the car, Buell Frazier asked, "What's the package, Lee?"

"Curtain rods," Oswald answered. Frazier also noticed his co-worker wasn't carrying a sack lunch as usual. Oswald said he planned to buy lunch that day.

The two men arrived for work at the depository by the 8:30 starting time.

Oswald's lunch break was supposed to last 45 minutes, but because no time clocks were used at the depository, it's not possible to pin when or if he broke for lunch.

He shot the president at 12:30, then stashed the Mannlicher-Carcano and headed downstairs. In the second floor lunchroom he discarded the dark blue jacket he'd worn to work that day. He also encountered Dallas Police Office Marrion Baker, who'd jumped off his motorcycle and run inside the book depository, with Roy Truly, the building superintendent.

In the lunchroom, Baker poked his sidearm in Oswald's stomach as he asked Truly, "Do you know this man? Does he work here?" Truly said Oswald did, and Baker let him go.

"Oswald looked a bit startled," the superintendent would recall, "as you or I would if someone threw a gun on you. But he didn't appear too nervous or panicky."

Moments later, as Oswald was departing the building, he crossed paths with a reporter , who was searching for a public telephone. (That reporter may have been NBC's Robert MacNeil.) Oswald told the reporter where to find a pay booth inside the building.

He was clear of the depository by 12:32, or about the time I had my makeshift reporting tools assembled and went to work interviewing. This is where the trail went cold.

Larry and I began by interviewing everybody we could think of at the depository, the sheriff's office, police department, federal law enforcement agencies, the DA's office—even some criminal lawyers we knew.

Nothing.

"Hell of a lot easier writing a column," Grove said in discouragement. "Do you do this kind of stuff all the time?"

Then we caught a break. Somehow, I ascertained that the mystery man we had photographed in Capt. Fritz's office on Friday evening was a bus driver named Cecil J. McWatters. I also had our picture of

McWatters, except I didn't know which one of two men it was. Jack Beers, the *News* photographer, had gotten McWatters's image all right as the witness was being escorted from city hall. But Beers had also photographed another witness leaving the building, and he didn't know which one was our bus driver.

Larry and I took the two photos with us on Saturday morning when we went downtown to visit the Dallas Transit Company. A supervisor there quickly picked out McWatters, checked the schedule, and said the driver would be back at work on Sunday. Around six o'clock that evening, as McWatters entered the office to check out for the day, we were waiting for him.

An 18-year veteran of the transit company, the 45-year-old McWatters, known as "Mac," remembered that he was steering his white, 44-passenger, No. 433 bus west on Elm Street when a traffic snarl brought him to a complete halt near Field Street, a few blocks east of the book depository. It was approximately 12:40.

"That's when I saw him," McWatters recalled as he enjoyed a cigar. "He beat pretty hard on the bus door and I let him in. The fare was 23 cents."

Oswald asked McWatters for a transfer, and took the second seat behind the driver. Had he remained aboard No. 433, the bus would have taken him directly past the corner of Elm and Houston, where ten minutes before he'd shot and killed President Kennedy.

Instead, said McWatters, as the bus slowed once more in traffic, Oswald abruptly arose and disembarked at Lamar Street, about halfway to the book depository.

To Cecil McWatters, Lee Harvey Oswald was just another anonymous fare. He was never able to conclusively identify Oswald as the slightly-built young man who rode his bus for about five minutes that Friday afternoon.

About five hours later that day, he told us, the police pulled him over near city hall and took him up to Capt. Fritz's office for questioning. Detectives told him they'd found the transfer ticket he'd issued Oswald in the suspect's clothing. It distinctly bore Cecil McWatters's stamp and was one of only two he gave out all day.

When the Dallas police showed him a line-up, he told officers that Oswald was the right height, weight and coloring, but he could not be absolutely certain.

"They sure wanted me to pick him out, without reservation,"

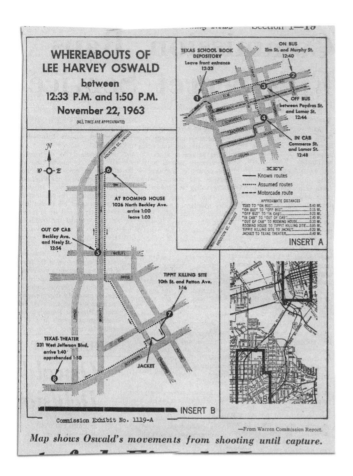

WHEREABOUTS OF LEE HARVEY OSWALD
between
12:33 P.M. and 1:50 P.M.
November 22, 1963
(ALL TIMES ARE APPROXIMATE)

AT ROOMING HOUSE
1026 North Beckley Ave.
arrive 1:00
leave 1:03

OUT OF CAB
Beckley Ave.
and Neely St.
12:54

TEXAS-THEATER
231 West Jefferson Blvd.
arrive 1:40'
apprehended 1:50

TIPPIT KILLING SITE
10th St. and Patton Ave.
1:16

JACKET

TEXAS SCHOOL BOOK DEPOSITORY
Leave front entrance
12:33

ON BUS
Elm St. and Murphy St.
12:40

OFF BUS
between Poydras St.
and Lamar St.
12:44

IN CAB
Commerce St.
and Lamar St.
12:48

KEY
— Known routes
······· Assumed routes
---- Motorcade route

APPROXIMATE DISTANCES
TSBD TO "ON BUS"..............0.40 MI.
"ON BUS" TO "OFF BUS"..........0.15 MI.
"OFF BUS" TO "IN CAB"..........0.25 MI.
"IN CAB" TO "OUT OF CAB".......2.40 MI.
"OUT OF CAB" TO ROOMING HOUSE..0.20 MI.
ROOMING HOUSE TO TIPPIT KILLING SITE...0.85 MI.
TIPPIT KILLING SITE TO JACKET..0.20 MI.
JACKET TO TEXAS THEATER........0.40 MI.

INSERT A

INSERT B

Commission Exhibit No. 1119-A

—From Warren Commission Report.

Map shows Oswald's movements from shooting until capture.

McWatters recalled to us. "I couldn't do that, not for positive."

Like all reporters, I had to hit it very hard sometimes, especially on the science and aviation beat. I covered all manned space activities for the paper, which meant dealing with a notoriously and annoyingly secretive government organization—NASA. On the aviation side, many of the really important stories were about mistakes and malfunctions— crashes and casualties—which required a lot of digging as well as assiduous cultivation of sources.

Now some of that hard work was going to pay off in an entirely unforeseeable way. I received a telephone call from a source I'd met at lunch the previous year with Lt. Col. John A. "Shorty" Powers, the famous onetime pilot and public affairs officer for NASA's original Mercury Program (and parenthetically the man who coined the term, A-OK).

"I live just a few houses from a guy who says he carried Oswald in his cab on Friday," the source told me. "I knew you'd know if he's lying or not."

Wow, I thought. Could this be real? Excited, I asked my new best friend for the cab driver's name and address and said I'd check it out.

"William Whaley," he said, and gave me an address in Lewisville, a little town about 18 miles northwest of Dallas. I grabbed Grove and off we went.

I hadn't risked telephoning Whaley in advance. If the cab driver didn't feel like talking it would be much easier for him to hang up the telephone than to banish my smiling face from his front door. I did call Whaley's employer to see if he was working that day. I was told the cab driver's wife was ill, and that he'd taken the day off to be with her. That explained why no one was home when we reached the Whaley address.

Larry and I drove around the neighborhood for a while, stopped for lunch at a decent barbecue spot, then returned to the still-empty house. We spotted a woman entering the house next door. She told us that Whaley's wife was at Flow Hospital in Denton, another 18 miles out, and that he probably was there with her.

So Larry and I rushed on out to Flow Hospital, where Mrs. Whaley indeed was a patient. She was asleep, we were told, and couldn't be disturbed. Several people had helpful guesses where her husband might be—the cafeteria, a convenience store down the street—but none panned out.

Back to Lewisville.

Mr. Whaley hadn't returned home, so I asked his neighbor what make and model of car he drove, thinking we might start checking the streets and lots surrounding Flow Hospital.

"Oh, he drives his cab," she said.

Larry and I exchanged a glance, feeling more than a little foolish, and thanked her.

Spotting his cab shouldn't be too tough, I thought, as we returned once again to Denton.

It was by now late afternoon. Whaley was not inside the hospital, and his yellow cab was not parked in any hospital lot. Just as I was about to take the Lord's name in vain, Larry grinned and said, "Hey, big Hugh, look over there," and he pointed at a yellow cab, apparently empty, parked about a block away, easily in sight of the hospital doors. I'd never make a good repo man.

We both ran to the cab, thinking we finally had Mr. Whaley cornered—sort of. He had to return to his cab at some time. As we drew closer, however, we saw a pair of legs dangling out one window. Attached to them was our quarry, sound asleep in his '61 Checker.

We awakened him, gently, and introduced ourselves. William Wayne Whaley, 58, known as "Chief," said that police detectives had been all over him since the assassination, and that he needed some time to himself, and for his sick wife. His boss had told him to take his cab and to take the day off, which he had.

So we moved ahead slowly. Whaley laughed to hear of our

adventures in search of him. He and Larry hit it off right away, especially when they discovered that both had served in the South Pacific during World War II. Whaley had been a Navy gunner and won a Navy Cross over Iwo Jima, he said. I was far too young to know anything about that.

Reporters sometimes forget the objective of any interview is to extract information. In this case, Larry was connecting with Whaley better than I, so he led the discussion. They talked about Mrs. Whaley's condition. They reminisced about the war. They even discussed the pros and cons of working for a cab company. Chief Whaley said he had put in 37 years behind the wheel; he was the senior driver at the company.

At last, we settled down to discuss Oswald. Whaley recollected that he'd dropped off a 55-cent fare at the Dallas Greyhound Bus Terminal on the corner of Lamar and Commerce sometime before noon, and was about to go inside to buy a pack of cigarettes when he saw a young man—Oswald—walking south on Lamar, approximately three blocks from where Oswald had departed Mac McWatters's city bus. He was waving at Whaley, trying to get his attention.

"He was very polite," according to Whaley, "said something like, 'May I have the cab, sir?' I told him, 'You sure can. Get in!'" Oswald climbed in the front seat.

"No sooner had he closed the door," Whaley continued, "when an old lady stuck her head through the window on his side and said, 'Driver, can you get me a cab down here? I've been waiting...'

"I guess I hadn't seen her in the doorway, and here he came walking. He opened his door a bit like he was going to get out, and he told her 'Here, I'll let you have this one.'

"She said, 'No, that's all right. He can get me another one.' So he settled back, looked at me and said, '500 North Beckley.'"

Sirens were screaming all over the area, Whaley said, "and I couldn't figure out why. Police cruisers were criss-crossing, making U-turns, then screeching off. I remember saying to him, 'What the hell's going on? I wonder what's happening.'"

Oswald looked at the cab driver, but didn't answer. "I just thought to myself, here's a guy who wants to be left alone," Whaley said. "So I left him alone."

Their route took them directly past 1026 N. Beckley and five blocks farther on, where Oswald gave Whaley a dollar for the 95-cent ride. "I pulled over to the curb and he got out, didn't say anything else," Whaley recalled.

What about the tip? we asked.

"Well, if you can call a nickel a tip, I guess he did," Whaley said.

According to the cab driver's logbook, he most likely picked up Oswald at approximately 12:45, and delivered him to his destination in Oak Cliff about ten minutes later.

Whaley was unaware he'd driven Lee Harvey Oswald's getaway car until the next morning when he saw Oswald's picture in the *News*. He told his boss about it, and within 20 minutes was on his way to a line-up, where he picked Oswald from among five or six other men.

One of my stories that appeared
in other news outlets.

New York

Journal American

NEW YORK'S WORLD'S FAIR NEWSPAPER

R

No. 27,765—DAILY   THURSDAY, OCTOBER 1, 1964   10 CENTS

LATEST
NEWS
(LATEST SCRATCHE

87,000 Children Adri

OCT 1 1964

chool Bus
rvices
t Down

"Outrage"
Page 20.

E PEARL
87,000 public
school chil-
many blind
d, were on
s the Chil-

Assassin's Dead Hand, Riches and Heartbreak

By HUGH AYNESWORTH
Special to The N. Y. Journal-American

DALLAS, Oct. 1.—This is the story of two women touched by history when assassin Lee Harvey Oswald's bullets took the life of President John F. Kennedy. As a result, one now never has had it so good, while the other would willingly trade her new riches for the return of her husband.

One woman is Marina Oswald, the assassin's widow who has been tranformed from a shy Russian girl into what some consider to be an aggressive, sure-of-herself woman who, when it is all over, is

great tragedy the money and letters were still trickling in from 17 nations.

Mrs. Jacqueline Kennedy wasn't sent money, for the wealth of the President's family long has been legend, but Mrs. Tippit and Mrs. Oswald have

Hugh Aynesworth, Dallas Morning News reporter, has practically lived with the story of the Kennedy assassination, and its aftermath, since that fateful day last Nov. 22. He believes he is the one man to have personally witnessed the assassination, the capture of Lee Harvey Oswald and the shooting of Oswald by Jack Ruby. This is his latest, intimate, behind-

Zapruder Film

Dress manufacturer Abraham Zapruder captured these images on his new 8mm Bell &
Howell home movie camera, a recent innovation. Notice that the image extends into the
"sprocket" area in what are now labeled Zapruder frames 230 and 274. If this were
played on a home projector, the image in the area of the sprocket, which allows the
film to be advanced, would not be seen—but was carefully examined by investigators.

CHAPTER SIX

Dallas: The Mood, the Realities

The Kennedy assassination was a watershed event for the news business. Up to then, television news was mostly a novelty. The era of the celebrity network anchor supplanting a kid on a bike as bearer of the evening news was not yet born. The national reflex habit of tuning to cable TV to follow any breaking story still was decades away. Daily newspapers were still the most common, and most trusted, source of news in the country.

But Nov. 22, 1963, went far to change all that, even if television coverage of the event and its immediate aftermath in Dallas was spotty and amateurish by today's standards. Only Abraham Zapruder, a local purveyor of women's fashions, caught the assassination itself on film, using his 8-mm Bell & Howell home movie camera.

The most vivid images of the weekend, in my view, were Jack Beers' great picture—showing Ruby moving toward Oswald—and the even greater Pulitzer Prize-winning still of the actual murder, taken by *Times Herald* photographer Bob Jackson.

At its best, however, the TV coverage (particularly of Oswald's murder) was more immediate and dramatic than anything you could put in a news column.

A revolution had begun.

The first victims of television's newly-discovered power to cover breaking stories would be the afternoon dailies. Yet on November 22nd in Dallas, it was the afternoon paper, the *Times Herald*, that scored a lot of the early newsbreaks.

The reason was simple. With an early afternoon copy deadline already in place (and much of the boilerplate reporting in hand), the paper could instantly mobilize.

The *Times Herald* got a special edition with a 150-point banner proclaiming PRESIDENT DEAD on the street by 2:30. The frightened, jittery Dallas citizenry, hungry for any information, paid as much as a dollar apiece for the nickel newspapers, a circulation department's dream.

Across the way in Fort Worth, the *Star-Telegram* began cranking out serial editions of its afternoon paper, remaking page one over and over as more news broke and Fort Worth readers lined up around the block to purchase the paper.

The *News* hit the streets overnight with a two-line banner:

Kennedy Slain
On Dallas Street

The *News* produced what I think was a comprehensive and balanced 12 pages of coverage devoted to the assassination, everything from a long Kennedy obituary to wire service reports from around the world to my interviews with Nick McDonald, Earlene Roberts, and others.

The centerpiece was a long narrative crafted from staff feeds by Paul Crume, the best front-page columnist then working west of the Mississippi, who was drafted into acting as a sort of super re-write man that day. Johnny King later told me that Crume filled three waste baskets with wadded balls of discarded copy as he labored over his typewriter to create as seamless a story as possible.

Unfortunately, two major errors crept into the piece; one, that Oswald's assassination weapon was a 6.5 Mauser rifle (actually Mannlicher-Carcano rifle, No. C2766) and, two, that Kennedy died in surgery on the sixth floor of Parkland Hospital (actually emergency ground floor, Trauma-1). Both mistakes soon were twisted to the uses of conspiracy theorists.

Ever since, stories have circulated that the president really didn't die that day, but survived and was placed on permanent life support systems in persistent vegetative state on Parkland's sixth floor.

Never mind that Parkland had no sixth floor. The story never went away.

Painful as the errors were, they were mistakes of inadvertence—Paul didn't mean to get it wrong. Not so our editorial that day, a

Front page of *The Dallas Morning News* for Nov. 23, 1963, the day after the assassination. It was not uncommon for several reporters to contribute to a story that another writer would compile. Here, the lead story was compiled by Paul Crume. It includes several inaccuracies, which often occurred in fast-breaking stories, especially in an age before instant telecommunication was possible. The first inaccuracy is that the murder weapon was misidentified. More important, for years afterward, many thought that Kennedy was kept in a secret room on the sixth floor of Parkland Hospital, even though there wasn't a sixth floor.

Largest Daily
Circulation
In Texas
230,421 WEEKDAYS
258,447 SUNDAYS

The Dallas Morning News

John F. Kennedy
Life History.
Pages 16 and 17

L. 115—NO. 54   TELEPHONE   DALLAS, TEXAS, SATURDAY, NOVEMBER 23, 1963—50 PAGES IN 4 SECTIONS   ★★★★   PRICE 5 CENTS

KENNEDY SLAIN ON DALLAS STREET

★ ★ ★ ★ ★   ★ ★ ★ ★ ★   ★ ★ ★ ★ ★   ★ ★ ★ ★ ★   ★ ★ ★ ★ ★

JOHNSON BECOMES PRESIDENT

Receives Oath on Aircraft

By ROBERT E. BASKIN
Washington Bureau of The News

In a solemn and sorrowful hour, with a nation mourning its dead president, Lyndon B. Johnson Friday took the executive of the United States.

Following custom, the taking took place only an hour and a half after the assassination of President —

Federal Judge Sarah Hughes of Dallas administered the oath in a hastily arranged ceremony at 2:39 p.m. aboard Air Force 1, the presidential plane that brought Kennedy on his ill-fated Texas trip and in which his body was flown back to Washington.

Mrs. Johnson and Mrs. Kennedy, her stockings flecked with blood of the assassination, flanked the vice-president as he raised his right hand in the forward compartment of the presidential jetliner at Love Field. About 25 White House staff members and friends were present as Johnson intoned the familiar oath:

"I do solemnly swear that I will perform the duties of President of the United States to the best of my ability, and protect and pre—

Lyndon B. Johnson

Gov. Connally Resting Well

By MIKE QUINN

Gov. John Connally — felled Friday by a sniper's bullet in the back—rested in "quite satisfactory" condition late Friday night at Parkland Hospital following nearly four hours of surgery in the afternoon.

An aide for the governor reported at 10:30 p.m. that the governor was asleep and resting comfortably following the incident which claimed Presi—

"After consulting with Mrs. Connally and others on the scene, the consensus is that the governor was quite fortunate that he turned to see what happened to the President. If he had not turned to his right, there is a good chance he probably would have been shot through the heart—as it was, the bullet caused a tangential wound."

Dr. Shires rushed to Dallas by

A 24-year-old pro-Communist who once tried to defect to Russia was charged shortly before midnight Friday with the murder in Dallas of President John F. Kennedy.

Kennedy was shot down about 12:20 p.m. Friday at the foot of Elm Street as the presidential car entered the approach to the Triple Underpass. The President died in a sixth-floor surgery room at Parkland Hospital about 1 p.m., though doctors said there was no chance for him to live when he reached the hospital.

Johnson was sworn in as the nation's 36th President inside the presidential plane before departing for Washington.

The gunman also seriously wounded Texas Gov. John Connally, who was riding with the President.

Four Hours in Surgery

Connally spent four hours on an operating table, but his condition was reported as "quite satisfactory" at midnight.

The assassin, firing from the sixth floor of the Texas School Book Depository Building near the Triple Underpass sent a Mauser 6.5 rifle bullet smashing into the President's head.

An hour after the President died, police hauled the 24-year-old suspect, Lee Harvey Oswald, out of an Oak Cliff movie house.

He had worked for a short time at the depository, and police had encountered him while searching the building shortly after the assassination. They turned him loose when he was identified as

Friendly Crowd Cheered Kennedy

Shockingly, the President was shot soon after driving the length of Main Street through a crowd termed the largest and friendliest of his 2-day Texas visit. It was a good-natured crowd that

---

[pull quote] Underpass. The President died in a sixth-floor surgery room at Parkland Hospital about 1 p.m., though doctors said there was no chance for him to live when he reached the hospital.

[pull quote] The assassin, firing from the sixth floor of the Texas School Book Depository Building near the Triple Underpass sent a Mauser 6.5 rifle bullet smashing into the President's head.

noxious blend of sanctimony and disingenuousness.

Calling the assassination a "shameful mark on this city's history," the writer loftily continued, "We join the rest of the nation in heartfelt sympathy and trust that the warped and distorted who become unstable in their opposition will retreat into darkness and not emerge until they regain the light of reasonableness and balance."

The *News'* editorialist seemed almost gleeful the following day for the chance to blame communists for Kennedy's death. "In the first agonizing hours after the assassination of President Kennedy," the editorial began, "the assumption was made by many and openly expressed by a few that the blame for this hideous crime rested at the doorstep of the 'radical right' in Dallas. Quite the opposite seems to be the case, making these assumptions and charges unfair. The man charged with the murder is pro-communist with strong 'radical left' ties."

The piece went on, "We have seen once again the murderous demonstration that the size of the domestic communist force is not the issue. Numbers mean very little in a conspiracy. Too many have scoffed at the danger by insisting that we have a mere 'handful' of domestic Reds—forgetting that a single determined pro-communist can murder the President of the United States and plunge an entire nation into serious crisis."

Relying on pitifully weak evidence to elevate a jack-leg Marxist such as Lee Harvey Oswald to membership in the supposed international communist conspiracy was precisely the sort of irresponsible straw man fabrication at which the *News* editorial writers excelled. No self-respecting communist would have wanted himself or his movement associated with the likes of Oswald.

Behind the *News'* editorial's bluster, however, lurked a different truth. It wasn't political conservatism, but intolerance—outright knee-jerk hostility to any opposing view—that characterized the thought of Ted Dealey and his fellow believers on the right. It was this brand of extremism that was discredited in Dallas by the events of November 22nd.

Fear for their own safety gripped some of the anti-communist crusaders after the shootings, possibly for good reason. Larry Schmidt and Bernard Weissman left town, the dust of The American Fact-Finding Committee settling to earth in their wake. Gen. Walker grabbed a plane for Shreveport, La., where he hunkered down for several days.

H. L. Hunt's daughter, Margaret Hunt Hill, later wrote that the Dallas police advised her father to decamp for safer precincts. "I do not get along well with being scared," the old man replied. "I am safe in my home."

Then the FBI called, "and warned him," Ms. Hill reported, "that mobs were singling out all conservatives who had been vocally anti-Kennedy, as Daddy had been in his radio broadcasts."

H. L. departed Dallas "within hours," she wrote.

The Hunt family went on high alert.

"We feared for anyone named Hunt. It was traumatic for the family to wonder if somebody was going to seek us out on revenge. In lock step, the media adhered to the story that Daddy had created an atmosphere of hate around Dallas toward Kennedy. It lasted two or three weeks. There were no attempts, though we did receive some hostile phone calls and a lot of hate mail, which naturally caused concern."

A more measured view of the assassination and its impact on Dallas came from Stanley Marcus, whom I interviewed in 1973 for a tenth-anniversary assassination retrospective in *Newsweek*.

Marcus was a marketing genius who transformed the store his father and aunt founded in Dallas in 1907 into a high-end retailing juggernaut. He was internationally respected as president of Neiman-Marcus and a pre-eminent local arbiter of taste. More important, his voice counted among members of the Citizens Council, wealthy Anglo-Christian oligarchs who then controlled every aspect of municipal affairs in Dallas.

I remember asking Marcus how a liberal Jew could flourish so in mid-century Dallas.

"The fact that I've been successful economically," he answered, gave him legitimacy in the Dallas business community. "If I hadn't been successful economically I'd have gotten the boot."

Marcus never shied from the fray. When it was announced in early Oct. 1963 that Ambassador Adali Stevenson would come to town on the 24th to address a UN Day celebration at the Memorial Theater, Gen. Walker immediately booked the facility for a "U.S. Day" rally on the 23rd, and even prevailed on Gov. Connally to proclaim Oct. 23, 1963, as "U.S. Day" in Texas.

Walker's event drew approximately 1,200 hard-right loyalists, whom the general enflamed with his rhetoric.

The UN Day organizers, led by local businessman Jack Goren, knew to expect trouble the next night after Walker practically equated attendance at the Stevenson rally with being a Communist. Worried about Stevenson's safety, Goren secured a promise from Chief Curry of added police security on the 24th.

Stanley Marcus accompanied Ambassador Stevenson to the meeting and introduced him to the large crowd.

TELEPHONE:
Riverside 7-611

DALLAS, TEXAS, FRIDAY, OCTOB

—Associated Press Photo by Carl Linde.
Ambassador Stevenson, flanked by police, shows shock after being hit on head by picket sign.

Stevenson Struck
With Sign, Booed

By MIKE QUINN   With an expression of shock on cratic candidate for president of

Businessman and icon of taste Stanley Marcus and others were concerned over the embarrassing assault on UN Ambassador Adlai Stevenson in October, prior to Kennedy's visit.

"Dallas was festering," he remembered. "There was tension, hate, and extreme bigotry."

The pickets who greeted Stevenson and Marcus outside the hall were noisy yet civil for the most part. But inside, as Stevenson began to speak, "there were hisses and grumbles and finally we thought we should end it and get out of there." said Marcus.

As they hurried to their car, placard-waving protesters chanted "US, not the UN! US not the UN!" A young student spat on the ambassador. When Stevenson broke from his police cordon to politely ask one woman why she was screaming at him, she hit him with her sign.

Once safely in the limo, Marcus recalled, Stevenson "was white as a sheet. His eyes bulged out. He said he couldn't understand this, not in America. He said he had been involved in many situations where pickets or opponents were present, but that this was different."

As the ambassador wiped away the spittle with his handkerchief, he turned to Marcus and wondered, "Are these people or are they animals?"

Mayor Earle Cabell and the Dallas City Council apologized to Stevenson and made it a crime in the city to curse or to shout obscenities during a public event. Congressman Alger thought that was overdoing things. He later said the boy who spat at the ambassador simply "lost his head because of his resentment against the UN that threatens his freedom and his country's freedom."

"I was physically afraid," Marcus told me. "I never want to go through anything like that again."

Yet he didn't back down.

On New Year's Day, 1964, Marcus bought half a page in the *News* and *Times Herald* for an open letter to the city, titled "What's Right With Dallas?"

The letter began by praising the city. "We think that our citizens are friendly and kind-hearted human beings who extend genuinely warm welcomes to newcomers to our city," Marcus wrote.

Then Marcus shifted gears: "That doesn't mean there aren't things about Dallas that couldn't be improved."

Turning to his real theme, he denounced political absolutism. "The rejection of this spirit of 'absolutism,'" he wrote, "and the acceptance and insistence by all citizens on toleration of differing points of view seem to us to be essential for the future health of our community,"

And he took a dig at the *News*. "We believe our newspapers have an important contribution to make in regard to this matter and we hope they will lead the way by the presentation of balanced points of view on controversial issues."

Stanley Marcus took a lot of pride in his letter. "I think [it] contributed to sobering the community," he told me. "I think it helped put things in perspective.

"The community as a whole appreciated the stance on that. But the fact was that we gave them hell without saying so. If we had said, 'What's Wrong With Dallas?' the bricks would have fallen down on me. But by saying, 'What's Right With Dallas?'—leading off with the positive and ending up with the negative—we got the message across in a sugar-coated form."

The ad prompted a rash of credit account cancellations at Neiman-Marcus, particularly from hard right Republicans in the West Texas oil towns of Midland and Odessa.

"Obviously, some preacher out there was dictating a letter because they were all the same," Marcus recollected. "They were saying I was a radical and had supported a man opposed to the free enterprise system. They were going to close their accounts.

"I wrote back to answer each, thanking them for writing, but telling them that I thought we had one thing in common and that was that we all believed in the democratic way of life and the free enterprise system. I expressed surprise that since we believed in the democratic form of government that they would take the role of the dictatorship countries by employing economic sanction.

"I didn't get any answer from most of them, but a couple wrote back and said they hadn't really looked at it that way before, and were now sorry that they'd written. Among those who closed their accounts, about 95 percent reopened them within three months."

In all, Marcus believed the assassination was a wake-up call that Dallas generally heeded. "I think the assassination brought about a spirit of moderation that wasn't there before," he said. "It had reached a point where when [Dallas conservatives] started talking about government, you wondered who the monster was that was about to devour you. The federal government was about to devour you. They built it up as a great big monster."

Bruce Alger, adamant as anyone on this point, would lose his congressional seat to Earle Cabell in 1964.

"The assassination sobered the community," said Marcus. "There was a recognition of the state of absolutism that had existed, and it gave way to more moderation."

An officer near the Texas Theater, the site of Oswald's arrest. *The Dallas Morning News'* editorial cartoon the day before the president's assassination, eerily showed Kennedy hunting with a scoped rifle.

CHAPTER SEVEN

Oswald: "I'm just a patsy"

Readers of the Sunday morning *News* were offered two distinct and contrasting views of accused assassin/cop killer Lee Harvey Oswald.

"He impressed me as a quiet, rather modest, nice-appearing chap who was doing an extremely good job as far as I could tell," Roy Truly, superintendent at the book depository, told *News* reporter Carlos Conde. "He gave us no trouble, was always on time and went about his work in such fashion that there was no indication there was anything wrong in his mind."

Directly adjacent to Conde's piece on page 10 of the front section, Bill Alexander, assistant district attorney, begged to differ. "He's the most arrogant person I ever met," Alexander told one of our reporters.

About seven on Friday night, Alexander represented the State of Texas before Justice of the Peace David L. Johnston at Oswald's arraignment for the murder of Officer J.D. Tippit in Oak Cliff. Before the court proceeding, the assistant DA informed Oswald of the charge in a brief meeting.

"Don't tell me about it," Oswald replied. "Tell my legal representative," even though he had none. In fact, Oswald asked repeatedly to be provided counsel, indicating his choice was either John J. Abt, a New York City attorney associated with left-wing causes, or perhaps a local ACLU lawyer. (Oswald applied for membership in the ACLU 18 days before the assassination.) He never was provided counsel, which could have caused headaches for the prosecution had Lee Harvey Oswald survived to stand trial.

Oswald at police headquarters on Nov. 23, 1963. Note (below) the photographer shooting news footage with a 16mm camera. This photo tells one story and the cropped version to the left, which focuses on a specific area of the image, tells another.

"I got the impression he enjoys being in the spotlight," Alexander said. "It's obvious he is a Communist sympathizer."

Oswald apparently disliked Alexander, too. At one point, according to the assistant prosecutor, the accused complained, "The way you're treating me, I'd might as well be in Russia."

Far trickier than the Tippit indictment would be charging Oswald with assassination. For one thing, at the time it was not a federal crime to kill the president, at least under most circumstances. (Oswald also had violated no federal or state law by bringing his rifle to work that morning.)

Dallas District Attorney Henry Wade surrounded by reporters. (Nov. 23, 1963)

Henry Wade, Dallas County district attorney from 1951 to 1987, probably is most widely remembered today as the Wade in *Roe v. Wade*, the 1973 Supreme Court case that made abortion legal in the United States. On Nov. 22, Henry Wade along with 2,500 other guests was just tucking into his steak lunch at the Trade Mart, looking forward to the first couple's imminent arrival, when news of the gunshots in Dealey Plaza reached them.

Rev. Luther Holcomb, president of the Dallas Ministerial Alliance, led the stunned assemblage in a brief prayer, then Henry Wade headed for his office.

"I didn't think I'd be involved in it," Wade later said to me. "About an hour after I got back to the office, I got a call from Barefoot Sanders, the U.S. attorney here. He said, 'Henry, do you

93

realize that the highest federal penalty for killing a president is for assault on a president, and it carries a penalty of just five years? This is going to be your baby.'"

The justice department for a time toyed with invoking a federal law against homicides committed on government property—the Lincoln Continental in which Kennedy rode. "It was a possibility," Wade told me, "but they decided it wouldn't cover this case." Just then Henry Wade's life was complicated by a radio report that the Dallas police, in a court filing, had somehow implicated the Soviets in Oswald's crimes. Moments later, the district attorney received a call from LBJ aide Cliff Carter in Washington.

"He said they were very concerned about how this kind of thing could affect our relations with Russia," Wade recollected. "I was concerned about it, too, because anything you allege in an indictment you have to prove." The DA headed for police headquarters, "to make sure they were filing just a straight murder case." He encountered "a wild scene," he remembered. "Newsmen, I would say, created most of it. They were running up and down the hall, trying to get in the room where Oswald was."

He recalled that the evidence against Oswald in the Tippit case was much stronger than for the Kennedy assassination. "The investigators told me that night they had evidence against Oswald that was stronger than it later turned out to be," he said. "They had a palm print on the gun, for example, and an expert who tentatively identified it [as Oswald's]. But I don't think the FBI ever did identify that palm print."

Wade filed his assassination charge against Oswald at approximately 1:30 a.m. on Saturday.

A prosecutor's best evidence usually is a confession, preferably on tape as well as signed. But if ever there was a chance of extracting the truth from Lee Harvey Oswald—a long-shot proposition—the Dallas police fumbled their opportunity.

Capt. Will Fritz, a 31-year veteran of the

Capt. Will Fritz, head of the Homicide and Robbery Bureau, interviewed by Bill Mercer of KRLD radio in Dallas.

police force, had been head of the Homicide and Robbery Bureau for at least a decade. Diminutive, low-key, given to mumbling, the captain had a well-deserved reputation as a brilliant interrogator. His forte was putting his subject at ease, developing trust, then gradually eliciting cooperation. Had Capt. Fritz carried out the questioning under rigidly-controlled conditions, Oswald might have been coaxed into damning disclosures.

Maybe.

Instead, a stream of cops, federal agents, and assorted law enforcement officials passed in and out of Fritz's office during the Oswald interrogation, including representatives from the FBI, Secret Service, Postal Service, U.S. Marshals, the Dallas police and the DA's office—even the DA himself. None of the conversations were tape recorded because the Dallas police department lacked the equipment to do so.

To his credit, Capt. Fritz understood the importance of creating such a reliable record of interrogations. He had included tape recorders in his budget requests for the past six years, at least, but always was turned down.

In any event, Oswald refused to crack, or even bend.

If, during approximately eleven hours of intermittent questioning conducted over two days, the prisoner was scared, confused, remorseful, or looking for some sort of deal, he never betrayed it. Instead, Oswald remained defiant throughout, by turns sarcastic or silent, apparently energized by this confrontation with authority figures, reveling in their undivided attention, delighting in their frustration.

This was Lee Harvey Oswald's moment.

Fritz later told me that he didn't consider the subject particularly troublesome. "If we would just talk to him quietly," said the captain, "he would respond. But every time I would ask a question that meant something, that would produce evidence, he immediately told me he wouldn't tell me about it. He seemed to anticipate what I was going to ask."

FBI Agent James W. Bookhout, who sat in on much of the interrogation, agreed. "You might say," Bookhout testified before the Warren Commission, "that any time you asked a question that would be pertinent to the investigation that would be the type of question he would refuse to discuss." Or simply lie about.

For example, Oswald vehemently denied owning a rifle.

Even when Capt. Fritz showed him a copy of the mail-order invoice that demonstrated he bought the Mannlicher-Carcano under his "Alek Hidell" alias, he claimed the information was false, that since leaving the Marines the only thing he'd fired was a little .22.

When detectives H.M. Moore, Gus Rose, and Richard Stovall exercised a search warrant on Saturday morning to examine Oswald's belongings in Ruth Paine's garage, they found two photos. Each clearly depicted him holding a rifle and a pistol. Fritz jammed the pictures at Oswald on Saturday night. "What about these?" the captain asked.

Oswald was not ruffled. "They're obviously fake photographs," he sneered. He cheekily accused the police of superimposing the weapons on pictures taken of him after his arrest. Fritz would produce the pictures once again on Sunday morning, but Oswald just laughed and said his non-existent lawyer would prove they'd been doctored.

(The pictures were later authenticated before the Warren Commission by photo experts and by Marina Oswald, who testified that she took the photos herself using Lee's Imperial Reflex camera.)

At the initial interrogation, Oswald admitted only to carrying a pistol and resisting arrest. When Fritz asked him why he had a handgun with him in the theater, Oswald replied, "Well, you know about a pistol. I just carried it."

He said he bought it in Fort Worth, which the cops already knew to be untrue. The pistol had been mail-ordered from a Los Angeles company.

Asked why he rented the North Beckley Street room under a false name, O. H. Lee, he said the landlady, Mrs. Johnson, just got it mixed up. He insisted he told her he was Lee, not Mr. Lee, even though he'd clearly printed O.H. Lee in the register I was shown by Earlene Roberts.

Oswald even lied about his reason for visiting Irving on the night before the assassination. He said he went there on Thursday, instead of Friday, because Ruth Paine's kids were planning a weekend party. He didn't want to be in the way. There actually was such a party; it had been held the previous weekend.

Oswald claimed he never mentioned curtain rods to Buell Frazier, adding that Frazier and his sister both were mistaken about him carrying a long package that morning. Oswald said the only sack he carried was his lunch.

Why did he leave the depository building?

Because foreman Bill Shelley told him there would be no more work, so he left. Shelley later testified he never saw Oswald after noon that day.

The interview sessions were punctuated by two arraignments and three fingerprinting and photographing sessions. Oswald also took part in four line-ups: at 4:35, 6:30, 7:55 and again on Saturday afternoon at 2:15.

Late, about midnight on Friday, as he was being led down the corridor from the final interrogation session of the night, he stopped to hold an impromptu press conference.

The brief encounter with reporters would be notable on three accounts. First, it was the single time Oswald spoke in public. When a newsman asked if he shot the president, he answered, "No, I have not been charged with that. In fact, nobody has said that to me yet. The first thing I heard about it was when the newspaper reporters in the hall asked me that question."

Second, there was his enigmatic remark to the crowd, "I'm just a patsy." I believe by "patsy" Oswald surely meant to portray himself as an innocent victim of what conspiracy theorist Mark Lane later would famously term the "rush to judgment." The remark has also been interpreted by assassination buffs to mean patsy in the more specific sense of fall guy, or scapegoat.

Third, there was a surprise presence at the midnight meeting, Jack Ruby. The club owner clearly can be seen in a film record of the session, standing on a table. That an unauthorized "civilian" at police headquarters should have such casual access to the world's most famous accused killer was just another of the many security screw-ups that characterized the assassination story. This official laxity certainly helped foster some of the darker conspiracy speculation that ever since has hung over Dallas.

At the very least, Chief Jesse Curry emerged from the saga as a well-meaning but weak and ill-prepared administrator whose shortcomings greatly exacerbated a national tragedy.

Harsh, though fair, in my view, that judgment nevertheless doesn't reach the heart of the matter.

Neither the DPD, nor the FBI, or even the Secret Service performed as it should have that weekend because no one really believed that such an act against the president was possible, not in the United States.

What you cannot conceive of is impossible to prevent. Stanley Marcus first expressed this insight to me in a different context.

"The assassination," he said, "was the beginning of a process that shattered some of the myths about the sanctity of the United States as something God had put on earth that was completely different from any other country. South Americans assassinated their presidents, but in the United States that never happened."

Of course it did, fairly frequently. Americans just have short memories. Lincoln in 1865. Garfield in 1881. McKinley in 1901. All were cut down. Targets of attempted assassinations include Andrew Jackson, Franklin Roosevelt, Harry Truman, Gerald Ford and Ronald Reagan. In each case the assailant acted alone, except for the 1950 attack on Truman, in which two would-be killers took part. Firearms always were the weapon of choice.

Marcus' point nevertheless was well taken. "The United States won every war, until we got to Vietnam," he continued. "Students never rioted here, until the mid-1960s. We've gone through these things ever since, and suddenly Americans have come to realize that the good Lord has not singled them out as a favorite people.

"America has taken a terrific ego beating, which it well deserved. It was good because we had expanded our ego beyond all sense of objective reality. We now know we are human beings with problems. That should give us a certain degree of humility."

Stanley Marcus died at 96, four months after the events of September 11, 2001.

•••••••••••••••••••••••••••••

Jesse Curry had much to be humble about. Just as the possibility of a Lee Harvey Oswald obviously didn't penetrate too deeply into the federal security agencies' thinking, Curry was blinded by his preconceptions.

"We knew some people here were really bitter and wanted Oswald dead," Curry later told me. "That was apparent from the phone calls and just the general mood of the community. But we never, not for a second, thought in terms of just one individual."

The only exception he considered, Curry said, was the possibility of a rogue cop murdering Oswald. "We discussed the fact that some

Two perspectives of Oswald during the "midnight walk," Nov. 23, 1963 (left). Sea of reporters (right) cram a hallway while Chief Curry is interviewed. Note the massive and heavy "new" video cameras (background) used to carry the story live.

Midnight walk

officer might become too emotionally aroused or upset that he might take things in his own hands," he explained. "That's why we were very careful about those officers we assigned to the basement."

Lee Harvey Oswald was to be loaded in the City Hall basement for transfer to Sheriff Bill Decker's custody at the county jail on Dealey Plaza, less than a mile away. The move was anticipated nearly from the moment Oswald first was brought to Capt. Fritz's office Friday afternoon.

On Saturday afternoon, Dan Rather, 32, did a CBS broadcast from the jail, advising viewers that Oswald was expected there "any time now."

Rather described a large wreath of mourning that had been placed on the grassy area just opposite the jail and the book depository. "All day long," said the newsman, "crowds have built up and waned and then again built up, as people came by just to look at the spot, walk around the wreath...The crowd now has moved to the sidewalk facing the county jail, facing the wreath. Not many people at this moment are looking at the building where the shot came; most of these people have seen it. Now they're waiting for a glimpse of Lee Harvey Oswald."

The crowds would be disappointed. Chief Curry canceled his original plan to move Oswald at 4 p.m. on Saturday after Will Fritz requested more time with Oswald. The captain mistakenly believed he was making progress.

Next morning, Curry reviewed his options with Capt. Fritz as well as Deputy Chief M.W. Stevenson and Assistant Chief Charles Batchelor. One idea they considered was to move Oswald in an armored truck. Unfortunately, the turreted models of the day wouldn't fit down the vehicle ramp into the basement.

Curry then called Sheriff Decker, whose department generally handled prisoner transfers from City Hall to the county jail. "I told him we were finished interrogating Oswald," Curry recalled to me, "that we weren't making any real strides. We chatted a bit about a couple of threats we had received by phone."

Decker, who had taken a late-night call from an individual promising "one hundred citizens, pure Americans" would grab Oswald and "kill that Communist son-of-a-bitch," seemed content to leave Chief Curry in charge of the matter.

"When I told him his boys could pick up the prisoner at any

time," Curry said, "he just sorta changed the subject. He wasn't in any real hurry. Looking back, I think he country-boyed me."

Jesse Curry bit the bullet. "So I told him I thought we had more manpower, and we'd bring him soon. I'd call him when we left the building." Curry hung up and turned to Stevenson and Batchelor.

"It's our deal," he said. "Let's get it done."

The Dallas Morning News

WHERE TO FIND
See Page
Announcements 1 18-19
Business 2   3
Classified 4 4-12
Comics 2   6-7
Crossword 4   2
Editorials 4   2

VOL. 115—NO. 56   TELEPHONE Riverside 7-811   DALLAS, TEXAS, MONDAY, NOVEMBER 25, 1963 — 52 PAGES IN 4 SECTIONS   ★★★★   PRICE 5 CENTS

Thousands Pay Homage to Martyred President   Story, Page 2

CLUB OWNER KILLS OSWALD   Story, Page 3

CHAPTER EIGHT

"Lee, what the Sam Hill's going on?"

After I saw Jack Ruby in the *News* cafeteria on Friday morning, he headed for our second-floor ad department to visit with Don Campbell, an ad salesman and another of my close friends on the paper's staff. I was married in Don's house the year before.

Ruby complained to Campbell that the two venues he operated, the Carousel Club, his strip joint on Commerce, and the Vegas Club, an after-hours destination in the city's Oak Lawn district, weren't doing well financially. He also bragged a bit about his prowess at breaking up fights and riding herd on the numerous drunken yahoos who frequented his establishments.

He told Campbell he recently had a major altercation, where he had to kick two or three customers out. "He said, 'They didn't know what hit them when I inserted myself,'" Don recalled. "He said it was a good thing he was in such good shape, because, 'you just can't find too many take-charge guys around.'"

Ruby was known to bully and abuse his patrons, especially if they were too tanked to fight back. In the spring of 1962 at the Carousel Club I saw him toss a drunk down the long flight of stairs to the street. Then he ran after the man and kicked him as he scrambled out the front door. I couldn't figure out why Ruby attacked this particular customer. The club was quiet, things seemed to be going smoothly and, as far as I could tell, the guy hadn't caused any trouble.

But Ruby had a hair-trigger temper. In seconds, he could change from easy-going to fists-in-your-face furious.

Campbell, the first witness to be called at Ruby's later murder trial, testified that the club owner behaved on Thursday as he normally did. He made no mention to Don of the president's visit.

Campbell departed the office at 12:25, leaving Ruby to work out his usual tiny notice for the weekend papers, usually a one-column ad, no more than three or four inches deep.

John Newnam, another News ad salesman, walked into the department about this time and noticed Ruby seated near Campbell's desk, reading the morning paper. "Look at this dirty ad," Ruby exclaimed in disgust as he pointed at the black-bordered announcement that Weissman and Schmidt had placed in the *News*.

Newnam would recall Ruby saying something to the effect he couldn't imagine a Jew promulgating such a message of hatred. "We've seen too much of that already," he said.

At that moment someone ran into the room, shouting, "The president's been shot! The president's been shot! I just heard it on the radio!"

Everyone gathered to watch the news on the television in promotion director Dick Jeffrey's office. The set was tuned of course to WFAA, where anchor Jay Watson had just broken into *The Julie Benell Show*, a local women's program, to break the news.

"You'll excuse the fact that I'm out of breath," said Watson, clearly befuddled, doing an impromptu stand-up from some anonymous corner of the WFAA newsroom. "But about ten or fifteen minutes ago a tragic thing—from all indications at this point—has happened to the city of Dallas."

Ad man Dick Saunders watched Ruby together with the others as Watson read United Press International's newsbreak on the assassination. "President Kennedy and Governor Connally have been cut down by assassin's bullets in Dallas."

"He sat there staring unbelieving at the television set," said Saunders of Ruby. "He was virtually speechless, quite unusual for Jack Ruby."

Ruby watched the unfolding tragedy

Rubenstein at News At Time of Shooting

By HUGH AYNESWORTH

Jack Rubenstein, whom police have charged with the vengance-killing of President Kennedy's assassin, was four blocks away when the President was shot last Friday.

Rubenstein, known as Jack Ruby since he came to Dallas approximately 10 years ago from Chicago, ate a late breakfast at approximately 11 a.m. Friday in The Dallas News cafeteria.

He pulled up a chair at a table about 15 feet from the cashier and sat for a length of time with two unidentified men.

He may have been there for more than an hour.

At 12:10 p.m., Ruby walked into The News' display advertising department and asked the whereabout of John Newnam, a News advertising man who had handled Ruby's account for several years.

The time was established because advertising representative Donald Campbell said he realized deadline time was at hand (deadline was noon, though Ruby was habitually late or close to deadline time).

For this reason, Campbell said he looked immediately at the clock. Campbell said he then called the layout department and reserved the usual ad space for Ruby, figuring that Newnam would return from lunch soon and work out the final arrangements.

"He was all wound up," Campbell said. "He remarked what a 'lousy business' he was in, but said, 'If I'd get in some other business I'd have the same headaches, or maybe more of them.'"

Campbell said Ruby talked "more than he has ever talked before. He just rambled on and on."

Campbell said he left the office about 12:20 p.m., leaving Ruby there.

Nobody would confirm seeing Ruby between 12:20 and about 12:45 p.m., though some persons vaguely said they believed Ruby sat down at Newnam's desk and began to lay out his own ad.

Newnam, who had watched the presidential parade from six or eight blocks away with some fellow News workers, said he returned "about 12:45" and noted Ruby sitting at his (Newnam's) desk, working on the ad.

One of the few stories that identified Ruby by his birth name and established his whereabouts at the time of the assassination. (*The Dallas Morning News*, Nov. 26, 1963)

for about 30 minutes, then he grabbed a telephone. His first call was to Andrew Armstrong, his assistant at the Carousel Club. "We're going to close the club," several ad salesmen overheard Ruby tell Armstrong. "I don't know what else to do."

Next, Ruby called his sister, Eva Grant, who seemed as devastated as her brother by the news. "My God, what do they want?!" she screamed into the receiver.

As Ruby put down the phone, he said to Newnam, "John, I will have to leave Dallas."

Members of the Warren Commission would ask Ruby what he meant by the remark.

"I don't know why I said that," he told them. "But it is a funny reaction you feel. The city is terribly let down by the tragedy that happened. And I said, 'John, I am not opening up tonight' And I don't know what else transpired. I know people were just heartbroken… I left the building and went down, and I got in my car and I couldn't stop crying."

There's no doubt that Jack Ruby was highly agitated in the wake of the assassination. For the next two days, he was a blur around Dallas. He arrived from the *News* at the Carousel Club about 1:45 on Friday, and set to work with Andrew Armstrong, notifying employees by telephone that the bar would be closed that night. A couple of hours later, Ruby decided to close the Carousel for three days, and instructed employee Larry Crafard to post a notice to that effect on the front door. "But don't put it out til dark," he ordered, "so they [his competitors] won't know in advance."

Ruby had a manic need to talk, if not listen, after the assassination. He called his friend Ralph Paul, who owned the Bull Pen Drive-In, a hamburger joint in Arlington, midway between Dallas and Fort Worth, and advised Paul to close his business, too. He tried repeatedly to reach Alice Nichols, a former girlfriend. He also called his youngest sister, Eileen Kaminsky, in Chicago. She later said her brother was "crying incessantly. He couldn't seem to stop. He told me he was going to leave Dallas, that he could never live this down."

As the hours passed, a crazed grandiosity crept into Ruby's remarks. He'd learned at the *News* that Bernard Weissman placed the offensive full-page ad and somehow connected that to the fact that he and Weissman both were Jews. The "dirty ad" upset him, Ruby told many of the people he telephoned.

He impulsively called Temple Shearith Israel in Dallas to inquire about the schedule of evening services, and then finally reached Alice Nichols to inform her he'd be attending at 8 p.m. He showed up for the final few minutes of the service. Afterward, Ruby spoke with Rabbi Hillel Silverman about his sister Eva's recent operation, but made no mention of the dead president.

The second theme of his conversations in these hours was "those poor Kennedy kids," several people recalled, as well as John Jr. and Caroline's widowed mother. Ruby later told me and other reporters that his motive for killing Lee Harvey Oswald was to spare Jacqueline Kennedy the pain of Oswald's trial, at which she'd likely be forced to testify.

After sharing a delicatessen dinner with Eva at her home on Friday evening, Ruby headed for city hall. He was a familiar figure to many cops in Dallas, and so it was not surprising (though appalling) that Jack Ruby could insinuate himself into the tumult on the third floor.

Following Oswald's midnight remarks to the press, Ruby edged up to District Attorney Wade. "Hi, Henry," he said, "don't you know me? I am Jack Ruby. I run the Vegas Club."

The next thing the DA knew, Ruby had reporter Ike Pappas from television station WNEW in New York in front of him, ready to conduct an exclusive interview. When Pappas was through, Ruby had a disc jockey from local radio station KLIF on the phone, also eager for an interview.

"I felt like he thought he was some kind of editor," Wade told me afterward. "It was hard to get rid of him."

Bob Jarboe, an Associated Press photographer sent to the station to get a photo of Wade, found that every time he got the DA centered in his lens, it seemed Jack Ruby would pop out of nowhere and put his chin on Wade's shoulder, ruining the shot.

"I sure wish I would have gone ahead and taken the picture anyway," says Jarboe.

From city hall, Ruby traveled over to KLIF with a bag of sandwiches for the staff. Then, about 4 a.m., he appeared at the *Times Herald*, where he spoke with Roy Pryor, an employee in the composing room who'd just completed his shift. Ruby told Pryor about attending Oswald's press conference. He called Oswald "a little weasel of a guy" and turned tearful and agitated when he talked of the now-fatherless

This Nov. 23 photograph in *The Dallas Times Herald* of Jack Ruby's Carousel Club was one of several photographs taken at random of businesses that closed because of the assassination. Ruby had not yet killed Oswald.

John Kennedy children.

A half hour later, Ruby went home to wake his roommate and employee, George Senator, and to call Larry Crafard at the club. He excitedly instructed Crafard to meet him and Senator at the Nichols Garage adjacent to the club, and to bring a Polaroid camera.

Ruby had just seen a billboard urging the impeachment of U.S. Supreme Court Chief Justice Earl Warren, and intended to take pictures of it. Senator later testified at trial that his roommate was upset both about the billboard's message and the Weissman ad in the *News*. "He said he couldn't understand anything of this nature being in the paper," said Senator in court. "He said it was a crime for something like this to appear in the paper. He said he thought the John Birch Society or the Communist Party or a combination of both were behind the billboard and the ad."

(Senator would later capitalize on his association with the soon-to-be-notorious club owner by selling off Ruby's wardrobe, and then some. Jack Ruby owned just two suits, for which he could not have paid more than $50 a piece. But his ex-roommate sold at least four "authentic" Ruby suits for as much $300 each.)

Recalling that the *News* ad had included a post office box address for Weissman's and Schmidt's "committee," Ruby's next and last stop on a long night of dashing around Dallas was the downtown post office, where an employee refused to provide the box holder's name.

He couldn't sleep, so Ruby watched television at home through the morning. By about one that afternoon he was seen in Dealey Plaza, walking around, talking to people, handling the wreaths. It is possible that Ruby had come to Dealey Plaza because, like Dan Rather and many other people, he expected Oswald to be transferred to the county jail that afternoon.

A policeman who pointed out Oswald's sixth-floor sniper's perch for Ruby said he was deeply morose, obviously troubled.

He seemed even more frenzied, as well. Saturday afternoon Ruby was repeatedly spotted at Sol's Turf Bar on Commerce, a favorite old haunt, as well as the Carousel Club and police headquarters at City Hall.

Frank Bellochio, a jewelry store owner Ruby encountered that day at Sol's, said that Ruby ranted on about the ad, declaring it was part of a plot against Jews in Dallas. As he showed his three Polaroids of the "Impeach Earl Warren" sign around the bar, a patron asked if he could have one of them. Ruby said no. According to this witness' later testimony, he "acted like it was a big scoop or something."

Ruby was still working the phones hard, too. In one call from the Nichols Garage to Ken Dowe, a KLIF announcer, Ruby discussed Oswald's coming transfer to the county jail. "You know I'll be there," he told Dowe.

About 4 p.m. on Saturday, Ruby called his lawyer, Stanley Kauffman. "He told me he had tried to get Weissman's address at the post office," Kauffman explained to me a few days later, "and said he was 'helping law enforcement.' He was rabid about the Weissman ad. He thought the black border had an inner meaning, proof that the man knew the president was going to be assassinated. I've seen him worked up lots of times, but on this afternoon he was really frantic."

Ruby appears to have spent most of the time between 4 and 8 o'clock that day at his sister Eva Grant's apartment, calling people, complaining to them about Weissman. When he and his sister couldn't find Weissman in the phone book, they concluded the name was an alias.

In the midst of it all, Ruby also called Russ Knight, a KLIF on-air personality known as "The Weird Beard," and talked to Knight about the billboard. According to Knight, Ruby asked him during this call, "Who *is* Earl Warren anyway?"

Ruby took a one-hour nap at his sister's apartment on Saturday evening—his first real rest since Thursday—and was back at his own apartment by 9:30 to take a call from 19-year-old Karen Bennett Carlin, one of his strippers. Carlin, who performed as "Little Lynn," needed money, a simple business problem for Jack Ruby that nonetheless would later bear critically on the issue of his frame of mind and intent the following morning.

According to George Senator, Ruby and Carlin exchanged angry words over the telephone, followed by Ruby's promise that he'd meet her at the Carousel Club in an hour.

Still another incidental character, Lawrence Meyers, a friend from Ruby's Chicago days, was in town on business, staying at a local hotel. Ruby called Meyers, who later reported his old friend was "incensed" that other strip-club owners were staying open over the weekend, which meant lost revenue. Ruby raged to Meyers about the ad, the billboard, and the harm they might do to local Jews.

"I've got to do something about this," he said. Meyers was unsure if his friend meant to "do something" about his competitors or Lee Harvey Oswald. He and Ruby agreed to meet for dinner on Sunday night.

Meantime, Karen Carlin and her husband were standing in front of the Carousel Club, impatient for their money. When Ruby didn't show, Little Lynn called him from the Nichols Garage next door, pleading

SHE WANTED TO HELP
Stripper Karen Lynn Bennett, 19, and her boss, Jack Ruby, were all smiles early in November when this photograph was taken. Miss Bennett, who worked at the Carousel Club under the name "Little Lynn," was released late Monday on $1,000 bond after searchers found a pistol in her purse when she appeared to testify at Ruby's bond hearing before Judge Joe B. Brown.—AP Photo.

Robert Oswald, who worked at a Denton brick factory.

for at least enough money for the two to get home to Fort Worth. At Ruby's request, garage worker Huey Reeves gave Carlin $5, made out a receipt for her to sign and time-stamped it at 10:33. Half an hour later, Ruby appeared at the garage, repaid Reeves his $5 and then, agitated as ever, went upstairs to make some calls from the Carousel Club phone.

Among those he reached was Breck Wall, who operated a popular revue called "Bottoms Up," then playing at the Adolphus Hotel, across Commerce Street from the Carousel. Since the show had been canceled because of the assassination, Wall was visiting relatives in Galveston, where he took Ruby's call. They discussed Oswald and the killings, Wall later remembered, but Ruby seemed more interested in discussing Dallas promoters Abe and Barney Weinstein, whose amateur strip shows were killing the Carousel Club's business, he complained. Ruby was trying everything he could to close down the Weinsteins' operation, and solicited Wall's views on whether the performers' union, the American Guild of Variety Artists (AGVA) would support or oppose him.

Ruby made one of his final calls of the night at 12:45, to check on his sister Eva. Then he went home and was asleep by 1:30, he later told police.

••••••••••••••••••••••••••••••

Robert Oswald's last moments with his younger brother Lee were spent in a small visiting room on the fifth floor of Dallas City Hall. Robert, 29, and Lee, 24, were separated by a Plexigas partition. They spoke to one another by telephone.

Robert Oswald worked in the marketing department at the Acme Brick Co. in Denton, the same little town where Larry Grove and I finally tracked down William Whaley, sleeping in his cab.

On Friday the 22nd, Robert and some business associates had just finished their regularly-scheduled luncheon meeting and were departing the restaurant when the cashier informed them the president had been shot. Back at his office, Robert turned on his radio to hear someone named Harvey Lee Oswald described as JFK's accused killer. The announcer soon added that a Dallas policeman had been shot dead as well. Then he repeated the suspect's name, getting it right this time: Lee Harvey Oswald.

"That's my kid brother," Robert mumbled in amazement to no one in particular. "Something must have shown on my face," he later told me. "Because the receptionist at the company began to cry."

About noon on Saturday, the 23rd, Robert arrived at City Hall to visit Lee. Jim Bowie, one of Henry Wade's top assistants, met with him beforehand, and laid out for Robert the already-persuasive case that his brother had killed both Kennedy and Officer Tippit.

Bowie raised the possibility that Lee might tell Robert exactly what his role had been in the killings, clearly hoping Robert would encourage Lee to do so and would report what he heard. Robert was noncommittal.

As Robert recalled their conversation to me, Lee spoke first. "How are you?"

"Fine," Robert answered.

He noted cuts and bruises on Lee's face, but his brother assured him the police were treating him all right.

"I cannot or would not say anything because the line is apparently tapped," Lee advised, then proceeded to monopolize the next two or three minutes, speaking in a strange, mechanical voice and saying, as Robert recalled to the Warren Commission, very little worth remembering.

"I was not talking to the Lee I knew," Robert later wrote in his diary.

He steered the conversation toward family matters, learning from Lee that he had a new niece, one-month-old Rachel. Lee said he'd wanted a boy, "but you know how that goes."

Eventually, Robert took up the big question.

"Lee, what the Sam Hill is going on?"

"What are you talking about?" he replied.

"They've got you charged with shooting a police officer and murdering the president. They've got your rifle and pistol."

"Do not," Lee cautioned, "form any opinion on the so-called evidence."

His tone was inappropriately flippant, which bothered Robert deeply. He later told me that he stared hard into Lee's eyes. "I was pretty intense. I was looking for some kind of reaction from him, anything at all. But there was absolutely no expression. He knew why I was looking so intensely at him. He said, 'Brother, you won't find anything there.' And he was right. There was nothing."

Later that afternoon, as Robert recounted the visit to his wife, Vada, and her parents, he suddenly broke into tears. "I didn't know exactly what to believe yet," he told me. "I thought there'd be time to talk more to him, to find out. But it wasn't to be."

Marina Oswald and her mother-in-law, 56-year-old Marguerite Oswald, came to visit Lee that afternoon, as well. Marina later told me her husband glowered when he saw his mother standing behind her. "Why did you bring that fool with you?" he snapped. "I don't want to talk to her."

"She's your mother," Marina informed him. "Of course she came."

Perhaps mindful of how prisoners routinely were treated in her home country, Marina's first concern was Lee's physical well-being. "Have they been beating you?" she asked.

"Don't worry about me," he answered, then quickly changed the subject, asking after his daughters. Marina told me she was fearful of saying anything that might get Lee into even deeper trouble. "I asked him if we could talk about things," she explained, "important things. Are they listening in?"

"Of course, we can't talk about anything important," he answered.

Unaware that the Mannlicher-Carcano already was in police custody, she asked him, "What about the gun?"

"It's a mistake," he answered with a smile. "I'm not guilty."

Marina also was unaware that Detectives Moore, Rose, and Stovall had recovered from Ruth Paine's garage that afternoon copies of the photo she'd taken of Lee with his gun. She had rounded up two other copies of the pictures, which she placed in her shoe that day and destroyed that night.

Lee again mentioned the New York attorney John Abt to Marina and said he still hoped to reach Abt. "He said, 'There are people who will help me,'" she recalled. "'We are not alone.'"

Marina Oswald began to cry. She later told me that she knew almost from his first words that Lee was guilty. The shock of that realization was compounded by worries that she and the two girls now had no money and no permanent place to live. Moreover, all three bore a universally infamous surname. Would someone try to hurt them? In the end, would U.S. authorities ship her and her daughters back to the Soviet Union?

Consumed by these fears, yet loyal in her way to her husband, Marina was deeply conflicted as the guards came to escort Lee away from the Plexiglas partition.

She told him for the last time ever that she loved him, and then he was gone.

••••••••••••••••••••••••••••••

Jesse Curry, who resigned as Dallas police chief in March 1966 and died of a heart attack 14 years later, was haunted to his grave by the events of Sunday morning, Nov. 24, 1963.

Marina Oswald escorted by Dallas Police. (Nov. 22, 1963)

The criticism that Curry and his department took for failing to adequately protect President Kennedy on Friday, the 22nd, was in part mitigated by the speed with which the Dallas police apprehended Lee Harvey Oswald and brought him in alive.

But then came the Sunday disaster. For years afterward, Curry received regular hate mail accusing him of everything from incompetency to complicity in Oswald's murder, often linking him to the Kennedy and Tippit killings, too.

He never shirked his responsibility for handling the transfer as he did, and never tried to weasel out of the decision, even as he freely conceded it was a bad choice. Had he the chance to do it again, the chief told me, "I would have cleared all the newsmen out of the building. I know that would have been very unpopular, but in view of what happened, it would have been the thing to do."

Curry denied that he was put under any official pressure to display his prisoner to the press, even though it was widely rumored that Dallas City Manager Elgin Crull instructed the chief to make Oswald's transfer "an open move, so people can see Oswald was not mistreated." (This was no trivial point at the time. Dallas County Medical Examiner Earl Rose reported that unnamed members of the Oswald family insisted on examining Lee's body for signs of injury before he was autopsied.)

Late on Saturday, over the vehement objections of his senior staff, Chief Curry told reporters they wouldn't miss anything next morning if they were on hand at City Hall by ten.

Captain Fritz didn't like the idea of a public transfer; he suggested using an armored car as a decoy.

Detective Jim Leavelle, forever famous in Beers and Jackson photographs as the cop in the light suit and Stetson who was handcuffed to Oswald, told me he advised Curry to "double-cross" the media, to move the suspect by surprise—a strategy that I personally expected Curry would carry out. It made no sense to move him in public.

But the chief was adamant. "I told them, promised them they'd see the man moved," Curry replied to Leavelle. "I want them to see we haven't abused him. And the only way to do that is to let them view the transfer."

································

There can be no doubt that Ruby knew of Chief Curry's plan to move Oswald on Sunday morning. It was announced on radio and television numerous times.

If, as some conspiracy theorists have surmised, Ruby was part of a plot to silence Oswald, it stands to reason that the club owner would have appeared with his gun at City Hall by the appointed hour, 10 a.m.

Instead, Ruby was awakened that morning by a call from his cleaning lady, Elnora Pitts. Apparently he was in no hurry to rise and consumed a leisurely breakfast.

George Senator told me his roommate headed to the apartment building laundry room with a load of wash about 9 o'clock. Telephone company records show that at exactly 10:19, a still-irate Karen Carlin called from Fort Worth, demanding $25 more that she needed for rent and groceries. Ruby told her he'd wire the money by Western Union later that morning.

I awoke about 9:30, turned on the television and was surprised to learn that Oswald was still at the police lock-up, still awaiting transfer that morning to Sheriff Decker's custody.

"Oh my God!" I thought. "Curry's taking a big risk."

"Look," I said to my wife. "We've got to get down there!" I didn't shave. I didn't eat. We just threw on some clothes and I drove like mad for City Hall.

Jack Ruby meanwhile had wired Karen Carlin her money from the nearest Western Union office and was walking back to his car, parked on Main Street, when he noticed a commotion a block away at city hall. Curious, Ruby detoured toward the crowd, joining the reporters who hoped to get into the basement to witness Oswald's transfer.

There was a lot of confusion, pushing and shoving, especially now that the huge out-of-town (and international) press contingent had arrived. Reporters from all over the world were in Dallas to cover the story, and I think every one of them was in the basement that morning.

Security was fairly tight. My wife was refused access. So she headed off for breakfast, where I planned to join her in a few minutes. Police guards checked my press credentials three times before allowing me into the area where Oswald was to be brought out of the elevator and escorted to the back of a waiting police cruiser.

I didn't see Ruby in the basement that morning. He was standing perhaps 15 feet from me as Detectives Leavelle and L.C. Graves brought their handcuffed prisoner toward the car. I remember a lot of talking and jostling and reporters trying to peer around other reporters, hoping for a glimpse of Oswald.

Then, in the midst of it all. came that *pop!* sound again. It was 11:21. Detective Thomas McMillon later testified that Ruby snarled "you rat son of a bitch" at Oswald as he shot him in the heart. But all I heard was that *pop!* Just once this time, and so faint and muffled that Jack Ruby's Colt Cobra .38 sounded like a toy.

In the *News*, first edition, Carl Freund's story featured an embarrassing misspelling in the headline. In a later four-star edition, "Roll" became "Role" and the updated piece featured a new byline, too.

Night Club Man Takes Role of An Executioner

By JAMES EWELL
and HUGH AYNESWORTH

A Dallas night club owner, who featured strip teasers in its shows, appointed himself an executioner Sunday and fired a lethal shot into the 24-year-old Communist sympathizer accused of murdering President Kennedy here.

Millions of TV viewers saw Lee Harvey Oswald slump to the floor as officers led him through the City Hall basement toward an armored car. It was to have carried him to the county jail.

Oswald died in Parkland Hospital at 1:07 p.m. although a 12-man surgical team massaged his heart in a desperate—but futile—attempt to save his life.

HIS SLAYING was believed the first in history witnessed by a nation-wide TV audience.

Dist. Atty. Henry Wade filed murder charges against Jack Leon Rubenstein, who used the name Jack Ruby. He owned the Carousel Club at 1312½ Commerce, which featured strippers.

The shooting of Oswald brought these developments:

Irving police increased their guard at the home of Oswald's family here and arrested a group of teen-agers with a rifle, but released them when they said they planned to use the weapon on a hunting trip.

—Mayor Earle Cabell's life was threatened and an airliner, which was to have taken him to Washington for President Kennedy's funeral, left without him. A spokesman said the mayor would fly to Washington later.

—MAYOR CABELL expressed admiration "for Chief Curry and his department" and urged Dallas residents to "resist hysteria". He said they should not seek a scapegoat.

stein as soon as he pulled the trigger. But, for "10 seconds which seemed like an eternity," he waved his pistol in an arc while officers tried to wrest it from him.

RUBENSTEIN'S roommate, George Senator, described the night club owner as a highly emotional man who "took the death of President Kennedy real hard."

"He's been going around the apartment saying 'Those poor kids . . . Those poor kids'," Senator related. "It bothered him tremendously."

As a result of Oswald's almost unbelievable death, there will never be a trial to prove he murdered President Kennedy. But detectives said their evidence left no doubt in their minds and Captain Fritz told reporters, "We now consider the case closed."

Justice of the Peace Pierce McBride ordered Rubenstein held without bond after Assistant Dist. Atty. William F. Alexander filed a murder charge against him.

Judge Joe B. Brown of Criminal District Court No. 3 scheduled a bond hearing for 11:30 a.m. Monday at the request of attorney Tom Howard.

Wade said he would ask Judge Brown to refuse bond. The judge could do so under Texas law if he believes a jury would assess the death penalty.

Police Chief Jesse Curry appeared stunned by the slaying of Oswald, who was in his custody.

FEARING THAT vengeance-seeking groups would try to harm Oswald, Curry had made elaborate plans for the transfer to the county jail.

He had arranged for a heavy guard to escort Oswald from the jail through the basement to an armored car. Police had roped

any incident. Six armed policemen surrounded the cart and attendants as it was moved to the green ambulance.

Funeral plans were incomplete.

One reporter said he heard the slayer add, "I did it for Jackie so she wouldn't have to go through all that . . . coming back here for the trial and everything."

But in Evansville, Ind., entertainer Bill Demar told the Associated Press he is positive Oswald was a patron in Rubenstein's night club nine days ago. Demar, who has a memory act, said Oswald was among those who called out an object for him to remember.

Detectives said Rubenstein may have carried photographic equipment and posed as a cameraman to gain admittance to the basement Sunday.

Officers checked Rubenstein's background.

They said he had come here from Chicago about 10 years ago and had confided in friends that he "had some trouble with racketeers" in the Illinois city.

His decision to become an executioner left the world with a mystery that may never be completely solved: If Lee Harvey Oswald did kill President Kennedy with a mail-order rifle—and officers say they are convinced he did—what was his motive for the crime that shocked the world and set in sequence an almost unbelievable chain of events?

—Dallas News Staff Photo.

Dallas News staff photographer Jack Beers took the Page 1 picture of assailant Jack Ruby holding a pistol at the stomach of Lee Oswald.

—Dallas News Staff Photo by Tom Dillard.

R OSWALD WAS SHOT

talks to
Harvey
of Presi-
ile under
ing trans-

ferred to the County Jail to await trial for murder. Police held nightclub operator Jack Ruby who fired the pistol blast that fatally wounded Oswald.

Front Page Photo Tells Grim Story

ve Bleeding

(Veteran Dallas News other than a squad car or paddy the man's movement, I tripped

Night Club Man Takes Roll of Executioner

By CARL FREUND

A Dallas night club owner, who featured strip teasers in its shows, appointed himself an executioner Sunday and fired a lethal shot into the 24-year-old Communist sympathizer accused of murdering President Kennedy here.

Millions of TV viewers saw Lee Harvey Oswald slump to the floor as officers led him through the City Hall basement toward an armored car. It was to have carried him to the county jail.

Oswald died in Parkland Hospital at 1:07 p.m. although a 12-man surgical team massaged his heart in a desperate—but futile—attempt to save his life.

HIS SLAYING was believed the first in history witnessed by a nation-wide TV audience.

Dist. Atty. Henry Wade filed murder charges against Jack Leon Rubinstein, who used the name Jack Ruby. He owned the Carousel Club at 1312½ Commerce, which featured strippers.

The shooting of Oswald brought these developments:

Irving police increased their guard at the home of Oswald's family here and arrested a group of teen-agers with a rifle, but released them when they said they planned to use the weapon on a hunting trip.

—Mayor Earle Cabell's life was threatened and an airliner, which was to have taken him to Washington for President Kennedy's funeral, left without him. A spokesman said the mayor would fly to Washington later.

—Mayor Cabell expressed admiration "for Chief Curry and his department" and urged Dallas residents to "resist hysteria". He said they should not seek a scapegoat.

—Twenty highway patrolmen from the Tyler district were ordered to Dallas on temporary assignment to guard Gov. Connally at Parkland Hospital. There were reports that patrolmen from other districts would

apartment saying 'Those poor kids . . . Those poor kids'," Senator related. "It bothered him tremendously."

As a result of Oswald's almost unbelievable death, there will be a trial to prove he murdered President Kennedy. But detectives said their evidence left no doubt in their minds and Captain Fritz told reporters, "We now consider that case closed."

The Justice Department announced in Washington that Assistant Atty. Gen. Jack Miller Jr., who heads its criminal division, was flying to Dallas to confer with U.S. Dist. Atty. Barefoot Sanders.

A SPOKESMAN refused to say whether the federal government considered the assassination case closed or whether there was a possibility others were involved.

Justice of the Peace Pierce McBride ordered Rubenstein held without bond after Assistant Dist. Atty. William F. Alexander filed a murder charge against him.

Judge Joe B. Brown of Criminal District Court No. 3 scheduled a bond hearing for 11:30 a.m. Monday at the request of attorney Tom Howard.

Wade said he would ask Judge Brown to refuse bond. The judge could do so under Texas law if he believes a jury would assess the death penalty.

Police Chief Jesse Curry appeared stunned by the slaying of Oswald, who was in his custody.

FEARING THAT vengeance-seeking groups would try to harm Oswald, Curry had made elaborate plans for the transfer to the county jail.

He had arranged for a heavy guard to escort Oswald from the jail through the basement to an armored car. Police had roped off Houston Street near the county jail as a precaution against violence there.

Chief Curry noted he could have moved Oswald secretly "in the dark of night" but had

Lee Harvey Oswald

Photographer Tells of Picture On Front Page

Veteran Dallas News staff photographer Jack Beers watched the fatal shooting of accused assassin Lee Harvey Oswald through the view finder of his camera in the police basement of the City Hall. Beers' camera captured the sensational photograph shown on Page 1. The

among the police and newsmen, a tenseness was apparent. Once, a glass bottle rolled out the back door of the armored car and shattered on the pavement. It startled the spectators.

Shortly before Oswald was to be brought down from his cell

BIG D

By PAUL CRUME

AS A TRIBUTE to John F. Kennedy, why don't we in Dallas set ourselves to behave in the next few days like John F. Kennedy?

Lee Harvey Oswald was accused of killing President Kennedy. Like every other person, though, he had a right to stand in an American court, unafraid of king or despot. He had a right to face his accusers and demand that they prove the case against him.

So does the man who shot Oswald.

These rights are the very reason President Kennedy lived and died. Seeing that they are granted to the weakest and the meanest persons is the reason we live as Americans.

Oswald never got his day in court, but each of us can shoulder our part of the burden of seeing that other men do.

We ought to get it clear in our minds whether it is better to be a John F. Kennedy or the kind of man Oswald was accused of being—and behave accordingly.

YOUTHS WHO pick up rifles and take after a human quarry should ask themselves whether they are behaving like John F. Kennedy or whether they are not, in fact behaving just as Lee Harvey Oswald did, assuming that he shot the President. If we had rid ourselves of this kind of impulsive violence, the President would still be alive.

Our boys and girls might further ask whether they want to live the rest of their lives like

---

County Jail to await er. Police held night Jack Ruby who fired that fatally wounded

Oswald ...jority

It's not the way to do it, it's a throwback to the old vigilante days."

"IT'S A BAD reflection on our

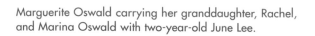
Marguerite Oswald carrying her granddaughter, Rachel,
and Marina Oswald with two-year-old June Lee.

CHAPTER NINE

Marguerite Oswald: A "Mercy Killing?"

The first person ever to be murdered on national television expired in Trauma Room No. 2 at Parkland Hospital at 1:07 p.m. that Sunday, directly across the hall from where President Kennedy died of his gunshot wounds 48 hours earlier. In fact, Oswald might have died on the same table as JFK had not hospital administrator Jack Price diverted his gurney from Trauma Room No. 1 at the last moment.

Next day, shortly after the nation watched the president's somber, dignified funeral on television, Oswald was buried in a gray casket on a barren hillside at Rose Hill Cemetery in Fort Worth. Two preachers who agreed to officiate failed to show, so the service was led by the Rev. Louis Saunders, a Disciple of Christ minister and executive secretary of the Fort Worth Council of Churches.

Marguerite Oswald and her son, Robert, who had made the funeral arrangements, were at the graveside, as were Marina and the girls. Six reporters served as pall-bearers, including Mike Cochran, the Associated Press correspondent.

Cochran at first refused. Then up stepped the competition, Preston McGraw of United Press International, who accepted the job. "At that point, I didn't have a choice," Mike remembers. Besides Cochran and McGraw, the other newsmen-pallbearers were Jerry Flemmons, Bunky McConal and Ed Horn from the *Fort Worth Star-Telegram*, and a sixth reporter from a Midwest newspaper.

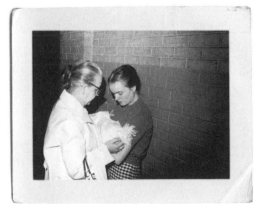

Marguerite with Marina and granddaughter.

Oswald's family at his graveside ceremony.

Perhaps two dozen more reporters and photographers stood 40 more-or-less respectful feet away as Rev. Saunders conducted Oswald's brief rites.

"We are not here to stand in judgment of him," the minister said to the press afterward. "We are here only to lay him to rest."

The press behaved in an uncommonly civil manner that day, says Cochran. "The media did not harass the family, not even the TV guys. Nobody intruded. It was respectful."

Later, when Jim Marrs, a well-known conspiracy theorist, sold a photo to the AP, claiming it was a shot of Oswald in his casket, Cochran did his best to screw up the deal for Marrs. "I guess it was Oswald," he remembers. "I don't know. I just said to the AP: 'It doesn't look like him at all."

•••••••••••••••••••••••••••••••

Given Lee Harvey Oswald's sorry life, his ignoble death and humble interment could be no surprise. It was easy to see him helplessly circling the drain almost from the start.

Born Oct. 18, 1939, in New Orleans, Oswald never knew his father, Robert Edward Lee Oswald, who was his mother Marguerite's second husband. An insurance premium collector, Robert E. Lee died of coronary thrombosis two months before Lee's birth.

According to several sources, the boy slept with Marguerite until he was eight—except for a few months when he was 4 or 5 and she placed him in the Bethlehem Orphanage Asylum with his brother Robert and their older half-brother, John Pic, from Marguerite's first marriage.

In 1945, Marguerite married a Boston industrial engineer, Edwin A. Ekdahl, and moved with Ekdahl to Dallas, where Lee began public school. John and Robert were sent off to military school in Mississippi. Ekdahl divorced Marguerite in 1948, claiming in court documents that she endlessly nagged about money and physically abused him.

John and Robert joined the armed services at their first chance, as would Lee, who by the age of 10 had attended six different public schools and was becoming a behavioral problem.

In the summer of 1952, Marguerite suddenly decided that she and Lee would move to New York to live with John Pic and his young wife, Margaret, who themselves were guests in a Bronx apartment Margaret's mother rented. Marguerite and Lee arrived unannounced and stayed with the Pics until John, annoyed that his mother refused to get a job or discipline his young half-brother, ordered them gone.

John Pic told the Warren Commission that his mother didn't think Margaret was good enough for him and told him so repeatedly. "Naturally, I resented this," he testified, "because I put my wife before my mother any day."

The flashpoint came one afternoon when Lee and Marguerite erupted into an argument over what channel to watch on the Pics' television. To Margaret Pic's horror, the 12-year-old hit his mother and menaced Marguerite with a pocketknife.

When Margaret told her husband of the incident that night, John Pic confronted his mother and half-brother. Marguerite downplayed the episode. Lee, according to John's testimony, "became real hostile toward me. When this happened it perturbed my wife so much that she told him they were going to leave whether they liked it or not."

The half-brothers never spoke to one another again.

Living with Marguerite in a tiny Bronx apartment, Lee seldom attended school, preferring instead to watch television, ride subways around town, and visit the zoo. Finally, truancy officials grabbed him and sent the 13-year-old to a youth facility for a six-week evaluation.

Psychiatrists there saw an intelligent non-conformist with a questionable role model, receiving unreliable adult supervision. Noted one of them, a Dr. Renatus Hartogs: "Lee is a youngster with superior mental endowments, functioning presently in the bright-normal range of mental efficiency. His abstract thinking and his vocabulary are well developed. No retardation in school subjects could be found despite truancy."

Oswald's IQ was measured at an above-average 118.

Evelyn Strickman, a social worker, wrote, "There is a pleasant, appealing quality about this emotionally-starved, affectionless youngster, which grows as one speaks to him." Lee told her his favorite television show was *I Led Three Lives,* a popular series based on the adventures of FBI double agent Herbert Philbrick. He also said he wanted more than anything to join the U.S. Marines, just like his big brother Robert.

When her youngest son was released, Marguerite moved with him to New Orleans, where his attitude did not improve. At 16, Lee forged her name to a note informing his school that he no longer would be attending classes inasmuch as the family was moving out of the district. Then he forged a second document attesting that he was 17 and thus eligible to join the military.

Oswald, a clean-cut teenage member of the Civil Air Patrol.

Marguerite signed the paper for him, but the Marines nonetheless refused him, telling Oswald to try again in a year. Finally, in 1956, his mother signed a proper permission waiver in Dallas and Lee at last was allowed to enlist.

This was a young man who most definitely wanted to get away from mom. And who could blame him?

But he hated discipline and the rigors of barracks life. His fellow Marines called him "Ozzie Rabbit" for the way his ears stuck out, and they derided him for reading a Russian-language newspaper. The other guys also made merciless fun of him when he accidentally shot himself in the arm.

He retreated into radical left wing ideology, and decided while still in the service that what he really wanted to do was visit the Soviet Union. With his mother's help—and the Marines' eager approval—he secured an early discharge.

Marguerite, who'd recently been injured in a fall, expected her boy to come stay with her in Fort Worth. But after two days, Lee announced he was headed for New Orleans to find work on a ship.

His mother was furious. "After all," she told me later, "I got him out so he could come and help me out financially."

A short while later, Lee put even more distance between himself and his mother. He defected to the Soviet Union.

•••••••••••••••••••••••••••••••

Few people have ever so deeply annoyed me as Marguerite Oswald. And of all the things I disliked about her, none irritated me more than her voice. It was strange—unique in my experience—a jarring combination of birdlike sing-song, childish whine, and predatory threat that invaded your head like a dental drill. She would not stop talking.

I first heard from Mrs. Oswald in early December 1963, when she called me at the *News* to complain about the escape route story I'd written with Larry Grove.

Obviously (her term), Larry and I got our information from a government leak, and she wanted to correct some mistakes.

Next (and this was typical of Marguerite Oswald) she suggested we call the *Star-Telegram* to arrange a car and driver for her to come visit us at the *News* in Dallas. It was a trick I would have loved to play on my friends in Fort Worth, but I told her instead that Larry and I would drive over to meet with her.

No photo ever really captured Marguerite Oswald. In pictures, she usually appeared behind a pair of dark-rimmed glasses, jaw set, moist eyes about to flood with tears, the very image of a doughty American mom fighting to clear her infamous son's name. In truth, she was supremely egotistical, combative, devious, and smart.

I knew before I met her that she already was selling interviews and artifacts to the highest bidder. In fact, she tried to open negotiations for a paid interview with *Life* magazine within 24 hours of Kennedy's death.

My single interest in her at the time was to learn if I could determine how Lee and Marina could afford their trip to Texas from the Soviet Union in the spring of 1962. I knew Oswald had little or no money and assumed the travel had been costly.

When Larry and I arrived at her tiny, cluttered house in Fort Worth, a pair of Japanese reporters, waiting for a cab, were sitting in her living room. They smiled a lot but seemed confused as Marguerite plunked news clips into their laps and proceeded to tell them who in the articles was a CIA agent or an FBI plant.

They greeted their cab's arrival with looks of genuine relief.

My first lesson in interviewing Marguerite Oswald was that you didn't, because you couldn't. She didn't exchange thoughts and ideas, but simply talked and talked and talked, oblivious to any distraction as she careened from subject to subject according to some interior logic that I never figured out.

The one subject Mrs. Oswald did not touch on in our first meeting was her son's very recent murder.

Instead, she ranted at length about Marina and Ruth Paine.

MOTHER FOR THE DEFENSE — Mrs. Marguerite Oswald, mother of accused assassin Lee Harvey Os-

Marguerite as the world saw her.

"Marina's mixed up in this," she said, "and that Paine woman. They conspired. I don't know the whole story, but I know enough."

She briefly turned her attention to our article, insisting we were wrong about her son taking a bus and then a cab. "And why would he go on past his rooming house?" she wanted to know. "And so he had a pistol! Half the young men in Dallas have a pistol!'

Then it was back to her daughter-in-law.

"Do you know why I didn't get to see my son for more than a year?" she complained. "Because of Marina. Marina wanted him away from me. Why, they didn't even tell me they were moving out of Fort Worth! I was with them the afternoon before they left and they never told me!"

Larry and I exchanged a glance. I was beginning to feel some compassion for Lee Harvey Oswald.

"Now she won't even talk to me," Marguerite continued. "She's in protected [sic] custody somewhere, but they won't tell me where." Somehow this fact reminded Mrs. Oswald that she once gave Marina a pocket watch that belonged to Lee's dad. "I guess she thinks that's hers now, too," she said with a huff.

Try as I might, I could not get her to focus on the single issue that interested me that day. After enduring her rambling tirade for an hour or so I frankly was content just to leave.

A short while she was back in my face again.

I did a radio show in which, as I recall, I mentioned that Oswald had purchased both his rifle and handgun by mail order, and that I thought it "interesting" how he and Marina seemed to get back from Russia to the United States so easily.

Marguerite called to complain, first of all, about how she, not her dead son, was being treated by the press. Almost every day, she said, there was some sort of attack on her in the papers or on television. Then she turned to my radio remarks, calling them "scurrilous, totally absurd, and ill-informed."

She was just warming up.

"As far as how he and Marina got back," Marguerite informed me, "I was the one. I sent him the money. Now what do you have to say about that?"

I believe I apologized to her, then asked how much the trip had cost her. "Oh, $800 or $900," she answered. "I don't remember." Much later I'd learn that she contributed nothing to her son's travel expenses. His brother Robert sent Lee several hundred dollars. The Red Cross and other agencies made up the rest.

"I guess you know my son was an agent for the federal government," she said, "and they just threw him away. I can prove that."

That's where I stopped Marguerite and said I'd like to come over and see her proof. In this period there were rumors everywhere that Oswald once worked for the FBI or the CIA as a paid informant. I was skeptical, but willing to be convinced.

One reporter who felt certain Oswald had worked for the government was Alonzo "Lonnie" Hudkins of the *Houston Post*. Lonnie called me constantly, hoping I'd uncovered

For years after the assassination, Marguerite continued to make outrageous claims.

Photograph

11-8-68
D.M. News

Marguerite Claims New Evidence

FORT WORTH (UPI) — Mrs. Marguerite Oswald, mother of the late Lee Harvey Oswald, said Thursday she is going to ask President-elect Richard Nixon to reopen her son's case.

Mrs. Oswald, sitting beneath a painting of "Whitsler's Mother," shower reporters an 8-by-10 glossy taken from a photograph taken in front of the Texas School Book Depository the day President John F. Kennedy was shot.

Mrs. Oswald said the original picture, which was not shown to the press, showed a clock which had the time as 12:40. The president was shot about 12:30.

She said in the glossy, which she said was new evidence to reopen the case, a man was standing in front of the depository.

"I would have to say this man in the white shirt is Lee Harvey Oswald, and this was taken 10 minutes after the assassination," Mrs. Oswald said.

OSWALD'S MOM ASKS

Laredo Times

AUDIENCE

6-29-67

FORT WORTH (UPI) —Mrs. Marguerite Oswald, mother of accused assassin Lee Harvey Oswald, said Wednesday she had sent a telegram to President Johnson asking that she be allowed to present evidence proving her son's innocence.

"I have sent a telegram to President Johnson saying that I am now ready to play the card that I have held for sometime," she said.

"The telegram states that I have in my possession evidence that can clear my late son's name and that he was not the killer of President Kennedy. I a s k respectfully to present this evidence and allow the American people to feel freer in their minds."

Mrs. Oswald said she had watched the CBS four-part series on the assassination and thought the television network did a "very, very good job." However, she said CBS made an error in stating her son was the assassin.

"Human beings are not infallible," she said. "They are subject to error. There was an error made on Sept. 23, 1963, that I, Marguerite O s w a l d, the mother of Lee Harvey Oswald, can prove wrong, can prove that my son's innocent."

something to move the story along. In time, I grew tired of Lonnie's queries, especially since I doubted his sources were that good.

So one day when I was busily juggling deadline stories for *Newsweek* and the *Times of London*, as well as a weekend piece for the *News*, Lonnie called once more, and asked me, "You hear anything about this FBI link with Oswald?" Tired of him bugging me, I said to him, "You got his payroll number, don't you?"

"Yeah, yeah," Lonnie said.

I reached over on my desk, and I read to him part of a Telex number on a telegram.

Yeah, yeah," he said, "that's it. That's the same one I've got." I knew that if Lonnie accepted the number as legitimate, he had nothing. He said he'd check his sources and get back to me.

Weeks passed and I forgot about the call until Jan. 1, 1964, when Hudkins published a front page article in the *Post*, alleging that Oswald may have been a federal operative.

Naturally, the story caused quite a stir. Members of the newly created Warren Commission summoned several top Texas law enforcement officials and advisers to Washington to discuss the development, including Waggoner Carr, the state Attorney General, Dallas DA Henry Wade, and his assistant Bill Alexander.

J. Edgar Hoover of course told them the story was not true. The Texas folk denied any knowledge of where Hudkins got his story and the story pretty much died—for a while.

Lonnie never disclosed his source for the bogus number, and I didn't admit to it for at least several years.

Marguerite Oswald didn't have any credible evidence her son worked as an informant for the government, either. On this visit she told me that she was writing a book about her son, a project that she'd originally embarked on over Lee's strong objections, when he first returned from the Soviet Union.

Before I was able to make my escape once more, she tried to sell me pictures of Lee, his letters from Russia, a couple of school report cards. When I tried to steer her back toward a substantive conversation, she snapped, "I guess you came here expecting me to tell you all I know without any payment. Well, those days are gone forever."

Thence forward Marguerite generally was upset at something in the *News* all the time, but she also freely berated me for pieces that

Opposite: The Hudkins' report: An example of
slipshod reporting that fueled conspiracy lore.

Oak St.—Post Photo

Oswald Rumored As Informant for U.S.

Federal Agent Approached Son, Mother Quoted as Saying

By LONNIE HUDKINS, Post Staff Correspondent

DALLAS — Was Lee Harvey Oswald a stool pigeon for a federal government agency? That's the question being asked by many people in responsible positions here.

If the answer is "yes," then the 24-year-old accused as the slayer of President Kennedy pulled one of the biggest and certainly the most embarrassing double-crosses in the nation's history.

AND IF THE answer is "no," it will go down as just another one of the fantastic rumors floating around in official and unofficial circles in Dallas.

Here are some of the facts and some of the opinions and the sources from which they came.

Oswald, who was later shot to death by night club operator Jack Ruby, did know of Joe Hosty, the FBI agent who handled subversive matters in the Dallas FBI office.

"He had Hosty's home phone, office phone and car license number," said Bill Alexander, assistant district attorney to Henry Wade and one of the state's most able prosecutors.

ALEXANDER was one of the men who got a chance to listen in on the grilling of Oswald on Nov. 22, the day the President was killed, and Nov. 23, the day before Oswald's life also came to an end.

Mrs. Marguerite Oswald, mother of Oswald, had a terse "no comment" when asked if her son had told her he was or had at least been asked to be an informant in antisubversive work. She did not deny it.

However, she was quoted in the Philadelphia Inquirer as saying her son had been approached by a government agent to be an informant and then had informed her about it.

INASMUCH AS she had no direct contact with her son after September of 1962, the contact, if made, would have been before she went to work for a Fort Worth matron in the same month and indicated to her employer

See OSWALD on Page 8

vestigating President Kennedy's death that states that "at 2:30 PM Friday, Nov. 22," an FBI agent told Dallas police that the FBI knew of Oswald and had conducted some surveillance of him.

IF THIS IS true, veteran police and sheriff investigators ask, then the FBI must have known they wanted his rifle to kill Connally, and that policeman have noticed the possible significance of his working in a building on the route of the motorcade.

"It is this point that has led to speculation by police and sheriff's deputies in Dallas that Oswald might have been an informant because, as one put it, "you just wouldn't think to check out one of your own stoolies.""

And it should also be pointed out that most of the people involved in the initial investigation of the case are reluctant to say much now that the case's subsequent developments are now in the hands of federal investigation.

BUT DISTRICT Atty Henry Wade, a former FBI agent himself and therefore a man who would know how such an agency would operate, does not discount the possibility that Oswald may have been an informant.

"It may be true," he said, "but I don't think it will ever be made public, if it is."

Another point of confusion involves Oswald's trip to Mexico City Sept 26 to Oct 3. Reliable sources in Dallas say he passed through Houston on Sept 26 en route to Mexico. One agency in Washington has "leaked" that Oswald was accompanied by two women and a man. But this

position — is if the government — any agency — knew about Oswald and had watched, why wasn't his name on the list of people for Dallas police to check before the President arrived?

And if Oswald was a government informant — and therefore

And if Oswald was a government informant — and therefore ignored, why?

SHE'S A BIG GIRL NOW

This time last year Maria Isabel Martinez, who was the first baby reported born in Houston after New Year's began, weighed 6 pounds and 3 ounces. This New Year's Day she was the eye-catching lyde bruncha weighs 17 pounds. She was born at Saint Joseph's Hospital just one second past midnight last Jan 1. Her parents are Mr and Mrs Felix Martinez of 425 North Live Oak St.—Post Photo

turned up elsewhere, such as *The New York Times* or *Detroit Free Press*.

I was hardly her only victim, though. She was a tireless adversary. One of her targets was Howard Brennan, the only eyewitness to the assassination.

Brennan said he watched Marguerite on *The Johnny Carson Show*, where she attacked him (Brennan)—not by name, but he felt everybody knew whom she was talking about.

"She impugned my integrity," he wrote in his memoir," and said, 'The witness is blind as a bat, he wears glasses.'" Actually, Brennan *did* wear glasses after January 1964. His eyes were injured in an industrial sand-blasting accident, which affected his eyesight. Still, he wrote in the mid-1980s, "After that my vision wasn't what it had been before the accident, yet even today I am not 'blind as a bat'; my vision is 20/20 with glasses. Before the accident my eyes were exceptional."

Although he received an avalanche of phone calls in the weeks after the assassination, one call that bugged the Brennans particularly was from a woman who would never give her name. The calls came every two or three weeks, he recalled. "Louise (Mrs. Brennan) said the woman's voice was familiar, though she couldn't place it.

"The caller adamantly refused to give her name, but she did her best to discredit me. She would say, 'How can your husband have the audacity to be so sure he saw the man that killed Kennedy?' Louise tried not to argue with her, though it was difficult because the caller questioned my eyesight as well as my integrity."

Finally, Brennan wrote, they just chalked it up as "another nut" and prepared to live with it.

Then one day she called and began the same tirade. "Then came a quick slip of the tongue as she snapped, 'My son didn't do it.' It was Marguerite Oswald!"

I heard from Marguerite again after I'd reviewed one of the earliest conspiracy books, a ridiculous volume that argued Lee Harvey Oswald worked for both the CIA and the FBI and was part of a crack undercover "hit" team. Burning up the telephone lines from Fort Worth to Dallas, she threatened to ruin me "as a journalist for taking such liberties," and again promised to produce hard evidence that Lee was indeed an agent. "You'll see," she screeched. "I can't wait to see you eat this crow."

I never saw her again, but I was party to a spectacularly strange episode in which Marguerite played the starring role.

On Mother's Day weekend, 1965, the writer Jean Stafford came to Dallas to do a major story on Mrs. Oswald for *McCall's* magazine. Jean was a wonderful writer—she'd win the Pulitzer Prize for fiction in 1970—and had been married to a couple of other literary lions, the poet Robert Lowell and journalist A. J. Liebling.

Stafford ran into trouble at the outset. When her limo driver delivered her to Marguerite's door on Friday, a loud voice from inside shouted, "I can't let you in. They are going to have to pay me a lot more. I've done some research on *McCall's*, and I know what they are worth."

Stafford didn't know what to do. She was told the magazine would pay Marguerite $800. "I wasn't the type to deal with the money, to make bids and the like," she later told me. "And I was taken aback, not by the coarseness of the demand, but by the voice itself. You have to hear that woman angered to understand what I mean."

I told Jean that I understood fully. I knew from long experience how absolutely eerie it could get with her. "How much do you want?" Stafford yelled back through the front door.

"Thirteen hundred and fifty," Marguerite shrieked, "and they've got it!"

Writer Jean Stafford

"Let me use the phone," Stafford replied. "I will call New York and see if they will agree to that."

Mrs. Oswald's truculence vanished at once. She opened the door and greeted Jean Stafford as she might an old friend. When the writer couldn't get anyone at *McCall's* to authorize the additional payment, she decided to guarantee the extra $550 Marguerite demanded herself. "I wasn't about to leave without something," Stafford explained. She soon had reason to rue her determination.

Stafford spent several hours with Marguerite that day, mostly discussing Lee. Mrs. Oswald stunned the writer several times with her bold, revisionist views on the saga, most particularly her avowed belief that since her son was a government agent, the assassination might have been an assignment, a mercy killing.

As Stafford later quoted Marguerite in her book, *A Mother in History*, "Now maybe Lee Harvey Oswald was the assassin. But does that make him a louse? No. No. Killing does not necessarily mean badness. You find killing in some very fine homes for one reason or another. And as we all know, President Kennedy was a dying man. So I say that it is possible that my son was chosen to shoot him in a mercy killing for the security of the country. And if this is true, it was a fine thing to do and my son is a hero."

Stafford was "staggered by this cluster of fictions stated as irrefutable fact."

"I had not heard that President Kennedy was dying," she managed edgewise into Mrs. Oswald's monologue.

"Oh yes," Marguerite said, explaining that Kennedy suffered from a kidney disease called "Atkinson's."

Purposefully or otherwise, she'd confused it with Addison's disease, a non-fatal malfunction of the adrenal gland for which Kennedy was treated for several years.

Friday evening, Stafford dined with me and Lon Tinkle, the venerable book editor at the *News*. "It scared the devil out of me," she told us. "All in all she was polite, but there's something deadly about that woman. Maybe I won't go back tomorrow."

Lon and I argued that she should, but as a safety measure maybe keep the car and driver waiting outside.

That idea seemed to reassure her a bit.

"I wish I could take pictures in that house," she said. "You won't believe what she's got over her desk."

"The plaque?" I smiled. "The hero plaque?"

"God! You've seen it!" Stafford gasped in mock horror. Lon looked puzzled, so Jean explained, reaching into her purse for a small notepad so she could get it exact.

"She's got this copper scroll, which says, 'My son, Lee Harvey Oswald, even after his death has done more for his country than any other living human being. Signed Marguerite C. Oswald."

Saturday, Stafford returned to Mrs. Oswald's house with two rented reel-to-reel tape machines. Marguerite had agreed to be recorded, but only if she got an original copy of the tape, too. I didn't envy Jean having to spend an entire, uninterrupted day with Marguerite, and wasn't surprised to hear by telephone on Saturday evening that she was completely spent.

"This is the toughest assignment I've ever had," she told me. "I don't feel like going back there tomorrow, but I left the tape recorders there, so I have to."

The third day, Mother's Day, at the front door she again heard

Marguerite's loud voice coming from within. This time it was recorded. "She had decided to tape record a couple of hours for me on her own," Jean later said. "I guess I wasn't asking the right questions."

The big finale to the grueling, three-day marathon was to be a trip to Lee's grave. Marguerite climbed into the new Buick Skylark she'd bought with proceeds of the sale to *Esquire* of Lee's letters to her from the Soviet Union, and Jean sat next to her. The rented limo trailed behind.

As they entered the turnpike, Marguerite leaned toward Stafford and held out her hand for the fifteen-cent fare. Jean dug a dime and a nickel from her purse. But Mrs. Oswald did not withdraw her hand. Stafford looked at her questioningly.

"Well," she said, "I have to return, Jean." So Stafford found a quarter and pressed it into Marguerite's palm.

"It seemed that everything she uttered got just a notch weirder," Stafford said over the telephone later that Sunday. "I found myself really afraid. She asked me if I would come back to Fort Worth and stay with her for the summer and write 'our' book together. When she asked me where I was staying tonight, I told her the SMU faculty club. I didn't know what she had in mind."

"Jean, SMU doesn't have a faculty club, at least not where guests stay," I said.

"I know. I know," she answered. "I just told her that. I'm flying out early tonight."

Stafford asked for an unusual favor.

"Hugh, I am not going back to the hotel," she said. "I have most of my clothes with me. I'm going straight to Love Field. Would you hold these tapes for me and send them to me when you can?"

I agreed, not quite getting why Stafford didn't want to travel with the reels of tape. Apparently, Jean had developed a Marguerite phobia, a deep dread not only of Mrs. Oswald, but of anything she'd even touched, including the reels of tape, which she left for me at the Braniff counter. I picked them up the next morning, and listened to them at home before forwarding them to Stafford in New York on Tuesday.

Six or seven years later, while I was living in Houston, working for *Newsweek*, I heard once more from Marguerite. She called me at home one Sunday about a story I'd just done on New Orleans District Attorney Jim Garrison and his sideshow investigation of the Kennedy assassination. I guess I was fairly curt with her; probably because she'd interrupted a football game I was watching on television.

In any event, she began shouting, as usual. "Your kids are gonna suffer," she railed. "I can guarantee you that."

We hung up and I thought about the conversation for a while. In my view, she was clearly disturbed and therefore probably capable of anything, if she was in the mood. It thus seemed prudent that if Marguerite was going to threaten me that I should get it on tape.

About an hour later I called her back, my tape machine recording the conversation. Her tone had changed completely. She was cordial. When I asked her bluntly if she'd meant the remark about my children as a threat, she said, "Oh, no. I will do more than that for you. I will make you eat the truth."

Then, as if we were lifelong pals, she cooed, "I'm going to do a town hall appearance in Los Angeles next weekend. Why don't you come out and debate me? We both could make some money out of it."

It was the last time we talked.

My exclusive first print interview with Marina Oswald.
Daughter June Lee is at Marina's feet in a newly
rented home in Richardson, a Dallas suburb.

The Dallas Morning News

DALLAS, TEXAS, SATURDAY, MARCH 7, 1964 ★★★★

HER THOUGHTS ON RUBY:

Marina Opposes Chair

By HUGH AYNESWORTH
© The Dallas Morning News, 1964

Marina Oswald doesn't want Jack Ruby sent to the electric
ʜair for killing _____

"It was not ____
ᴏr the right w____
ᴏ the law.

"I just do ____

The remarꜰ ____
ᴠe interview ____
y a newspapeꝛ ____
ʜan who killed it.

"When the ____
ʜe right to tal____

MARINA ____
ᴡhen news of ____
ɴg it all the w____
Marina s____
"very badly"____
"I am as ____
She said ____
ᴇturn for th____
Speaking ____
English on ____
ʜat I can u____
She hope____

ASKED ____
ꜱaying she ____
ꜱoftly, "Fir____
ʜing I can ____
ᴡay of life.____
Q.—But ____
A.—(Sʜ____
Marina ____
ʜany lette____
"But I ____
and a gestꜱ____
Marina wanted to talk about what____
expressions of love from the American people."

This money, she said, is "under the complete control" of James
Martin and John Thorne, the business adviser and lawyer Marina
hired while being held in protective custody at Inn of the Six Flags
at Arlington.

____ __ said as if she didn't quite ____

She told of one letter in particular that touched her. It was, she
said, from a church in New Jersey and it contained a small amount
of money.

"The children in the Sunday School baked and sold cakes to
raise the money. I almost cried when I read it," Marina said.

A friend of Marina's interjected, "You did cry. I saw you."
_____ "_____tly relieved" to have settled

A.—I just couldn't believe it. I thought this must be a very bad
man to do something like that. Then I thought of poor Mrs. Kennedy and how those children would have to grow up without a father. I've thought about them many times since, too . . . and Mrs.
Tippit and her children, too.

Q.—WHAT DO YOU think most about these days?

C H A P T E R   T E N

Marina Oswald: An Affair to Remember

On Saturday, November 23, *Life* reporter Tommy Thompson and photographer Allan Grant quietly sneaked Marina Oswald and her mother-in-law to one of Dallas' best hotels, the Adolphus, directly across the street from Jack Ruby's Carousel Club. But, as Grant recalled later, other reporters quickly discovered their coup, necessitating them to spirit the Oswalds out of the downtown area and to the Executive Inn near Love Field.

Life executives in New York had turned down Marguerite's insistence they be paid, but Grant said he gave her $200 as they were registered under his name. Lee's brother, Robert, had agreed to accompany government agents to the hotel, where they wanted to interrogate Marina. Then he planned to drive her, Marguerite and the little girls to the safety of his in-laws' farm a few miles outside Ft. Worth.

Robert, the agents and translator Peter Gregory arrived there just after eleven. As they approached, the agents were notified by radios that Oswald had been shot. "Now don't get excited," one of them said to Robert, "but we've just got word that Lee's been shot."

Robert jumped back in his car and headed for Parkland Hospital, instructing the agents as he departed to take everyone inside the motel to the farm. Instead, they drove Marina and Marguerite around town without informing either of the homicide just committed in the basement at City Hall. Eventually, they did tell Marina that Lee had been shot, but said he was not seriously hurt.

For reasons I've never ascertained, the group eventually ended up at Chief Curry's house, of all places. Marina told me that the Currys were very welcoming, offered them drinks and made small talk. It was there, she said, that Peter Gregory finally broke the news. "Get hold of yourself," Gregory said. "He's dead."

••••••••••••••••••••••••••••••

At the time of her husband's murder, Marina Oswald, then just 22, had known Lee for less than three years—all but a few weeks of that time as his wife. Like Oswald, she never met her father, whom her mother cryptically indicated had "disappeared" soon after Marina's birth in 1941. Then her mother died when Marina was 16.

Despite stern disapproval of relatives, the teen-ager began spending more and more time with a friendly prostitute named Irina. In his book, *Oswald's Tale*, Norman Mailer recounts the story of Irina's Afghan "client" who rapes Marina, then demands his money back after learning from Marina that she was a virgin.

When Marina complains of the assault, Irina says, "What do you expect? Do you think you can go around forever and eat and do nothing for it?"

Marina was tiny, about five-two, weighed less than 100 pounds and wore a size five dress. She was conventionally pretty, despite bad teeth. She drank heavily, chain smoked and, according to Mailer, was rumored to have worked as a street hooker in her native Leningrad.

She met Lee Oswald on March 17, 1961, at a student party in Minsk, where he worked for 23 months in a radio factory, and she studied to become a pharmacist.

In his secret "Historic Diary," Oswald described the occasion. "Boring, but at the last hour I am introduced to a girl with a French hairdo and red dress with white slippers.

"I dance with her, and then ask to show her home."

Marina didn't lack for admirers at the party; Oswald counted five other guys also eager to escort her into the night. "Her name is Marina," he continued. "We like each other right away. She gives me her phone number and departs home with a not-so-new friend in a taxi. I walk home."

The courtship revved up quickly and blossomed into marriage on May 1st, *the* red letter day in any communist land, as Lee Harvey Oswald most definitely was aware. Yet in the diary Oswald dates his wedding day as April 31st, which I doubt was a mistake. More likely it was a deliberate, veiled reflection of his gathering disenchantment with Soviet life. For months he'd been plotting his return to the United States.

Nor was Marina the first girl Oswald proposed to that year. Ella Germain, whom he described as "a very attractive Russian Jew," also worked in the Minsk radio plant. Ella caught his eye around the start of the year.

"I think I'm in love with her," he wrote. "She has refused my more dishonorable advances." On January 2nd, he proposed to Ella and was rejected. "My love is real," he noted forlornly, "but she has none for me."

After wedding Marina, he admitted in the diary that his motive in marriage was to "hurt" Ella Germain, but that he'd also grown to love Marina—who in any case was "madly in love with me from the very start."

According to Marina, this was typical self-flattery. "I felt sorry for him," Bob Fenley quoted her in the *Times Herald*, "because everybody hated him—even in Russia."

Whatever Marina's reason for marrying Lee, or her hopes for their union, she was to be thoroughly disappointed. Oswald was a violent, petty tyrant who neither smoked nor drank and forbade his wife from doing so, either. He even banned lipstick.

Once they arrived in Texas, she was not allowed to speak any language in his presence except Russian, even though Marina longed to practice English as part of her desire to secure U.S. citizenship. She and Lee fought frequently. Acquaintances reported that Marina often was covered with bruises left by her husband's fists.

After his murder, legions of generous strangers stepped forward to help Marina address her main concern: how to care for two small children with very little money and no safe, permanent shelter.

At our first meeting in March 1964, Marina told me that she feared presuming any further on Ruth Paine's charity. "The Secret Service people told me to stay away from her," she reported. "They said the Paines had been put through enough already, and they said I had enough money to easily live. I didn't know. I wasn't sure."

The Feds were right about the money part. But they also made a second recommendation, that Marina seek help with the management of her money from an individual named James Herbert Martin.

In light of Marina's experience, the agents' counsel of disengaging from Ruth Paine while engaging with Jim Martin had a disagreeable

My notes from the first interview with Marina.

Marina chats about the small details of her life...

...and about adjusting to U.S. life.

Marina tells me about Oswald's Nixon threats.

A kitten named Kisa interrupted the interview during a tense moment.

first night she was afraid
— actually wasnt
afraid of kill her

no furni^ture — hear every
sound — weird
floors cracking."

wants do all she can to
help the Commission

dehs comm^ission people
dihes partuculer Dulles

she came by mrs Paine.
once of n a visit

feeling better now
cant live over →
knows stay w/ her
long time

She touches on the ill effects of Oswald's behavior.

change a little

never in U.S.

silver ring — no other ring
on left →

friend isnt afraid to write
Russian just wont let letters
through →

like to find what
eating at home

too costly
here
"dont write this"

finds →

Red caviar →
reasonable in Russia
fresh over there

before
Easter — Blinzes
red caviar inside
cream over it

"delicious
now"

doesn't eat very

Marina asks me not to mention that
she liked expensive red cavier.

141

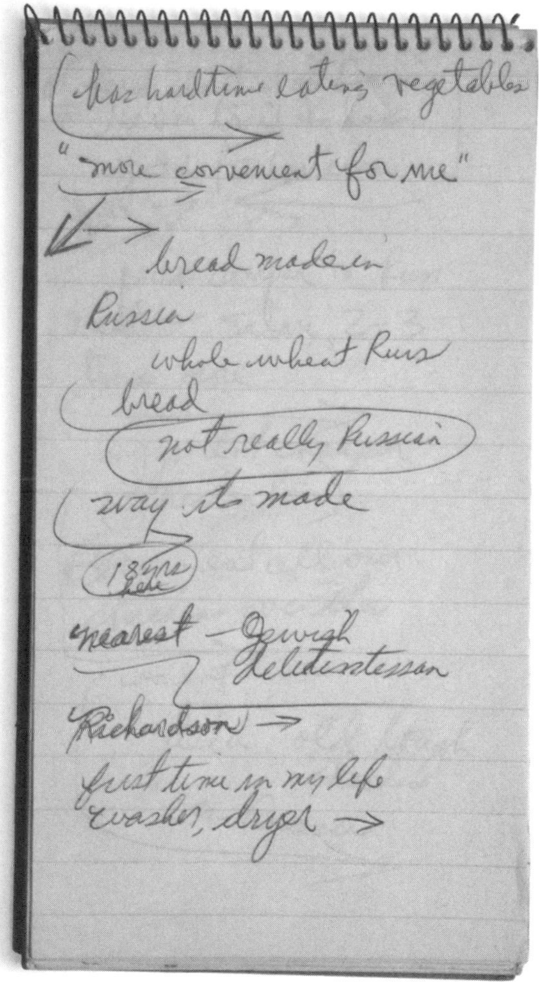

[handwritten notebook notes, left page]

has hardtime eating vegetables →

"more convenient for me"

→

bread made in
Russia
    whole wheat Russ
bread
    (not really Russian)
way its made
(18 yrs here)

nearest — Jewish
        Delicatessen

Richardson →

first time in my life
washer, dryer →

[handwritten notebook notes, right page]

pay

somethin happ
1st thing you think about →

she — lied — didn
lie to her.
covered up →

thought
she was big shot
she below himself

Marina was pleased that for the first time
in her life, she had a washer and dryer.

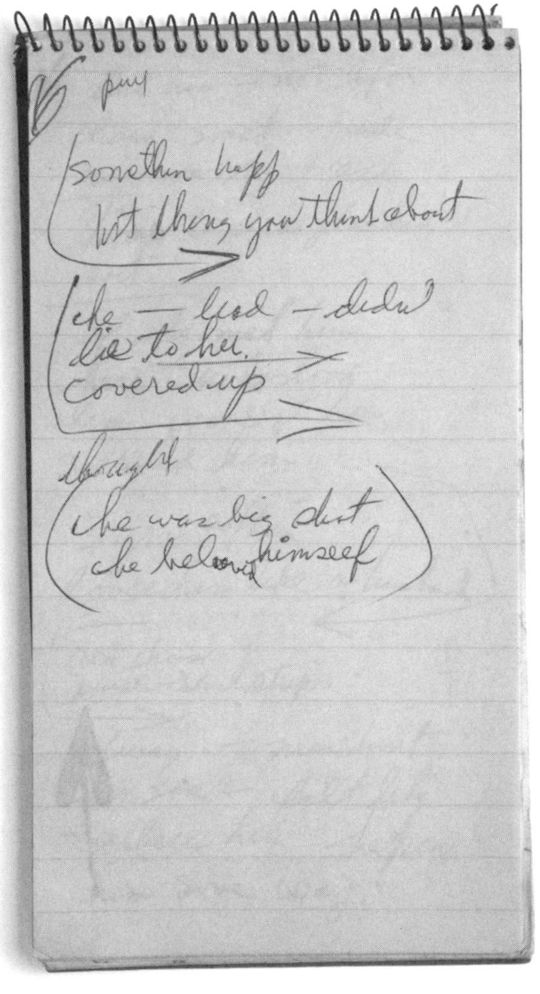

Lee "thought he was a big shot," Marina told me.

smell to it.

The first financial help Marina received was a check for $25,000. from a Philadelphia publisher. A river of money from all over the world would follow.

Some foreign news organizations compensated her in cash. Two whom I ushered into her presence told me they forked over $12,000 and $8,000 respectively for the pleasure of her company. *Life* may have balked at paying for an interview, but the magazine ponied up $20,000 for her permission to republish the "Historic Diary" that I obtained.

There was no public accounting of the sums Marina received from donors, but I know it came to at least $200,000. She did even better once she got a firmer grasp of Western capitalism. In the end, her total haul greatly exceeded Marguerite's, but was dwarfed by the mountain of money collected by J. D. Tippit's widow, Marie. Published accounts pegged that amount at $750,000, which probably was a low estimate. Mrs. Tippit also benefited from the investment advice of several Dallas financial experts, who established a fortune in trusts for her at local banks.

•••••••••••••••••••••••••••••

The largely untold story of Marina's path from destitution to solvency was not without its share of intrigue, drama, fear, and pain.

It began at a motel, the Inn at Six Flags in Arlington, where for a time the Secret Service kept her in protective custody. There Marina met Jim Martin, an assistant manager at the inn. Marina later claimed to the FBI that at first she believed Martin simply was in charge of cleaning her room.

Her relationship with him began six days after the assassination, when Martin asked her to Thanksgiving dinner with his wife, Wanda, and children at their home in suburban Garland. Before the meal was over, the Martins had invited Marina to come live with them. She moved in a day or so later.

(Marina's Dallas police protection squad followed her. She apparently was unaware that one member of her security detail was Nick McDonald, the cop who helped capture Lee at the Texas Theater.)

"He seemed nice," she said of Jim Martin to FBI agents Gobo Bogoslav and Wallace Heitman, "and I realized he knew more about money than I did."

Martin went right to work. Since her English was still quite shaky, he communicated with Marina via a Russian-speaking Secret Service agent, Leo Gopadze. Wheeling and dealing, her new business manager set up several paid press interviews, negotiated with movie companies and explored other possible sources of income on her behalf. He also introduced her to lawyer John Thorne of nearby Grand Prairie. Thorne soon became Marina's attorney.

Jim Martin had other designs on Marina Oswald as well. She later told the FBI that he pursued her romantically almost from the moment they met. He teased her, courted her, touched her, and begged her to love him. On New Year's Day, for example, he played a record by Mario Lanza and sang "some tunes of love" as Marina remembered, while Martin's "eyes ate me up."

Marina told Martin that she'd never marry him, but she would be his lover if he liked. "Jim and I discussed plans," she told the bureau agents. "We planned that I would have my own house and he would come to visit me and we would be lovers."

She claimed that particular part of their relationship was consummated just once, on Friday night, Feb. 7, 1964, at the Willard Hotel in Washington D.C., where they had traveled for her to testify before the Warren Commission.

The biggest hurdle to the union was the Secret Service agents camped in the room next to hers. They made it difficult for Martin to sneak in and out. So Marina requested that the agents be removed. Within hours, Jim Martin and John Thorne took over the vacated room.

That night, she and Martin and little June Lee went to dinner, arriving back at the Willard about 8 o'clock. When John Thorne finally fell asleep, Jim Martin slipped next door.

"I took a bath," Marina told the FBI, "and was partly dressed when I re-entered the bedroom. Jim finished undressing me, and thereafter we had sexual intercourse. It was with my consent, and I did not resist. Martin did not make me perform any unnatural sex acts."

Marina returned with Martin and Thorne to Dallas the next day, and spent Saturday night at Jim Martin's house. Sunday, on a visit with Robert and Vada Oswald to Lee's grave, "she spilled the beans," as Robert later put it. "She was under tremendous pressure," he told me. "I knew I had to get her out of there."

Her disclosure did not come as a complete surprise to Robert. He said that he hadn't trusted either Martin or Thorne since December. Just a week before Marina's graveside admission, Vada told Robert that Marina had discussed Jim Martin's sexual advances with her and confided in Vada that she felted threatened by the situation.

"You're going home to my house," Robert said to Marina at Lee's grave.

She agreed.

Next day, Vada Oswald took Marina to a doctor's appointment, then they stopped by the Martin house to pick up the rest of her clothes and belongings. As they were preparing to depart, Marina said, Jim Martin called from his office. They discussed her decision to move out, and she made a suggestion that seemed to stun Martin.

"I told him that he and I and Wanda should get together to talk the whole affair over, and that his wife should know the whole truth," Marina reported. A meeting to address those issues was set for Robert and Vada's house the next day, but the Martins did not show.

So Marina telephoned them that night. "His wife was on the extension," she recalled, "and we had a three-way conversation. I told Martin I was ending his services as my business manager and my lover."

Earlier, Wanda Martin had informed Marina that if ever Jim found another woman he loved, she would divorce him. The subject arose during their phone chat. "Wanda said she now knew that Jim loved her," Marina remembered, "and that she would not divorce him."

There was stickiness still ahead, however. Neither Jim Martin nor John Thorne would willingly back out of contracts they'd signed in December with Marina, guaranteeing them a 25 percent cut of her income, from any source, for the next ten years. With Robert's help, she engaged Dallas attorney William McKenzie and sued Martin and Thorne in April 1964.

Three months later, Martin and Thorne walked away from the deal in a $12,500 settlement.

••••••••••••••••••••••••••••

The person most damaged by Marina's dalliance with Jim Martin probably was Ruth Paine. She was Marina's big sister, willing to fetch a very pregnant Marina and her daughter, June Lee, from New Orleans in the fall of 1963, then happy to let them and the new baby live with her in Irving without charge.

Statement of Marina Oswald, given Feb. 19, 1964 at Dallas, Texas.

I, Marina Oswald, give the following voluntary statement to Anatol A. Bogoslav and Wallace Heitman whom I know to be special agents of the Federal Bureau of Investigation, Dallas, Texas.

On about Nov. 25, 1963 while I was residing at the Inn of the Six Flags, Arlington, Texas, under the security of the Secret Service, I was told by one of the Secret Service agents that James Herbert Martin, whom I knew as Jim Martin, had invited me and my two daughters to reside at his home as guests. I was invited to the Martin home for Thanksgiving dinner and I accepted this invitation. I had seen Jim Martin at the Inn of the Six Flags and at first thought he had something to do with cleaning up the room, but later I learned he had some position with the Inn.

During my visit at the Martin residence on Thanksgiving, 1963, Mr. and Mrs. Martin told me that they would like for me and my daughters to reside with them as guests. I agreed to do so and offered to pay my share of the expenses.

I moved into the Martin home on about Nov. 29 or 30, 1963. About two weeks after I moved into the Martin residence, I was told by Special Agent Leon Gopadze of the U.S. Secret Service that Martin had advised that I needed an attorney and Martin had a good friend named Thorne who was an attorney.

At the same time Gopadze, the special agent, told me for Martin that I needed a business agent manager too. I suggested that one of my Russian-speaking friends in Dallas would be a good business manager, Martin asked, through Gopadze, if he would be available if he could serve as my business manager and I said that would be okay. I never requested Martin to be my business manager because I thought he was working at a steady job and would not have the time.

Early in 19 December, 1963 I signed contracts with Jim Martin and John M. Thorne,

Later on that day Martin caught me in a hallway when I went to atight**
children and told me he loved me and he kissed me. I told him he** g of love
Martin replied that I should not worry and he would not harm me.
morning on New Year's Day, Martin put on a Mario Lanza record anty
me if
of love and while the record played, Martin's eyes "ate me up."

Later on that day Martin caught me in a hallway when I went to attend to one of my children and told me he loved me and he kissed me. I told him he should not kiss me. Martin replied that I should not worry and he would not harm me. During this early morning on New Year's Day, Martin put on a Mario Lanza record and sang some tunes of love and while the record played, Martin's eyes "ate me up."

I felt flattered by his attention but felt that Jim probably did it because he thought I was alone on this day. Jim had been drinking and I thought he would forget the whole thing in the morning. The days after, while I was at the Martin house, Martin spoke of his love for me almost daily. He never missed a chance to hug me or kiss me. He always hugged me and kissed me when his wife or children or the Secret Service agents were not around. I recall on one occasion, Martin had brought a phonograph record and he came to my bedroom and told me to come into the living room to listen to the record, particularly the second tune, which he said was for me.

Excerpt from transcript of a Feb. 19, 1964, FBI interview with
Marina Oswald in which she details her brief affair with Jim Martin.

Mrs. Paine, who loathed Lee Harvey Oswald, nonetheless found him the job at the book depository.

When Rachel was about to arrive, Ruth donated blood at least twice so that Marina qualified for a free delivery at Parkland Hospital. After the shootings, Mrs. Paine showed up with cookies, clothes, and other gifts for the girls, thinking that if anybody needed a friend just then, it was the Russian girl.

Ruth never got past the door. The last time I inquired, she and Marina had not exchanged a word in 39 years.

In contrast to Mrs. Paine's experience, I was an unwitting beneficiary of Marina's personal and business problems. The February 1964 press stories in which she appeared to be fighting over money with her business partners didn't bolster the image that her new lawyer, Bill McKenzie, had in mind for his client. He wanted the world to see the young widow's compassionate side.

So in early March 1964, McKenzie decided to arrange a newspaper interview in which Marina asked mercy for Jack Ruby, whose murder trial was underway.

As it happened, I was at the time discussing with McKenzie a possible interview with his new client. Marina's views on Ruby were one of the topics I said I'd like to explore. My broader agenda was to open a line of communication with Marina, since anything she had to say was going to make news for a long time.

So far, she'd done a single television interview with Eddie Barker of KDFW-TV in Dallas, which didn't work out too well because of Marina's broken English. She did acknowledge Lee's culpability in the Kennedy assassination, however, an acknowledgment she would renounce many years later.

My 40-minute interview with her, published March 7, 1964, was her first unpaid print interview. Under the headline "Her Thoughts On Ruby: Marina Opposes Chair," I reported: "Marina Oswald doesn't want Jack Ruby sent to the electric chair for killing her husband, Lee Harvey Oswald."

"It was not right, what he did," she said slowly as she searched for the right words, "but I think he should be punished according to the law. I just do not believe in capital punishment."

From a news-gathering point of view, probably the second most important thing she offered was an apology for Lee. Marina said she wanted all Americans to know how "very badly" she felt about the assassination. "I am ashamed and sorry," she added. Another time, she went into more detail about Oswald. "He had this strangeness about him," she told me. "He had strong political beliefs, but rarely talked to me about them. He considered most women unable to understand or maybe to add anything to such conversation.

"He always seemed like a man deeply hurt by something," she continued, "and I always felt somewhat like a mother to him, felt I was helping him in some way. I've always thought what a shame that something or somebody had made him the way that he was. If I had met him in the United States, and understood him, I probably would not have married him."

Marina blamed herself, in part, for the assassination, believing that had she been more welcoming, more loving, on the night of November 21st then Lee's anger and frustration might not have boiled over as it did the next afternoon in Dealey Plaza.

The prelude to their last argument came earlier in the week when she tried to reach him at the rooming house.

"Lee Oswald? No, nobody here by that name," a man said over the phone.

Lee had neglected to tell her that he was Mr. O. H. Lee on North Beckley. Next day he called Marina and chewed her out for blowing his cover. She screamed back at him and hung up, and then hung up three more times when he called to try to smooth over the spat.

She told me that she worried, "What will Ruth think? What kind of nut will she think he is?"

Marina said she was surprised when Lee showed up that Thursday night, instead of Friday as usual. "Then I became angry," she explained. "He knew he wasn't to come out there without Ruth's permission. And he knew he was supposed to telephone first."

This argument did not seem different in tone or intensity from any of the scores of scraps that the battling Oswalds constantly were getting into. Yet Lee seemed especially vulnerable this time. "He kept talking, kept talking, trying to make me feel sorry for him," she remembered. "He said he missed me and the children and was very lonely."

Marina only glared at her husband, and would not speak.

Pretty soon, Mrs. Paine drove up and noticed Lee playing with his older daughter. "Marina sat apart from him, pouting," she told me.

Marina later described the evening to the Warren Commission.

"He was upset over the fact I would not answer him," she testified. "He tried to start a conversation with me several times, but I would not answer and he said he did not want me to be angry with him because this upsets him. On that day he suggested that we rent an apartment in Dallas. He said he was tired of living alone and perhaps the reason for my being so angry was the fact that we were not living together, that if I wanted to he would rent an apartment in Dallas tomorrow, that he didn't want me to remain with Ruth any longer, but wanted me to live with him in Dallas.

"He repeated this not once, but several times. But I refused. And he said that once again I preferred my friends to him, and that I didn't need him." She told her husband that it was best for her to stay with Mrs. Paine in order to save money.

"What did he say to that?" Marina was asked.

"He said he would buy me a washing machine."

"And what did you say to that?"

"Thank you. That it would be better if he bought something for himself, that I would manage."

"That may have been the breaking point for Oswald," wrote William Manchester in *The Death of the President*. "He had nothing left, not even pride."

While surprised at Oswald's presence, Mrs. Paine made no particular mention of it that evening. Instead, she tried and failed to draw Oswald into a conversation about President Kennedy's pending visit. He said nothing to her.

Dinner at 6:30 was tense. Lee, still unable to connect with Marina, watched television for a while, then ducked out into the garage where, while the women were busy with household chores, he undoubtedly disassembled the Mannlicher-Carcano for transport to the book depository next morning.

When Mrs. Paine went to the garage at 9 p.m., she noticed he'd left the overhead light on. When Marina later went to bed, she sensed that Lee was still awake, but did not speak to him.

•••••••••••••••••••••••••••••

Marina did not believe there was any genuine ideological component in her husband's decision to assassinate the president. She understood that Lee had psychological, not intellectual, problems, and probably

Papers across the United States picked up the
Nixon story and applied their own treatment.

The Detroit Free Press

METRO FINAL

EXTRA

Ten Cents

On Guard for 133 Years

Friday, June 12, 1964

Vol. 134—No. 39

MARINA OSWALD'S STORY: PLOT ON NIXON

BY HUGH AYNESWORTH

DALLAS—Marina Oswald thinks she may have argued her husband Lee out of trying to kill former Vice President Richard Nixon in early 1963, she told me in an exclusive interview before she left to testify before the Warren Commission Thursday.

She also disclosed:

● That Oswald considered Gen. Edwin A. Walker an "extremist" and believed he had done the right thing when he shot at the onetime army officer April 10, 1963.

● That regardless of her feelings toward her husband, she probably wouldn't have married him had they met in the United States and had she understood him.

● That she feels certain that Lee was the lone assassin who killed President John F. Kennedy and wounded Texas Gov. John Connally, but that it was just because "he wanted to be a big shot," not because of hatred for Kennedy.

Exclusive

Much of the material discussed in the lengthy interview also had told to the Warren Commission in her more than 20 hours with the investigators in February. She returned there Thursday to go over more details for the probers.

THE NIXON THREAT CAME in April or May of 1963, shortly before the Oswalds left for New Orleans to live. (She spent two weeks with Mrs. Ruth Paine in the Dallas suburb of Irving before joining him there.)

Marina said she could not pinpoint the exact date, but said: "He came walking into the room, all dressed up, and had a gun in his

hand. I asked him what he was doing, where he was going."

"I'm going to see Richard Nixon," she quoted Oswald as replying. This was within a few days of the attempt on Walker's life.

Marina said she was afraid and tried to get Lee to talk about it.

When James Martin, Marina's former business manager, testified before the Warren investigators, he told them Marina locked Lee in a room to keep him from going after Nixon. Martin made the statement just a few days after he had been fired by Marina.

Marina made no mention of this in the interview, but she described the scene as "a heated argument."

"We argued plenty," Marina said, "and he didn't go. I didn't know anything about Mr. Nixon. I didn't know if he was in Dallas or where he was."

SHE ADDED: "It didn't matter to him who he killed, he just wanted to become popular."

She hesitated here as she realized, despite her limited English, that the word "popular" wasn't the one she

Marina Oswald   Lee Harvey Oswald   Richard Nixon

Cavanagh Men Seek Dem Reins

BY HAL COHEN AND GENE ROBERTS
Free Press Staff writers

The possibility of a citywide struggle between Detroit labor and Mayor Cavanagh's political forces arose Wednesday when Cavanagh's supporters confirmed they have entered more than 300 candidates in this race for Democratic precinct delegates.

The mayor's delegates—if a majority of them were elected

Scranton Reported Set

THOUSANDS of paratroopers were dropped into Normandy to seize vital road crossings and battle up German reinforcements while Allied troops secured their invasion beachhead. Stars on map indicate where paratroopers of the 82nd and 101st airborne divisions landed.

If Invasion Had Failed, Ike Wanted All the Blame

CRONKITE: General Eisenhower, did your staff have a plan for evacuating the invasion beaches in case of failure?

EISENHOWER: No. If we had to do any evacuating—God forbid—that would have been a terrible thing. But if there had been no more hope, the ships were there to take them off.

QUESTION: Just a matter of sending a message to get off the beach?

EISENHOWER: That's right. Well, I'll tell you. I talked to one of the invasion units and to Gen. Bradley's headquarters staff, and what I said was, "This operation is not being planned with any alternatives." This operation is planned as a victory, and that's the way it's going to be. We're going down there, and we're throwing everything we have into it, and we're going to make it a success.

So we just really didn't have anything planned for the last minute. But, of course, the naval commanders would have done their best to get the men off. They would have covered an evacuation with a tremendous bombardment. They would have tried to get everything back if a disaster had occurred. Only in the Omaha area did we really have real trouble. The Germans had their 352d Division at Omaha, and it was an active outfit and a very good one.

QUESTION: The German 352d?

EISENHOWER: Yes. Though our intelligence finally confirmed its

D-DAY PLUS 20

Ike's Own Story

Twenty years after D-Day, Gen. Dwight D. Eisenhower, in exclusive conversations with Walter Cronkite of CBS News, recounted the historic moments of the Normandy invasion. This sixth of 16 instalments is based on a talk in the war room at Eisenhower's old Portsmouth, England, command post.

presence at Omaha, they did so only at the last minute. Too late to make changes, to tell our people going in. "Maybe you ought to go in elsewhere." So they went right in and had a real fight.

CRONKITE: General Eisenhower, I gather that at one point you wrote a message that you were prepared to send if there had been a disaster on the beaches.

EISENHOWER: Walter, let me tell you something. What I did was this.
Turn to Page 2A, Column 1

ARGUMENTS DISSUADED MATE

JUN 1 2 1964

Marina Recalls Threat to Ni[x]

(c) The Dallas Morning News, 1964
By HUGH AYNESWORTH

Marina Oswald thinks she may have argued Lee Harvey Oswald out of trying to kill former Vice-President Richard M. Nixon in early 1963, she has told The Dallas News in an exclusive interview.

Before leaving for Washington to testify before the Warren Commission, Oswald's widow also disclosed:

—That Oswald considered Edwin A. Walker an "extremist" and he believed he had done the right thing last April 10 when he shot at the onetime Army general.

—That regardless of her feelings toward her husband, she probably wouldn't have

Attack on Polio
—See Back Page

A full report on the second instalment of "Operation Sugar Cube," the three-county attack on polio, is on the Back Page today. For the second time, the Free Press publishes the complete list of centers where the dis-

"popular" wasn't the one she wanted to use.

"TO BE recognized . . ." her interpreter, Mrs. Declan Ford of Dallas, corrected with a smile.

"He played the big shot so much I'm sure he believed it himself," Marina recalled.

Nixon wasn't in Dallas at that time, but on April 21 (about a week before Oswald left Dallas for New Orleans), The Dallas Morning News printed these bold headlines on the lead story last Sunday:

"NIXON CALLS FOR DECISION TO FORCE REDS OUT OF CUBA."

Oswald was an avid newspaper reader. If he picked up a paper that day

hurt has been allowed to rub off on the little ones.

We asked if Junie missed her father.

"I think she was affected by all that happened," Marina said, "but I don't think she understood it all. She was sick and very nervous during all the happenings, though." Marina added with a smile:

"She calls every man she sees 'Daddy' now."

JUNIE PULLED herself into Marina's lap as her mother recalled how she had met Lee in Minsk, Russia, at a dance.

"I was with a friend who was a medical student," Marina said,

warm. When we arrived near noon, Junie burst into the living room sans clothes, just as Marina was offering us a soft drink. Marina was slightly embarrassed. "Help yourself," please," she smiled, pointing to the refrigerator as she herded the 3-year-old back into the bedroom for some panties.

MARINA HAS a washer and a dryer, of which she is very proud. "The women in Russia don't have such things," she said wistfully.

"I think American women have a much better life," she said. "Their load is much lighter."

E. R. Robnett, manager of a Wyatt's store about a block from Marina's

here, so that's cheap."

THE RUSSIA much more in than her Amer Marina explaine

"Everybody her she smiled. "No coal from downsa

We noted the some dental wo had last seen seriously:

"It's so diff They never w personal things. about who has h

"The Russian on, "didn't even

NEW YORK—[A]—The nude look in fashion, threatened or promised in 5 to 10 years, is here now.

Nobody is more surprised than the designers and buyers.

"IT'S INCREDIBLE," sighs weary Rudi Gernreich after a hectic day of taking orders for his topless ladies' bathing suit model, orders from such high-fashion stores across the country

King
Attorney Gen Warren of Day-

jury to investigate the racial turmoil in St. Augustine.

Circuit Judge Howell Melton signal an order summoning the grand jury into special session Friday at the request of State

the key impulse behind pulling the trigger was a pathological hunger to be recognized. "Sometimes he was a little bit sick," she told the Warren Commission. "He was a normal man, but sometimes people don't understand him. And sometimes I didn't know—he want to be popular, so everyone know who is Lee Harvey Oswald."

From Oswald's point of view, then, the single significant difference between the Kennedy assassination and his two previous attempts was that killing Kennedy finally made him famous.

His bungled assault on Gen. Walker came to light in early December 1963, after Ruth Paine turned over to police a box of Oswald's possessions. The materials included an undated note to Marina, written in Russian, instructing her what to do if he was arrested. The note assured her that he had paid the rent and utility bills. She was to send any news clippings about him to "the embassy," so they could help her. He also left a mailbox key, asked her to hold on to his personal papers and to contact the American Red Cross for help if she needed it.

Confronted with the note, Marina conceded she was familiar with it and the reasons Lee wrote it.

On April 10th of 1963, the Oswalds were living in an apartment on Neely Street in Dallas. That evening, according to Marina, Lee went out alone shortly after dinner. She thought he'd gone to his nightly typing class. But when he didn't return by 10 o'clock, she grew nervous and went to the small enclosure he used as an office, where she discovered the note.

Finally, a couple of hours later Lee came in the door panting, his clothes in disarray. "He came in all pale and I could see he was nervous," she later told me. "I asked him where he had been and he told me, 'I just tried to kill Gen. Walker.'"

In fact, he had barely missed. The slug ripped through a window casing, skimmed Walker's scalp, and then tore a golfball-size hole in the wall behind him, penetrating nine inches before coming to rest on a stack of pamphlets in the adjoining room.

Marina said she didn't know who Walker was. "Who is Gen. Walker?" she asked. "Does he have a wife and family?"

"He's a fascist," Lee snapped back.

According to Marina, Lee later told her he planned the shooting for two months. He showed her a notebook with photos of the Walker house in Dallas' exclusive Turtle Creek area, and a map to find the residence.

A source I developed on the Warren Commission added a bit more to the story. He told me that after that night Marina apparently used the Russian-language note Oswald left her as leverage. Whenever Lee started to abuse her, Marina would mention the letter and scare him into worrying that she'd turn him in, and therefore leave her alone.

The tale of Oswald's second alleged target that April is somewhat murkier. On Jan.13, 1964, Jim Martin informed Robert Oswald that Marina had recently told him that Lee threatened to shoot former Vice President Richard Nixon.

"He said Marina had locked Lee in the bathroom for the entire day," Robert then told the Warren Commission on February 20th. According to Robert's diary, Marina also confirmed the story to him, once again in conjunction with a trip to the cemetery.

"We had been talking about the children," Robert testified. "And at a pause in this conversation, she started relating to me this incident. 'Robert, Lee also wanted to shoot Mr. Nixon' she told me. I replied, 'Yes, Jim told me about this when we were sitting in the den that afternoon.'"

Marina explained to Robert that his younger brother had been angry, but calmed down after his stay in the bathroom.

Warren Commission assistant counsel Alfred Jenner was incredulous. "Did it occur to you that it might be quite difficult for a 98-pound woman to lock your brother in a bathroom?"

"Yes, sir," Robert answered, "it has occurred to me exactly how this was possible, to an extent that a bathroom usually has a lock on the inside and not on the outside."

Marina later repeated the story in general to me, but not the stuff about locking Lee in the bathroom. This public disclosure got her into trouble. Back in February when she testified before the Warren Commission about the Gen. Walker episode, commission member John Sherman Cooper, a GOP senator from Kentucky, asked her, "Did he express to you any hostility toward any particular official of the United States?"

Marina said no.

I don't know whether the commission members simply overlooked Robert Oswald's later testimony on the subject, but they made a lot of threatening sounds and recalled Marina to Washington for further testimony after my story appeared on June 12th.

Marina was furious with me.

"What do you know about all this?" she demanded over the phone. "You have caused me hurt! Caused me to have government people calling me a liar! Do you know what you've done? Isn't anything private?"

I began to speak, then thought better of it.

"Think of my children! Your story is wrong."

I asked her what part was wrong.

"The whole thing! And the way you slanted at me as if I was a criminal." Then she hung up.

The story was absolutely accurate, and when she reappeared before the commission that month, the mood was not warm.

Marina was asked why she hadn't mentioned the Nixon story in February.

"There were an awful lot of questions at that time," she answered. "And I was very tired and I felt that I had told everything. And I don't remember. I can't understand why I didn't mention this. It would have been better for me to mention it the first time than to make you all do more work on it."

She told the committee that Lee came in the apartment dressed in his suit and said, "Today, Nixon is coming. I want to go out and have a look at him."

"I know how you look," Marina remembered replying.

"You have already promised me not to play anymore with that thing," meaning the handgun Oswald carried. Marina testified that they argued for perhaps a half hour before her husband finally left. "I am going to go out and find out if there will be an appropriate opportunity," he said, "and if there is I will use the pistol."

"Didn't that statement he made about Vice President Nixon make a strong impression on you?" asked Allen Dulles.

"I don't know," Marina answered. "I was pregnant at the time. I had a lot of other things to worry about. I was getting pretty well tired of all these escapades of his."

Marina and her children.

Oswald's self-styled "Historic Diary" in *Life* Magazine.

C H A P T E R   E L E V E N

"We'd like for you to tell us where you obtained the Russian diary"

There have been four occasions in my professional life when government officials wanted to know what I knew, but I wouldn't tell them, so they tapped my phone. I don't think such a measure has ever been justified in my case, and I also doubt that it ever was worth their trouble.

The first time I suspected that my phone was tapped was in late June of 1964, when I obtained what Lee Harvey Oswald styled his "Historic Diary," otherwise known as his Russian diary, together with a number of his personal effects, photos, and documents.

The diary, about 5,000 handwritten words in all, covered his life from Oct. 16, 1959, the day he arrived in the Soviet Union, to March 27, 1962, just after he and Marina had flown with one-month-old June Lee from Minsk to Dallas.

This was a major newsbreak and ran on page one of practically every American daily—and overseas papers as well. Our first-day headline:

SECRET DIARY
Oswald's Thoughts Bared

Among our many disclosures, we told the world that Oswald said he had been on the Soviet secret police payroll.

"When I went to Russia in the winter of 1959 my funds were very limited," he wrote. "So after a certain time, after the Russians had assured themselves that I was really the naive American who believed in communism, they arranged for me to receive a certain amount of money every month.

"Oh, it came technically through the Red Cross as financial help to a poor political immigrant, but it was arranged by the MVD."

He reported that once he lost faith with communist society and started to negotiate his exit from the Soviet Union "my 'Red Cross' allotment was cut off."

Early in the diary he also described his attempted suicide when he believed he would not be allowed to stay in the country.

"7:00 p.m. I decide to end it. Soak wrist in cold water to numb the pain. Then slash my left wrist. Then place into bathtub of hot water."

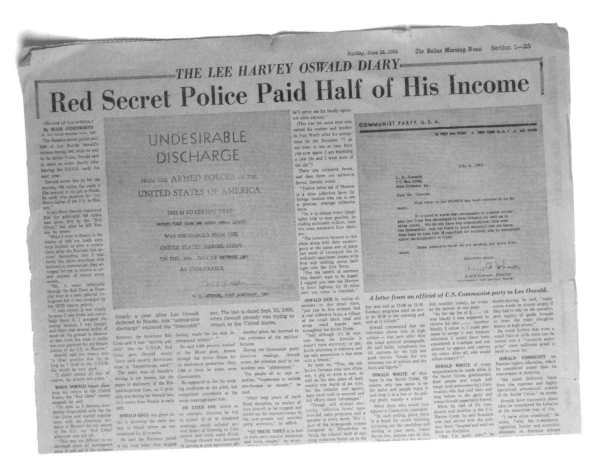

One of a series of stories I wrote about Oswald's Russian diary, which he called the "Historic Diary"—the title Oswald himself gave his diary.

Rimma Sherikova, Oswald's Intourist guide, discovered him on the bathroom floor and summoned an ambulance, which rushed Oswald to the hospital, where five stitches were taken in his left wrist.

The diary's sudden appearance in *The Dallas Morning News* caught everybody by surprise, and there were a number of people who were very angry with me. The FBI was quickly dispatched to find out where I got the material and, if possible, whether more was coming.

"An embarrassment," commission member and former CIA Director Allen Dulles later told me. "If the lawyers could have gotten hold of you," Dulles added, "I hesitate to think what might have become of you."

He told me the publication of the diary hadn't bothered him personally. "You just released the facts," Dulles explained. "You didn't attempt to color it as some would have done."

J. Edgar Hoover took a dimmer view of my work.

Within hours of the first story's appearance on Saturday, June 27, 1964, Hoover ordered Gordon Shanklin to sniff out the leak. Shanklin dispatched two agents to interview me, several times, as well as several editors at the *News*, to whom I had not disclosed my source's identity. I knew better.

Ted Dealey called me from his office after the agents departed. "The FBI just left my office trying to get me to tell them where you got Oswald's diary," he growled. "I told them I wasn't going to tell them anything, and I showed them the way to the newsroom and told them they could interview you. They'll be there momentarily. I hope you don't tell them a damned thing either."

Minutes later Johnny King swung by my desk, wearing a large grin.

"May I present these two men from the FBI," King said. "They think you might have some business with them."

He introduced Manny Clements and another agent whose name I have forgotten, then moved off a few feet—close enough to monitor the conversation but not close enough to be part of an arrest.

"We'd like for you to tell us where you obtained the Russian diary," agent Clements began in a friendly manner as he and his partner pulled up a couple of reporters' chairs close to my messy workplace.

"You see, to you this is just a news story," he went on, "but to us it's much more. Somebody is leaking material that shouldn't be released. We've got to find out who is dealing in this material and why."

FROM OCT. 16 1959 ARRIVAL —

1959   LEAVEING

1ST PAGE

OCT. 16. ARRIVE FROM HELSINKI BY TRAIN; AM MET BY INTOURES REPRE. AND IN CAR TO HOTEL "BERLIN". REGES. AS "STUDET" 5 DAY LUX. TOURIST. TICKET.) MEET MY INTOURIST GUIED RIMMA SHERIKOVA, I EXPLAIN TO HER I WISH TO APPLI: FOR RUS. CITIZENSHIP. SHE IS FLABBERGASSED BUT AGGREES TO HELP, SHE CHECKS WITH HER BOSS, MAIN OFFICE INTOUR; THAN HELPS ME ADD. A LETTER TO SUP. SOV.T. ASKING FOR CITIZENSHIP MEAN WHILE BOSS TELEPHONS PASSPORT & VISA OFFIC AND NOTIFIES THEM ABOUT ME.

OCT. 17- RIMMA MEETS ME FOR INTOURIST SIGHTSEEING SAYS WE MUST CONTIN. WITH THIS ALTHOUGH I AM TOO NEVUOS SHE IS "SURE" ILL HAVE AN ANSEWER. SOON. ASKS ME ABOUT MYSELF AND MY REASONS FOR DOING THIS I EXPLAINE I AM A COMMUNIST. ECT. SHE IS ADITLY SYM. BUT UNEASY NOW, SHE TRIES TO BE A FRIEND TO ME. SHE FEELS SORRY FOR ME I AM SOMETH. NEW.

SUND OCT. 18. MY 20TH BIRTHDAY, WE VIST EXHIB. IN MORNING AND IN THE AFTER NOON THE LEAIN-STALIN TOMB. SHE GIVES ME A PRESENT BOOK "IDEOT" BY DOSTOEVSKI.

OCT. 19. TOURISM. AM ANXIOUS SINCE MY VISA IS GOOD FOR FIVE DAYS ONLY AND STILL NO WIRD FROM AUTH. ABOUT MY REQEST.

OCT. 20 RIMMER IN THE AFTER NOON SAYS INTOURIST WAS NOTIFIED BY THE PASS. & VISA DEPT. THAT THEY WANT TO SEE ME I AM EXCITED GREATLY BY THIS NEWS.

OCT. 21 (MOR) MEETING WITH SIGLE OFFIAL. BALDING STOUT, BLACK SUIT FAIRLY. GOOD ENGLISH, ASKES WHAT DO I WANT? I SAY SOV.TE CITIZENSHIP, HE ASK WHY I GIVE VAGUE ANSEWERS ABOUT "GREAT SOVIET UNION" HE TELLS ME "USSR ONLY GREAT IN LITERATURE WANTS ME TO GO BACK HOME" I AM STUNDED I REITERATE, HE SAYS HE SHALL CHECK AND LET ME KNOW WEATHER MY VISA WILL BE (EXTENDED IT EXIPIERS TODAY)

EVE. 6.00 REVIVE WORD FROM POLICE OFFICIAL. I MUST LEAVE COUNTRY TONIGHT AT 8.00 P.M. AS VISA EXPIRES. I AM SHOCKED!! MY DREAMS! I RETIRE TO MY ROOM. I HAVE $100. LEFT. I HAVE WAITED FOR 2 YEAR TO BE ACCEPTED MY FONDLE DREAMS ARE SHATTERED BECAUSE OF A PETTY OFFIAL, BECAUSE OF BAD PIANNING I PLANNED SO MUCH! 7.00 P.M. I DECIDE TO END IT. SOAK RIST IN COLD WATER TO NUMB THE PAIN. THAN SLASH MY LEFT WRIST, THAN PLAUG WRIST INTO BATHTUM OF HOT WATER. I THINK "WHEN RIMMA COMES AT 8. TO FIND ME DEAD IT WILL BE A GREAT SHOCK. SOMEWHERE, A VIOLIN PLAYS, AS I

"You sound like you think I bribed somebody to get into the commission archives," I replied. "Or that somebody is selling this information. I don't like that perception. It's totally untrue."

We parried in this way for a few minutes to nobody's advantage. I told them that I expected to work as a journalist the rest of my life. To divulge information that could—undoubtedly would—be detrimental to my source or sources was not something I would ever do.

Clements said something like, "Well, we intend to find out."

I answered "Good luck," or whatever, and the interview ended.

The magnitude of the story—the *News* fielded at least 75 queries from all over the world, publications asking if there was more to come, could they reprint the entire piece—caused some uproar in the newsroom. A couple of my colleagues disappointed me when they warned that my life would never be the same if I didn't cooperate and tell the FBI everything. My only answer was that my life would never be the same if I did. I don't rat out my sources.

The best advice came from Harry McCormick. "Listen, Kissy," he said (I don't know where Harry came up with that nickname, which he used with a half dozen or so young reporters), "don't tell 'em anything. They don't really expect you to tell 'em."

Harry did warn me that I could expect a tap on my phone.

"They've already been embarrassed enough by the assassination," he said. "They won't want to admit they can't find out where a reporter scooped them. But don't say anything on your phone for a few days that you wouldn't want to become a part of a report somewhere down the line."

The next afternoon I received another call from Manny Clements.

"You ready to tell us now?" he asked.

"No, nothing has changed."

"Well, if you're going to be in tomorrow morning, I'd like to run something by you. Eleven o'clock agreeable?"

That night I discussed the bureau probe with my wife, when suddenly I had an inspiration.

"I'll call you tomorrow morning as soon as I get to the office," I told her, "and I'll set a trap for them. If the FBI is listening, I'll know it when they come by at eleven."

"You're going to get in deeper trouble," she warned me.

This was the fun part. At the office next morning I telephoned home, ostensibly to discuss my concerns over the FBI investigation.

Opposite:
First page of
Oswald's diary.

160

"I'm a little worried they are going to find out where I got the diary," I said gravely, "that Shanklin slipped it to me. He could lose his job."

All I had to do was wait. A short time later Clements and his partner reappeared at the paper.

Manny tried as usual to be friendly, persuasive. "We don't want to hurt anybody here," he said, "but just like you, we have a job to do. We know where the diary is and how many copies are available and where they are. All we need to know is where you obtained your copy."

Then he tipped his hand. "What we are seriously concerned about is that somebody official is involved here."

I stifled a smirk.

"Can we be reasonably assured that nobody in the U.S. attorney's office gave you this material? Can you assure us nobody employed by the Federal Bureau of Investigation allowed you to see it or copy it?"

"Sorry," I said, absolutely delighted with myself and my little strategem. I imagined Gordon Shanklin with steam coming out his ears. "But I am not going to exclude anybody. What you have to do is your job and what I must do is mine. I am not going to tell you."

Manny's partner stooped to intimidation. "You familiar with federal grand juries?" he snarled at me as they left.

Afterward, crusty old Ted Dealey summoned me up to the executive floor and shook my hand. "Damn fine job, Hugh. Glad you didn't break down and tell 'em.

I was persistently investigated by the FBI after *The Dallas Morning News'* release of the diary.

"They won't be forgetting your name soon around here, young man," he added.

Two years later, when he presented me a five-year

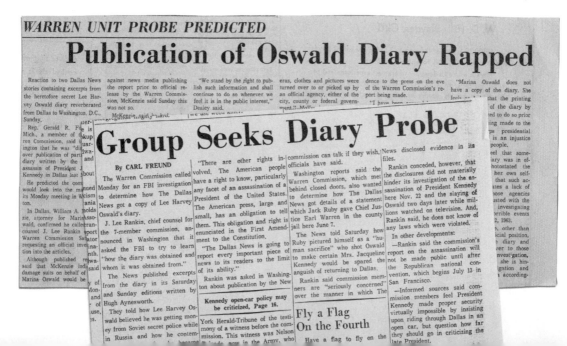

service pin, Dealey called me Frank Reece.

Actually, for all his tough talk and bluster, Dealey was fairly easily panicked. Following our first two installments of Oswald's diary, Dallas lawyer William McKenzie threatened a lawsuit against the *News* on Marina's behalf. When it appeared that the mere chance of being sued might scuttle our third and final installment, I lit a backfire, telling my editors that the *Detroit Free Press* had gotten hold of the material, and was poised to scoop our scoop. This of course was not true, but it did persuade the *News* to proceed with the third article.

Nothing came of Marina's threatened suit, but the diary case did not improve my relations with her. Nor did a front-page story I wrote for the *New York Journal-American* in which I mentioned her heavy smoking and drinking. (A television reporter once told me he watched Marina finish off a fifth of Bailey's Bristol Crème, washing the stuff down with beer, in two hours "and still she didn't seem drunk!" he said.) My article also described how Marina had become "very Americanized" in the savvy way she peddled interviews and the like.

For years thereafter, Marina considered me her enemy.

Oddly, it would take another newspaper article to undo her animosity.

Marina married Ken Porter and gradually faded into relative obscurity in Rockwall, a little town east of Dallas. From time to time she'd meet with conspiracy theorists, some of whom took advantage of her. At last, and who knows why, she announced that her slain husband hadn't killed anyone. I tried to get in touch with her a couple of times during this period, but Marina told me she had nothing to say to me.

Then, after a silence of more than a decade, my telephone rang one morning, and there she was.

"Is this Hugh Aynesworth, my enemy?"

"Well, it's me, Marina," I replied. "But I'm not your enemy. How are you?"

She went straight to the point.

"Do you read the *National Enquirer?*"

"Not if I can avoid it."

"Well, please get one and read a story in this edition. It's about me and the children, and it's really horrible for them. I need your help. I have nobody else to turn to."

I figured that no doubt was so, given her deep dislike for me. But I was curious to see what kind of article it took for Marina Oswald Porter to reach out to me for help. So I went to the grocery store, bought the *Enquirer*, and immediately understood why she was so upset. It was a really nasty article, purporting to tell how June Lee and Rachel were hated and taunted in their neighborhood.

This was not the picture I'd received over the years. From all reports, Marina and Ken Porter had been great parents and the girls were doing extremely well, especially in view of the past.

I called Marina back and emphatically recommended that she sue the tabloid.

"I can't afford a lawyer," she said. "Do you know anyone?"

"Not many that know libel law well," I said, "but give me a few hours to check around."

My choice was Frank Jackson, a former NFL running back who'd played for the Kansas City Chiefs and Miami Dolphins and now was very successfully practicing criminal defense law in Dallas.

"I'll do what I can," Frank said when I explained the situation. That turned out to be quite a lot. Jackson determined that Marguerite was partly behind the mischief; she helped plant the story through a friend who had neither met nor even seen her grandchildren. In the end, the *Enquirer* settled for more than $50,000, most of which I hoped would be put away for June Lee and Rachel's college educations.

Marina graciously thanked me for my help and asked me to lunch with her daughters.

We talked warmly, like old friends, not enemies. A year or so later, however, when I called to ask for a comment on an aspect of the assassination story, she told me she was under contract and could not be quoted.

Since then she worked as a clerk in a north Dallas Army-Navy surplus store. I haven't seen her for many years now, but am told that she retired at 62 in August 2003.

Ruby with his attorneys Joe Tonahill (left), Melvin Belli (right),
and investigator for the defense team, Bob Denson (center).

CHAPTER TWELVE

"He wanted to be a hero"

Jack Ruby was the quintessential wanna-be but never-was. Full of big stories, bigger dreams and lusty braggadocio, the strip show operator was first and foremost a lowlife, a man who searched for class as though he understood what it was.

Often he would tell his pals that someday he'd have a club in Las Vegas. That, to him, was class. Once he told his lawyer Stanley Kauffman that when he made it big in the Nevada city, he wouldn't have to worry any more about years and years of difficulties with the Internal Revenue Service. "He said, 'They never bother the big, important guys. You don't see guys hassled once they become somebody in show business.'"

Hardly a week went by in Dallas when you wouldn't see Ruby promoting some inane product, chasing fire trucks, pushing himself into public displays or passing out his Carousel Club calling cards at the fights, in the bars, or on downtown streets.

One time it might be promoting a young black singer/dancer, another time an exercise board, or a potion "sure to make you thinner and more powerful." Once he touted a gangly Arkansas girl as a "dancer," predicting she would be a smash hit at the Carousel. "She'll be the only Jewish stripper Dallas has ever seen," he told Don Campbell, the *News* ad executive. The girl never graced his stage.

Ruby never married, was somewhat of a health nut, and I never found a person who recalled his drinking alcohol. Because he was at times almost prissy and had a very slight lisp, some thought he was homosexual. For several years, he dated a shy, pretty woman named Alice Nichols, but by November 1963, they hadn't been together in months. Their usual dates, only periodic, meant dinner and a movie.

Mrs. Nichols testified briefly at his trial, but then faded into obscurity as the media, showing more sensitivity than usual, left her alone.

Even those who should have known him well usually admitted they didn't. "He had this big, big heart," said sister Eva. Sister Eileen Kaminsky once described him to me as "this great big puppy dog. He might slobber all over you, but you couldn't dislike him."

Fact was, I and many others disliked him intensely.

Bob Larkin, once Ruby's bouncer and later a club owner on his own, said that while Jack was warm-hearted to many, he had a "weird, unusual" bent. He said that one time he had been stabbed in the stomach and was writhing on the sidewalk—not dangerously injured but in a lot of pain—when Ruby walked up to him.

He said Ruby kicked him. "And kept saying, 'Get up Bob. Get up.'"

Melvin Belli, during his first weeks as Ruby's lawyer, got in trouble with the local bar association (and the Ruby family) for describing his client as "a Damon Runyon character, a scrounger with a million and one different ventures. He builds up in his own mind all sorts of grandiose ideas."

Carl Freund, the *News'* main courthouse reporter, a prolific contributor and fast writer, had stepped into the role that Paul Crume had played with the Nov. 22 JFK murder story. He processed and fine-tuned reportage from several reporters handling various aspects of Ruby's thrust into history that Sunday.

Jubilant Dallas bystander the day of Oswald's murder.

Freund dropped by my desk the following morning to apologize for not using more of my file in the Nov. 25 story. And in the course of discussing the possibility of my doing a feature on Tom Howard, Ruby's initial lawyer, another reporter dropped by, grinning, with Freund's story in hand. "Look at this," he said to Freund, tossing down the newspaper and walking away.

Freund looked, and read a little bit—then it hit him. The headline read: "Nightclub Man Takes Roll of Executioner."

I had not noticed the misspelling

of "role," nor had anyone else that I saw that morning.

••••••••••••••••••••••••••••

In the immediate aftermath of the Oswald murder, within minutes of an ambulance wheeling him off to Parkland a number of reporters, including me, headed upstairs at City Hall to ferret out what we could. There wasn't much to learn at first, but several of us noted a small-time local defense lawyer named Tom Howard arriving for a meeting with Ruby's sister, Eva Grant, and one other person I couldn't identify.

Melvin Belli interviewed by media, including Dorothy Kilgallen (to Belli's right) and me (far left).

Jim Underwood, a KRLD reporter, was greeted warmly by Eva, and I think he was privy to the brief meeting they had in a police station anteroom that afternoon. I don't think they met with Ruby himself at that time, but I am not sure. Some elevators in that building ended up in strange places.

As Howard headed back to his office—directly across Akard Street—a short while later, several of us trailed him. "Are you gonna plead insanity?" one newsman shouted.

Howard stopped, grinned and replied: "Well, I guess you'd say that anybody who'd kill a man in the police station might just be crazy, but that's something we will have to decide at a later point." Tom, a country-talkin' good ole boy popular with the courthouse guys, said he had to talk with family members and would be glad to answer questions, possibly later that day.

In a few minutes, the other reporters peeled off in search of better copy, but I had noticed that the last person into Howard's office door had left it slightly ajar. So, after waiting for what seemed an eternity, but was probably four or five minutes—and when I could be sure none of the other reporters could see me, I slipped inside.

It was late afternoon on Sunday. There were no secretaries; the

Eva Grant, Ruby's sister (top center). Notice the news cameraman in formal attire, common in the 1960s.

lights were dimmed. I didn't see anyone in the office, but I heard voices—Howard's and others—on the other side of an office wall.

Someone said, "Well, hell, just call him" and they chatted a moment or two about how to approach whomever they were planning to call. I heard Eva say, "Well, tell him right off, we don't have any money."

They put through the call, and on a receptionist's desk near me a telephone clicked—which gave me an idea. Maybe I could ease the receiver off the hook—they were big, black and heavy then—and find out who was on the other end.

But I hesitated, scared to death somebody would bolt out of Howard's office and catch me. Still, I needed to know what was happening. Knowing and understanding defense lawyers even then, I knew that if I waited for an explanation, (1) it might never be forthcoming; and (2) if it was, it might be colored to benefit the client.

Though I could hear Howard's booming voice, I still needed the other side of that conversation.

Just behind that desk was another office. I had already been through so much emotionally that weekend, I doubt I consciously considered what might happen if I got caught. I just sidled into the office, slowly lifted the receiver, and listened. Unlike two days before, when I had stumbled on the scene with nothing to write upon, this time I had several index cards stuffed in my pocket.

I heard a woman saying, "Oh, here he is, hold on a minute." Then boomed a deep, drawling voice I thought I recognized. A couple of

comments later, and I was sure. It was Percy Foreman—
undoubtedly the most famous criminal lawyer in Texas history,
an old-time orator and spellbinder. Percy had won something
like 300 straight murder cases.

I had known him only casually, but had heard myriad tales about
how Foreman was so good that sometimes prosecutors tried to avoid
trying cases against him. His presence in a case—always expensive—
usually changed many aspects of a murder trial. He was said to be
absolutely phenomenal at jury selection—which he onetime later
told me was "more than half the battle."

In the other room they got to discussing an insanity plea for Ruby.
"You've got to build a strong case—believable witnesses who will say
this man was so upset at Kennedy's killing that he couldn't operate
normally," Foreman suggested. "Hell, everybody in the country was
upset. I was. Weren't you, Tom?"

"Now if it was me trying this…" Foreman began—and Howard
cut him off. "Percy, that's why I'm calling you. The family wants you
to help us, to help me."

A man I had never seen before, possibly one of Howard's
law partners, swept out of the closed office and hurried down to
a restroom on the south side of the offices. I jumped just in time,
slipping under the desk. It seemed a lifetime till I heard the man
walk back in and close the door. I was really afraid. I knew that if
the session in Howard's office ended abruptly, I was done for.
They'd be visiting me down the row from Jack Ruby.

But the temptation was too great. I needed to know if Foreman
was going to represent Ruby. I needed to know how much money he
was going to charge. I needed to know so many things—things
nobody else in the media would know.

I had stopped sweating, and I eased the receiver up again. This
time an agitated, Midwestern accent almost screamed, "I don't care
what he wants. Don't deal with the son-of-a-bitch one more minute."

"I'll be there as soon as I can," said the voice. "You see that he's
treated okay and look after Eva." I quickly hung up the phone and
crept out into the late afternoon—and ran back across the street to
City Hall, where I called the newspaper office.

One of the assistant city editors asked me if I had filed my first-
person stuff from seeing Ruby shoot Oswald, and I said I had called in
hours before. "Well, I don't see it anywhere," he told me. "Better come

on in and make sure we have it all."

It was several weeks before I got the entire story of those phone calls from Howard and Earl Ruby. It had been Earl on the other end of that phone call that first afternoon, irate—he told me later—that Foreman wanted a guarantee of $75,000 before he would get involved.

That contact between Howard and Foreman with Earl Ruby (who'd bankroll his brother's defense) changed many things about Jack Ruby and Dallas—perhaps even history. For one thing, Earl took such an instant dislike to Foreman that he questioned Howard's judgment in soliciting Foreman's opinions. And Earl—who owned a thriving cleaning establishment in Detroit's Cobo Hall, immediately flew to California, where he watched Melvin Belli in trial—and within hours hired him to represent Jack.

When Belli arrived in Dallas, with his long-time pal Joe Tonahill of Jasper, Texas, in tow, it was just a matter of time before Howard was scuttled.

"I would have put Jack on the stand and gotten him to tell the jury how he felt, how he hurt, how he bled when that communist killed our president," Howard told reporters after he was replaced. "I know enough about Jack Ruby that he would have cried, wailed, blubbered all over himself. They couldn't have put a man like this to death.

"After all," Howard added, "how many of them (jurors) might have felt the same way?"

Howard wasn't the only one who believed that Howard's strategy might have worked.

"If they had moved the trial out of Dallas, we could have come close to walking him," Foreman later told me.

When he finally was hired as an appeals expert in late 1964, he didn't last long. Foreman and Earl still couldn't abide each other. Foreman said he finally quit because "the family can't agree on anything."

But back to Belli. Though he was a wonderfully adept personal injury lawyer, the San Francisco lawyer had never tried a murder defense before. He was something of a "dandy," a flashy dresser, snappy with the repartee, and vicious with his criticism—which was often directed at Dallas authorities and the *News*.

From the moment Belli hit town and Bill Alexander laughed publicly at his fur-lined briefcase, it was all about the courthouse crowd making fun of the silver-haired interloper, while Belli daily berated the *News,* the city itself, and all it stood for.

The Dallas establishment found much to dislike in Melvin Belli.

Though there was a cadre of people in Dallas who probably deserved comeuppance for their blatant bigotry and insensitivity, most of the citizenry considered itself fair and open-minded. And Belli didn't wear well with them.

"If he had been able to get a change of venue, all this folderol might have been of value," said Charles Tessmer, one of Dallas' most talented criminal lawyers, "but when poor Jack had to face a jury that had already endured weeks of taunting, anti-Dallas rhetoric, there was no way he would win.

"Of course," Tessmer added wryly, "that defense didn't help much either."

District Judge Joe B. Brown was a friendly, outgoing character, a man who loved the press—that is, until he took a harsh dose of out-of-town media abuse, some deserved, most not. Belli, behind his back, used to chortle and call the judge, "Necessity." Asked why he called Brown that, Belli would slap his leg and drop his punch-line, "Because necessity knows no law."

Brown decided early on he wasn't going to allow a defense move to take the trial elsewhere. That was apparent by his rulings in a change of venue hearing.

I once asked him if he didn't think it would be better for all (what naiveté!) if he moved the trial somewhere else in Texas. "Where the hell else?" Brown snapped. "Everybody in Texas saw what he did. Everybody in the world had seen it ten times since then. A change of venue is for when the move can assure a jury panel would not be tainted by publicity or intense prejudice. This case doesn't qualify."

A few days later Brown called me into his chambers at a noon break and told me with a big smile: "Hey, I found the perfect place."

Sensing I did not understand, he said, "the place to move to trial to, you know."

"Yeah," he continued, "it's Mentone, Texas. There are only 51 people in the whole county (Loving County in deep west Texas) and only two of 'em have television sets."

I wasn't sure where he was heading.

"But where in hell would I sequester the jury," he said as we walked out together.

Notice Ruby's middle finger used to pull the trigger, which became the basis for the Ruby defense.

•••••••••••••••••••••••••••

So, when Brown ruled they would hold the trial in Dallas, Belli began to build a defense. Joe Tonahill told me in 1999 that Belli was so certain he would be able to obtain a change of venue, that little had been done to build a secondary line of defense.

And, within a few weeks, the Ruby family in particular became extremely worried.

"I don't know what they're doing," Earl told me one afternoon. "They meet and eat and drink and spend money, but here it is nine days before trial and Belli won't even tell me what witnesses he wants to use and when he wants them to testify."

Unbeknownst to brother Earl, Belli and Tonahill had just hatched an esoteric plan to prove to jurors that Ruby had been unable to control his impulses that morning in the police basement. It was called the "psychomotor epilepsy" defense, and it originated one late evening as Belli and some of the national media guys who regularly partied with the defense were whooping it up at the Statler Hilton Hotel. Present that night, Bob Considine said later, was his co-Journal American star columnist Dorothy Kilgallan.

"She said Belli and a couple others were closely examining various pictures of Ruby in their suite when Belli noted something he thought strange about the Bob Jackson photo— the one that showed Oswald grimacing as he was shot," Considine recalled. "Dorothy said Belli leaped up and said, 'By God! That's it. That's it!'"

Belli later told me that it was indeed at this moment that he first noticed Ruby pulled the trigger on his black Colt .38 with his middle finger, instead of his forefinger. That gave

Belli his idea. The use of the middle finger was a symptom of a psychiatric problem, he decided.

So was born the psychomotor epilepsy defense.

Then, since he was unaware of anybody who had ever used that tactic in a murder defense, Belli had to hustle to find expert witnesses to lay the predicate, the possibility, before the jury.

The next few days were frantic, for both sides. Belli collected a powerful team of psychiatric experts—persons who would testify that Ruby seemed to have suffered a momentary lapse of some sort, psychomotor epilepsy perhaps—and Henry Wade and Bill Alexander would hit the books on the subject and contact every expert they could find to rebut Belli's experts.

It came down to a University of Texas psychiatrist, Dr. Martin Towler, and a Baltimore psychiatric legend, Dr. Manfred Guttmacher, for the defendant.

Towler testified strongly that Ruby had been in a seizure mode and said a person in the midst of such a seizure would move like an automaton, oblivious to what he was doing. He suggested that the scores of brawls that

Assistant District Attorneys Bill Alexander (left) and Jim Bowie (center) with District Attorney Henry Wade.

Ruby had been involved in over the years—especially where he had been hit in the head—could have caused irreparable psychiatric damage. He described it as "a seizure disorder" and later said, "It falls into the category of a psychomotor variant."

Guttmacher, who had written several books on various forms of psychiatric abnormality, said Ruby was under some sort of extreme strain, but he ruled out schizophrenia or paranoia. Ruby, he testified, seemed "unable to tolerate anxiety" and was "a very unstable individual."

Belli tried to steer Guttmacher to use the phrase "psychomotor epilepsy" but the Baltimore doctor wouldn't. John Kaplan and Jon R. Waltz, in their book, *The Trial of Jack Ruby*, commented:

"No matter how hard Belli had tried, through his questioning to force the witness to hew to the defense's preordained line,

174

psychomotor epilepsy had gotten lost. The jurors would soon know, if they did not already realize, that the defense's chief attorney and his principal expert had passed like ships in the night."

Later it was revealed why Belli and Guttmacher weren't ever on the same page.

Guttmacher had delivered a memo to Belli on March 3, the day the 12th juror was chosen. Simply put he told Belli he couldn't testify for certain that Ruby had suffered a psychotic attack at the time he killed Oswald.

It was too late for Belli to go shopping for another expert.

Guttmacher later told reporters in Baltimore he was discouraged at how Belli used him and complained that he seldom had a chance to explain anything pertinent to the San Francisco lawyer. Belli, claimed Guttmacher, "surrounded himself with all sorts of characters, even a movie crew. They were actually filming how he tried the case. He was never available to me."

Tonahill, in a rare moment of reflection about his friend Belli in 1999, said though he hated to admit it, all those psychiatric witnesses had been somewhat negated by the preparation done by the DA's office. "Henry and even more so, Alexander, had really done their homework," Tonahill said.

But in the end, it didn't matter whether Jack Ruby was a blathering idiot, a man stricken with a sudden urge to kill, or a demonic wannabe who thought he might end up as a hero, technically he died an innocent man.

The jurors agreed that Jack Ruby should die for killing Lee Harvey Oswald, but the Texas Court of Criminal Appeals reversed that judgment and a new trial was scheduled for Wichita Falls. Ruby's death from cancer intervened.

Many legal experts from around the country expected the trial would be moved from Dallas, which at the time was being terribly vilified throughout the world. But, at a pre-trial hearing, several business leaders and authorities testified that Dallas could give the defendant a fair and just trial.

Though the failure to take the trial to another city was mentioned as one of two main reasons the judgment was soon overturned, the most damning reason was that the tribunal did not believe the testimony of one Dallas cop—the man who gave the prosecution a reason to believe that Ruby's act was not a sudden urge, but one

Policeman Testifies Ruby Admitted Mulling Oswald Slaying for 2 Days

State Rests Case In Murder Trial

By BOB FENLEY and JIM LEHRER, Staff Writers
A police sergeant testified Friday that Jack Ruby said he first thought of killing ...

Sgt. Patrick Dean, the prosecution's strongest witness, who was later discredited. Note byline by current PBS news anchor Jim Lehrer.

harbored for two days.

On Friday, March 6, 1964, the final day of the prosecution's case, Sgt. Patrick Dean "stunned the courtroom," as Bob Fenley and Jim Lehrer reported in the *Times Herald*, "when he said the nightclub owner told him he thought of killing Oswald when he noticed the 'sarcastic sneer' on the accused assassin's face."

As Fenley and Lehrer went on to report, "Over strenuous defense objections, the officer related his conversation with Ruby in the fifth floor city jail approximately 10 minutes after Oswald was shot.

"He said something to the effect he had thought about this two nights prior when he saw him (Oswald) on the show-up stand," the officer related.

"Sgt. Dean said Ruby told him he 'wanted the world to know that Jews do have guts.'"

Dean's testimony of clear premeditation punched a devastating hole in the defense contention—to come later—that Ruby was in a "fugue state" at the moment he shot Oswald. Belli objected heatedly to Dean's testimony on the grounds that no foundation had been laid for it. He moved for a mistrial, which Judge Brown overruled.

What no one on the defense team then realized was that Sgt. Dean's alleged conversation with Ruby could not have occurred as Dean testified it had.

This information came to me in June from a Dallas police department source. I didn't write about it at the time because all my attention was then devoted to reporting the story of Oswald's diary. And after its publication, the tight scrutiny I was getting from the FBI

(DN12)DALLAS,TEX. MAR. 6—TESTIFIES—Sgt. P. T. Dean, of the Dallas Police Department, enters court where Jack Ruby is on trial. Dean told the court that Jack Ruby told him he (Ruby) thought of killing Lee Harvey Oswald, accused assassin of President Kennedy, on Friday night, Nov. 22, when Kennedy was assassinated. (See AP Wire Story) (AP Wirephoto)(db61500stf) 1964

During his dramatic appearance on the stand for direct examination, Sgt. Dean gave a running commentary on Ruby's remarks to him during their conversation in the jail.

"He said he believed in due process of law . . . but he was so torn up and emotional about this event, he and his sister both . . . she had been in the hospital . . .," the officer related.

"He said this man (Oswald) not only killed the President but also shot Officer Tippit . . . and that the outcome of the trial would be that he (Oswald) would be given the death penalty inevita-

Largest Daily
Circulation
In Texas
220,831 WEEKDAYS
253,935 SUNDAYS
ABC Publisher's Statement
September 30, 1963

The Dallas Morning News

7 Break Out of County Jail, Creating Havoc Outside Ruby Trial Courtroom

Hostage Taken; Four Captured

By DON MILLSAP

Seven prisoners using a fake pistol and razor blades overpowered three unarmed jailers and broke out of the Dallas County jail about 3:30 p.m. Friday, creating havoc outside the courtroom where the Jack Ruby murder trial was under way.

The prisoners, all either convicted or awaiting trial for robbery, burst out of the locked door leading to the jail elevator on the second floor of the Criminal Courts Building and scattered among a confused horde of spectators, witnesses, reporters and deputies attending the Ruby trial.

Charles David Gregory, 20, identified as the man carrying the fake pistol, grabbed a woman hostage in a nearby court office, bluffed his way past waiting spectators and escaped through the front door of the courts building.

He was captured moments later by Deputy Sheriff Charles Polk Player, who grabbed the bogus gun from Gregory as he shoved the hostage, Mrs. Ruth Thornton, about 60, east on Elm near Record.

Player was unarmed at the time.

Another escapee, Johnny Robert Jenkins, 31, was captured as he went down a stairway in the Records Building Annex.

Third Man Nabbed Hour Later

A third prisoner, Herschell Alvin Crocker, 26, was captured about an hour later on the porch of a house near Eighth and Polk in Oak Cliff by County Fire Marshal Hal Hood.

Tommy Powell Calverly, 29, was the fourth escapee captured. Deputies Allan Sweatt, A. D. McCauley and H. E. McHugh overpowered him in the 3500 block of S. Lamar about 5:20 p.m.

Still at large were Leonard Franklin Driggers, 25, awaiting trial for robbery by assault and theft over $50; Billy Ray Brock, 35, under a 15-year sentence for robbery, and Randolph Richardson Hudnall, 26, awaiting trial on two counts of robbery with firearms.

[...] driver reported to deputies [...] identified as Crocker and Drig[...] commerce, near the new cen[...]

[...]them to a location on Beck[...] [...]jumped out and fled without[...]

[...]charged with robbery, Croc[...] [...]ery, and Calverly faces a 15-year[...]

[...]n Sixth Floor

[...]men, confined on the sixth [...]caffic A. S. Greer as the distribu[...] [...]t to a jail elevator.

[...] visitor's elevator operated by [...]ought attorney G. Ray Lee Jo

[...]reet's back, forced Strehley in [...]they encountered jailer Leroy [...]his keys.

[...]n they learned he did not give [...] was not injured, however, as [...]et.

[...]kins started toward the Elm [...]bbed Edna Biggs, a clerk in [...]he offices of Criminal Dist.

[...] Page 8.

Jailbreaker Charles Gregory flees with hostage Mrs. Ruth Thornton, ca[...]

BIGGEST BLOW SWUNG

State Rests Case Against Jack Ruby

By CARL FREUND
and HUGH AYNESWORTH

Dist. Atty. Henry Wade swung his biggest blow in the Jack Ruby murder trial Friday, minutes before a jail break threw corridors outside the courtroom into a turmoil.

Before resting his case, Wade presented testimony that Ruby "thought about" killing Lee Harvey Oswald for two days.

Judge Joe B. Brown admitted the testimony by Police Sgt. P. T. Dean despite heated objections from defense lawyers. They shouted that it violated Ruby's constitutional rights.

Ruby slipped into the City Hall basement Nov. 24 and fired a single bullet from his Colt Cobra .38-caliber revolver into Oswald while network television cameras recorded the scene.

DEAN QUOTED Ruby as saying he saw Oswald two days earlier "with a sneer on his face" and thought at that time about killing him. Officers were holding Oswald, a 24-year-old Communist sympathizer, as the

was sure to bring the death penalty.

—He wanted to spare President Kennedy's widow the mental anguish of returning to Dallas to testify against Oswald.

DEFENSE lawyers charged angrily that prosecutors told Dean what to say while on the stand.

The lawyers noted also that Dean testified he questioned Ruby about 11:30 a.m. Nov. 24, but stated in a report that he interviewed the slayer at "approximately 12 noon." They emphasized this discrepancy, but prosecutors said they regarded it as a minor point.

As Dean left the stand, Wade arose and announced, "Your honor, ladies and gentlemen of the jury, the State rests at this time."

This meant Wade and his assistants—A. D. Jim Bowie, William F. Alexander and Frank Watts—had completed the basic case with which they hope to convince jurors that Ruby is a coldblooded killer who should

If jurors accept the defense theory, they must find Ruby innocent of murdering Oswald.

After Wade's announcement, defense lawyers asked Judge Brown to order the jury to find Ruby innocent.

Belli and two other defense lawyers, Joe Tonahill and Phil Burleson, contended prosecutors failed to make out a case.

JUDGE BROWN quickly rejected the request.

They also asked Judge Brown to order jurors not to consider testimony by Dean and other officers about statements which Ruby made while under arrest.

The defense lawyers claimed the statements violated Ruby's constitutional rights since the slayer was under arrest, but had not been warned he was not required to make any statement.

Judge Brown agreed with prosecutors that the officers could relate Ruby's statements under the res gestae rule. This legal rule holds that statements [...]

Above: Public waits in line for courtroom seats to Ruby trial.
Opposite: Bizarre jailbreak interrupted the Ruby proceedings.
The gunmen fashioned the replica of a pistol from a bar of soap.

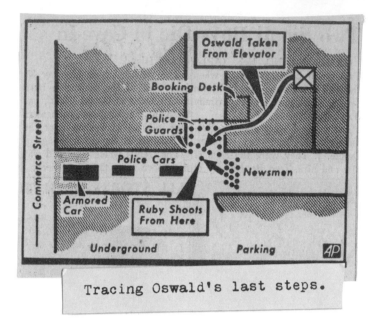

made it difficult to work with certain sensitive sources.

I learned that Warren Commission investigators had come to doubt Sgt. Dean's word back in April, after Ruby was convicted. In fact, according to my source, they confronted Dean and accused him of lying under oath.

They caught him while in search of something else entirely, a possible accomplice who might have helped Jack Ruby penetrate police security that morning in the City Hall basement. Federal investigators and a contingent of local cops reviewed every available image taken in the basement before and after Oswald's death—television footage and stills. Though they found no evidence that Ruby had a helper, they kept seeing Sgt. Dean pop up when, according to his testimony, he was upstairs in the jail, listening to Ruby admit that he planned the Oswald murder.

This knowledge placed me in a quandary. Belli was angry at me over an article I had written in late March that made him look like a liar for the way he waited until after the guilty verdict to object about a possibly tainted juror. I liked his second lead counsel, Joe Tonahill, but Joe was too close to Belli.

Yet I felt certain the truth about Dean's testimony would be a strong point for Ruby's appeals team, and I felt obligated to get it to them in some fashion. I still was no fonder of Jack Ruby than I had been in the past, but possible perjury was not something to ignore.

So I went to Phil Burleson, then a young former prosecutor who'd handled much of the organizational work for Belli in the original trial. With my source's permission I told Phil what I knew and how I knew it—as well as who else knew it, including Henry Wade, Jim Bowie, and possibly Bill Alexander.

Phil Burleson at some point told the Ruby family that he received the original tip about Sgt. Dean from me. Both of Ruby's sisters, Eileen Kaminsky in Chicago and Eva Grant in Dallas, telephoned me to express their appreciation. From that moment on, I was well connected inside the Ruby camp, especially through Eva.

••••••••••••••••••••••••••••••

Jack Ruby never was emotionally stable, not in my opinion anyway, but the assassination and Oswald's murder seemed to further destabilize him, mentally.

Dr. Robert Beavers, then director of the psychiatric hospital at Southwestern Medical School, was asked by one of Ruby's lawyers, Clayton "Red" Fowler, and the court to mentally evaluate the convicted killer in the summer and fall of 1964. Ruby had been acting strangely, talking of suicide and hearing voices.

He spent numerous lengthy sessions with Ruby over the next six months and said he found the strip joint owner "bedeviled by demons—a very unstable, tormented person."

"Basically I had thought it was a farce, an embarrassing farce, the whole psychiatric bullshit during the trial," said Dr. Beavers. "I felt that here was a sick guy, in jail and I thought it was a way of making a statement that psychiatrists are doctors and they see people just like in the case of a person who had broken his leg, an orthopedist would go do something to help the person in jail."

Unable to move Ruby to a psyche ward because of regulations which did not allow a convicted felon to be treated there, Beavers said he found the only way to try to help his new patient was to visit him in his jail cell regularly—which he did.

"When I saw him he was psychotic, there's no doubt about that. He'd be flipping off alternately claiming he heard from 'I'm hearing the Jews being killed in the street' to 'It's all my fault' and like that," recalled Beavers. "Then he would discuss something rational, normal."

I asked Beavers if Ruby seemed aware that many Americans thought he did what he did as part of a conspiracy.

"You got to remember," the psychiatrist said, "this guy really was crazy. The outside world doesn't become that significant when you're in a 6 by 9 cell and you can only hear noises—and you're crazy to boot."

Dr. Beavers said in his opinion Ruby wasn't psychotic on Nov. 24, 1963. "That's why," he went on, "I was embarrassed as a psychiatrist with all that nonsense, that psychomotor epilepsy defense. To my

COBO CLEANERS, INC.
18135 Livernois Avenue
DETROIT, MICHIGAN 48221

Message Reply

DATE: 5-5-70

PRIORITY
☑ URGENT!
☐ SOON AS POSSIBLE
☐ NO REPLY NEEDED

Phone 863-0400

TO: *Hugh Aynesworth*
1259 Tennessee Bldg.
1010 Milam St.
Houston, Texas 77002

Dear Hugh:
Please see what you can do about closing Jack's Estate in Dallas.
You must know someone who can help us. What about some help from one of the newspapers in Dallas? Perhaps one of the reporters.
Sincerely
Earl Ruby

SIGNED: *Earl Ruby*

DATE OF REPLY: 7-23-70 REPLY TO: Mr. Earl Ruby

Dear Earl:
    I have made several calls to Dallas in hopes of clarifying the situation of Jack's will. First, a new judge has taken over and he knows little about the situation and doesn't particularly seem to care what happens. Second, Jules Mayer is in no hurry to settle the estate. I get the feel he is dickering with people on certain items to get more money, so his fee will be greater. Perhaps this is an unfair judgment; I'm not sure. Will call you soon.

SIGNED: *Hugh Aynesworth*

SENDER: MAIL RECIPIENT WHITE AND PINK SHEETS.

Above: Personal note sent to me from Earl Ruby. Note old carbon copy format with space provided for reply.

Below: Subpoena requiring me to appear at a Ruby hearing.

Opposite: A "backgrounder" is information provided to an editor for consideration.

No. E-4010-J

IN THE DISTRICT COURT

OF_____Dallas_____COUNTY

THE STATE OF TEXAS
vs.

Jack Ruby

SUBPOENA
FELONY

Issued ____27th____ day of ____April____ 19_64_

BILL SHAW ____Clerk

By____R. ALIPRANDI____Deputy.

Returned and filed this the_____day of

_____19____

_____

Clerk_____Court

By_____Deputy

THE STATE OF TEXAS,

To the Sheriff or any Constable of____Dallas____County, Greeting:
    You are Hereby Commanded to summon Hugh Aynesworth, Dallas Morning News, Dallas, Texas,
_____to be and appear before the Honorable Criminal District Court of No. 3 of Dallas County, Texas, to be held at the Court House of said County, in Dallas, Texas, at 9:00 A. M. on the 29th day of April, 1964

_____then and there to testify as witness____in behalf of the defendant in a criminal action pending in said Court, entitled and numbered on the Criminal Docket of said Court, The State of Texas vs. Jack Ruby____No. E-4010-J, and there remain from day to day, and from term to term, until discharged by due course of law.
Returnable____April 29, 1964 at 9:00 A. M.
    Herein Fail Not, and make due return hereof, showing how you have executed the same.
    Witness my official signature, at Dallas, Tex. this 27th day of Dallas A. D. 19 64.

BILL SHAW ____Clerk
Dallas ____County.

By____R. ALIPRANDI____Deputy.   District Court

Jack Ruby backgrounder:

The 7-man, 5-woman jury this week determined that Jack Ruby was sane. Now the Ruby appeal lodged with the Texas Court of Criminal Appeals (the highest court in the state) will be considered again. The Court of Criminal Appeals instructed several months ago that before it could consider the briefs prepared by the several Ruby lawyers, it would have to be determined by the district court in Dallas as to the convicted man's sanity.

Mrs. Eva Grant, Ruby's red-haired and occasionally wild (curses, rants, throws her XXXXXXXXXX purse, shouts in the courtroom, etc.) sister actually set the stage for the sanity hearing when she filed an affadavit of insanity on April 27, 1964, just six weeks after Ruby was convicted of killing Oswald. She withdrew this affadavit and motion for a sanity trial June 9, 1966 when Ruby's lawyers determined he would be better off if the state appeals court were heard first.

Best bet is that if it isn't reversed, John Connally will commute it to life. Connally, an extremely popular governor with eyes farther north, holds a unique place in all this too.

I covered the entire Ruby business and I'd bet all my xxxxxxxxxxxxthat Jack Ruby will live to be free again. I don't know but if he hasn't already gone through enough to pay for his crime.

regards, hugh aynesworth (dallas)

Apparently this is true. Justice Tom Clark, in writing the majority opinion in the Sheppard case (he's from Dallas incidently), claimed the press was allowed to run wild at the Sheppard trial, making justice impossible. Obviously the Ruby trial was this way too--maybe even more so.

The Texas "supreme" court has said it will render a speedy decision, within weeks. It will likely uphold the verdict. Few cases are reversed in this co Of course, few offer the myriad complexities of this one.

There is no other legal filings binding. On June 1, 1966 Kunstler asked Supreme Court Justice Hugo Black for a stay of the June 13 sanity trial, contending mainly that Ruby could not have any kind of a fair representation while there was still in-fighting between lawyers. Kunstler's petition sha attacked the Texas Court of Crominal Appeal's ruling of several months ago that Tonahill, the huge Jasper, Texas lawyer, should be retained as a Ruby counselor. **MORE**

(more)

mind that was an attorney-developed concept."

Beavers said his theory was admittedly "a little shaky" because he had not seen Ruby immediately after the murder, but, he added, "You don't get rid of psychomotor epilepsy, and in my opinion, he had no evidences of it at the time I was interviewing him."

"He thought he was going to be a hero. That's what he talked about when he flipped to the sanity. He thought everybody would think he was great."

Ruby was kept in the Dallas county lock-up pending his appeal, and almost every night he would telephone his sister Eva. As the months passed, his conversation grew stranger and stranger, less coherent, and reportedly quite wild. Eva told me her brother would rant that all the Jews in America were being killed, and how she and others were in particular danger. Somewhere he got the idea that his brother Earl had lost both his legs. Once he screamed, she said, and said he would hear "them, coming for me now!"

During one of our discussions, Eva suggested I listen to Jack for myself. "Why don't you come over tonight and you can hear," she said.

What a great opportunity! I thought.

I arrived at her apartment and soon the phone rang. It was Jack.

"How are you feeling?" Eva gushed. "Did you get what Hyman sent you? Are you sleeping better?"

After a moment she placed her hand over the receiver, looked at me, and rolled her eyes. Jack was off on some tirade.

"Jack...Jack...Jack!" she said into the phone, trying to get his attention. "Hugh Aynesworth is here. You remember him. Ask him what you just asked me. He is a reporter. He will be truthful with you."

"Hi, Jack," I began. How are you?"

Nothing.

"Hey, I talked to a good friend of yours today."

Still nothing.

"Yeah, George Senator called me. Said he was going to try to get in to see you."

As if I'd said nothing about his old roommate—who'd called to ask me if I knew anyone who'd like to buy Jack's suits—Ruby suddenly spoke up, heading off in several directions at once.

"I've got this bad headache, never stops," he said. "You'd think they'd give me something for it. But they won't. They want me to suffer."

Pause.

"This place stinks. You come down and see. Bill Decker will let you in."

I tried with no luck to pose a couple of questions, and Ruby gave me no indication that he even knew with whom he was speaking. He complained about the medicines he was receiving and said he had stomach pains.

"Are you Jewish?"

"No, I'm not."

"Well, you wouldn't understand what we are going through, then. Do you know I'm the only Jew in this jail?"

I doubted that, and was pondering my reply when Eva motioned for me to return the receiver to her. "They only allow so much time," she explained.

After she hung up, we visited for a few minutes. Eva promised I could return again later in the week. But when I called her, she was ill. Other matters intruded, and I didn't see her again until Jack's death.

That was quite an occasion.

In late December 1966, Jack Ruby lay in Parkland Hospital in Dallas, dying of stomach cancer. At the time, I was briefly out of journalism, working as the public relations director for the George A. Fuller Co., a major international builder.

The job had been interesting and far better-paid than journalism, yet I missed the news business. After a few months among the suits, I had just agreed to go to work for *Newsweek* in its Houston bureau.

On Jan. 3, 1967, as I was having a cup of coffee in a cafeteria along Stemmons Freeway (I-35) just northwest of downtown Dallas, I heard the report on a local radio news program: "Jack Ruby is dead. Authorities at Parkland Hospital announced that the former nightclub owner died of cancer this morning."

Now, I officially was still a PR man; the *Newsweek* gig wasn't to start for three weeks. But I called New York anyway and spoke to the magazine's chief of correspondents, Rod Gander.

"Do you want me to handle it?" I asked a little breathlessly.

"Yes, of course," Gander told me.

A journalist once more, I drove like crazy for Parkland. As I pulled up to the front entrance, Earl Ruby, together with Eva Grant and Eileen Kaminsky, hustled out the door.

"Come with us!" Earl said, taking my arm. "I'll bring you back later."

"Yes! Yes! Hugh can help us," said Mrs. Kaminsky.

1940 → scuffle, man shot
and killed
mourned for months
(how he got the name Leon

1950 - business active
    club lost money
    7 mths - depression
    holed up in hotel for weeks
        apathetic
    suicidal ideas
    went back to Chicago
"7 mths 'til he was himself"

depression is a
    psychosis mental illness

came out gradually

3rd - prior to Nov. 22
depression

agitated by
    Impeach Warren
        ads + signs
    ad in paper

he was in depressed state

knew nature & quality
of his acts
at time of shooting

"knowledge
did not know
precisely"

Above and opposite: Testimony of
psychiatric observations at Ruby trial.

"knew rt/ffbom"

"emot. state was such
he didn't know right
from wrong."

every little movement
Thurs thru Sunday

Severe emotional shock
feeling of frenzy
confusion, agitation
restlessness,

excitement
depress, agitation
excite all combined
(fugued state)

---

more instinctive
& automata
w/out conscious knowledge

(cross at 2:24 p.m.)

pages Walter Bromberg, M.D.

recall of event?

no recall up to
gaining entrance
"walked down ramp"

where lose recall?
(if he did go down ramp)

on floor, other men on
top of him.
(on concrete floor)
(1 or 2 minutes)

Continued testimony at Ruby trial.
Chief Curry takes the stand.

at time functional

organic damage to
    brain

tripped off

more in minds of defense
(attorneys than in
floor to exam?

    Why are you doing this, I'm
Jack Ruby

    day or two later he
resumed recall.

"I hope the S.O.B. dies"
I think he did remember

where carrying gun?

unconsciousperiods
from cerebral trauma
diagnosed as a
    brain concussion

Chief Curry at 3:11
        50

know Oswald?
during lifetime?

no previous
what he might be?
    where he was, etc.

know he was in Dallas
before city hall?

    "no"

haven't any doubt
about that

FBI report to you
that Oswald
& was a Comm
sympathy

+ info that they knew
it — wasn't my own
personal Knowledge +

"no bearing in hearing" +
Brown

satisfied (inves) that
FBI did not Know
Oswald was in
Dallas?

objection! —
sustained
⟶ notes
objection

make your questions
relevant to hearing
Mr. Tonahill Brown

arranged transfer
of Oswald

who responsible
" I was the man in charge"

ordered armored car?
"I requested it"

for safety of prisoner
why

what so different
about Oswald?

Because he was a
Communist? — Tona

objection

My notes from the Ruby background testimony.

atmosphere in Dallas
one of mixed
emotion
    weeping, crying
    & bitterness

"let's get on something
else besides Oswald
Case — Brown"

"I didn't know Jack Ruby
Hundreds there. To my
personal knowledge too."

Did not make 10 a.m.
announcement.

has nothing to do with
bond hearing

at 3:30 (Thanks Chief.
You're very nice

I think you'd tell us the
truth if they'd let you
    Tonahill

"Oh ya"
  said Wade

Sat aft. rm. + I see newsman
            Roe Dow
Sat nt. w/ w.Beard — Russ Knight
Dr. John P. Holbrook
        1353 Westmorelan
    Beverly Hills
            Calming him
  /psychiatrist

← Dec. X 2nd visit

"I can't see how he can, he [re]members when they bought & paid for him." (Tonahill)

→ about general — born in Chicago → his personality as he saw it.

very poor district
father alcoholic
8 children
he had been considered
black sheep — always able
to make a fast buck

→ scrounging for a buck

involved in labor unions
his best friend killed there

buying & renting billboards
Bob Wills — promoter

→ drifted — unable to
"dog it" or back down
from situations

occasions to get in fights,
frequently got into them

small man — labor union
beat him up — tracked
him down & beat him up.

prob because of his
Jewish

"had to show Gentiles
to show [they] Jews
were pretty nice
guys anyway.

→ peculiar — "they often
fused him"

he had promotional ability
salvation, sisters &
brothers.

I had no idea how that might be so, but was more than happy to accompany them.

Earl drove us to the Weiland-Merritt funeral home just east of downtown, on Live Oak Street. Two photographers were right behind us.

On the way, Eva began to sob. "Jack's gone! Jack's gone!" She wiped her tears with a multi-colored handkerchief. Of them all, Eva was closest to Jack. She often helped him manage his Dallas clubs and frequently offered business advice, which he followed. "He didn't act like he knew he was dying," she said. "He called me a couple of nights ago, and we had the best talk."

"But he still believed in this conspiracy stuff, didn't he?" asked Eileen. "Last time I talked to Jack he told me that unless I could pretend I wasn't Jewish, I'd be killed. I told him I didn't know how to do that."

When we got to the funeral home, Earl pulled around back and the four of us hurried into a bare anteroom.

A covey of reporters and photographers soon was outside, most of them my close acquaintances, some of them pounding on the doors. One photographer scrambled up the side of the building to reach a ledge from where he could shoot pictures down into the room. I hoped no one suggested that I go outside to join my unruly friends.

Earl and Eva broke into an argument over whether or not their dead brother, an army veteran, qualified for a government-paid funeral. Eileen excused herself and headed for a telephone. "Have to alert so many people in Chicago," she said.

The funeral home director, trying to keep the group calm, assured Earl and Eva that he could check out any possible benefit. He sat them down and asked to which Chicago funeral home Mr. Ruby's body was to be sent.

"Old Original Weinstein & Sons," said Earl. "We go back a long way with them."

"Okay. Let's start with his birth date."

That was a problem. None of the three siblings knew the date; all three guessed different days.

"It was March 25, 1911," I spoke up for the first time. (In fact, according to the Warren Commission report, nobody knows precisely what day Jacob Rubenstein was born in Chicago; March 25, 1911, was the date Ruby himself most often gave.)

Then Earl and the funeral executive began to discuss the costs of preparing and shipping Jack home for burial. The price of the casket nearly choked poor Earl, who had good reason to wish that costs were kept down. I know he had spent $100,000 or so of his own money paying for Jack's legal defense. Earl was not a rich man.

And unlike Lee Harvey Oswald's wife and mother, the Ruby clan was no good at making crime pay. One sorry attempt I know of involved smuggling a tape machine into Jack's hospital room to capture his voice for a phonograph record they hoped to sell in cahoots with some operator from California.

They got the recorder into the room all right, but made the mistake of resting the machine on a radiator. The record that was ultimately produced and sold in vanishingly small quantities included the radiator's full metallic repertoire in the background, from steamy hisses to angry bangs.

"But you will want a nice casket," the funeral man pressed on. He said he could offer Earl a good deal. That's when a thought occurred to me. I'd read somewhere that some states required a locally-sold casket when a body is shipped in from out of state. So I motioned to Earl that I'd like a private word with him and shared what I knew.

Maybe all they needed to get Jack to Chicago was a simple pine box.

"Oh yes! I was going to mention that to you, Mr. Ruby," the annoyed funeral man said. "No need buying an expensive casket here in Texas."

Business finished, we made our escape out the back.

On the way to my car, Earl turned and said, "Hugh, you're going to be with us, aren't you?"

I said I'd have to check with *Newsweek*.

"My God, yes," Rod Gander said over the phone. "Call when you hit the ground."

Phil Burleson, another invitee, and I checked into a motel close to the Weinstein funeral home in Chicago, then took a cab together to Eileen's house. We'd been asked to join the family the night before the funeral…I was a bit apprehensive, since I'd never been inside a Jewish temple, much less attended a Jewish funeral.

But I sure wasn't going to miss it.

As we were instructed, Phil and I washed our hands in a pan just outside the door, then walked inside Eileen's modest south side residence. The interior was sparsely furnished. Pictures were turned to the wall. People sat quietly on benches and crates. Some prayed. I was self-conscious that I didn't misplace my yarmulke, the Jewish skullcap. (Oddly, earlier in the day, a Catholic nun appeared at Weistein's and requested to see the body. When refused, she left without signing the register. Three priests came the night before with the same request—when cordially denied, they knelt in the snow outside, briefly prayed, and departed.)

Later that evening, a problem arose. One of Ruby's pallbearers became ill and could not make the service the next day. A cousin suggested they contact one of Jack's boyhood friends, now in the upholstery business. But then someone else informed the group that Sid, the upholsterer, had been dead himself for five years.

Earl took me aside. "Could you do it?" he asked quietly.

I was torn. The Rubys were a decent family, compassionate and loving. They did not deserve the pain that Jack caused them. What Earl asked was a simple favor that I'd be happy to do under any other circumstances. However, it seemed hypocritical if I, who genuinely disliked Jack Ruby, helped carry him to his grave.

"I don't think I'm the proper man," I told Earl.

"Why not?"

"Because while I like all of you, I did not like Jack, and I knew him pretty well. Any person has the right to have those who loved and respected him carry him those last few yards."

Luckily, Eileen and Eva soon found an old ex-schoolmate to fill in.

"Damn, Hugh, why did you turn 'em down?" asked Burleson, who would be one of the pallbearers, as we rode back to the motel that night. "I thought Eileen was going to cry."

I think I told Phil that *Newsweek* might frown on a correspondent's becoming part of a story he covered, which I guess was probably true, but it wasn't the reason I refused. It was my call, and I didn't think I should do it.

The next morning was cold and snowy.

Scores of reporters showed up to cover the funeral, but were kept behind police barricades. I was the only member of the press allowed inside the sanctuary, where a brief service was held.

Before the rites, I voiced a concern to Earl and his brother Hyman. With all the conspiracy talk already around, I worried that someday someone would say that the man in Jack Ruby's grave was not Jack Ruby.

The family of
Jack Ruby
acknowledges with deep appreciation
your kind expression of sympathy

Dear Paula and Hugh,
*   I'm taking the liberty of*
addressing you by your first
names to thank you for the
really beautiful flowers and
the delicious fudge. How
very thoughtful of you.
*   Sincerely*
*   Jack Ruby's Family*

Thank you note from the Ruby family.

This was not an idle fear. A British barrister named Michael Eddowes later argued in a book that Lee Harvey Oswald was not buried in his grave. Some Russian spy supposedly was moldering there. Eddowes agitated to have Oswald exhumed. Robert Oswald was horrified by the idea. Marina, after the application of a certain amount of cash, approved the deal. In 1981, Lee was dug up. A team of scientists led by Dallas forensic pathologist Linda Norton examined the remains, declared they were Oswald's, and the assassin was reinterred with a casket upgrade. The old one apparently leaked.

My proposal to the Ruby family was to allow a pool of reporters into the sanctuary just before they closed Jack's casket for the last time, in order to attest that Jack Ruby actually was in it. That way no one, ever, should concoct some phony excuse for disinterring Ruby.

"That would be so horrible," said Eileen.

"OK, we'll do it," Earl said. "I'll work it out some way." He conferred with a lawyer friend, Alan Adelson, who agreed it was a sound idea.

So for a couple of minutes, three Chicago reporters came into the cemetery sanctuary, viewed Jack Ruby in his casket, and left. The only one of the three I now remember was Nelson Benton of CBS.

Eva and I stayed in touch for a while, until she decided to move to California and live with her son. Just before she left, she called me to say she wanted to give me something "for being so kind to the Ruby family."

She had two of Jack's neckties, "and I want you to have them," she said. It was a touching gesture, which I deeply appreciated, and said so. I told Eva that I'd stop by her apartment for them soon.

But I never did.

Statement Recorded By Ruby

Dallas Times Herald
1-3-67

A commercial recording, taped by Jack Ruby in his room at Parkland Hospital without consent of Sheriff Bill Decker, apparently will contain the Dallas nightclub owner's last words on the shooting of Lee Harvey Oswald.

Ruby died of cancer at 10:30 a.m. Tuesday. He had been in Parkland since Dec. 9.

The recording, made during a conference between Ruby and his lawyer, was revealed in an Associated Press sotry quoting attorney Elmer Gertz of Chicago. Gertz told The Associated Press the three-minute recording was made for Capital Records as part of a 46-minute album entitled "The Assassination."

OTHER VOICES reportedly included in the album are those of the late President John F. Kennedy, accused presidential assassin Lee Harvey Oswald, several Dallas policemen, and Gov. John Connally, who was wounded by the rain of bullets which killed Kennedy.

Ruby reportedly said in the recording—as he has all along—that he was not part of a conspiracy but shot Oswald on a sudden

See RUBY on Page 19

Dallas Morning News entertainment columnist Tony Zoppi reported that Earl Ruby and his attorney made a secret recording of Ruby the day before he died. During that visit, Ruby lamented making a fateful U-turn.

18—Section 1   The Dallas Morning News

DALLAS AFTER DARK:

JFK Was Host To Show Folk

By TONY ZOPPI

Less than 24 hours before President Kennedy's arrival in Dallas, Joan Crawford was telling Dallas newspapermen of a meeting with the chief executive in his White House offices.

"I'd known Jack Kennedy for years, and that's why I couldn't

Washington armory. He lined up a show of stars which was probably unprecedented in the history of the trade. Everyone cooperated but the weatherman, and the affair was a dismal flop.

Yet it set a sort of precedent as the first family took show business to its heart and elevated its image

"If I hadn't made the U-turn on Main Street that morning none of this would have happened."

- Jack Ruby

Dallas Morning News photographer Jack Beers captured his photo (below left) just before Oswald was shot, while *Dallas Times Herald* photographer Bob Jackson shot his photo six-tenths of a second later. Jackson's photo of Oswald being hit won the Pulitzer Prize. Ironically, Beers' photograph was printed in The *Fort Worth Star-Telegram* before the *News* printed it because it was sent out on the AP wire and the *Star-Telegram* used it before the *News* hit the street. (*The Denver Post*, Nov. 25, 1963)

16 **THE DENVER POST Monday, Nov. 25, 1963

CHATTED WITH POST PHOTOGRAPHER

Ruby Was in a Position to Shoot Oswald on Friday Night

By CHARLES ROOS
Denver Post Staff Writer

DALLAS—Jack Ruby, 52, Dallas nightclub operator who shot and killed Lee Oswald Sunday, was close enough to Oswald to have done the same thing in Police Headquarters Friday night.

Denver Post photographer Cloyd Teter can testify to that. Official security in Dallas had already been questioned as a result of the assassination of President John F. Kennedy Friday.

But the President was slain as he rode along a downtown street beside a tall building in an open limousine, as presidents have done for years in every major city in the United States.

Oswald, heavily guarded since his arrest Friday, was shot down Sunday in the basement of Police Headquarters as he walked through a garage area from an elevator to an armored car that was to haul him to Dallas County Jail to await trial.

Newspapermen recalled then that Sunday was not the first time Ruby had bent security regulations. Ruby's name is Jack Leon Rubenstein but he was known as Jack Ruby.

He has frequented police hallways since Oswald's arrest—hallways supposedly off limits to all but law enforcement officers, witnesses and the press.

On Friday night Dallas police held an unusual press conference in a basement squad room. At the request of photographers, Oswald was brought down from jail and displayed to the press.

Ruby was there then. He stood with reporters and photographers as though he were one of them. Before Oswald appeared Friday night, Ruby spoke to Teter, standing on a table next to him.

"Do you think this (Kennedy's assassination) will hurt Dallas?" he asked.

"Sure it will for a while," Teter replied.

Ruby then handed The Post photographer a business card advertising girlie shows at his downtown strip tease club, the Carousel.

"This will explain why I'm interested in whether it (the assassination) will hurt business here," Ruby said.

When Oswald was led into the room by detectives, the prisoner stood about 15 feet from Ruby. No one knows whether Ruby was armed then.

Ruby knew top police officers. He named some of them for Teter and wrote out several names for another photographer.

Teter put Ruby's business card in his pocket and forgot it until he was told the name of the man arrested for the shooting of Oswald Sunday.

Ruby apparently had been admitted to the Police Building without question because police knew him. He reportedly was there again Saturday.

On Sunday, just before Oswald was brought down from City Jail to be transported to County Jail, Ruby apparently slipped into a large basement room from an outside entrance.

Police officials said the room and the surrounding area had been searched twice earlier.

Police Sgt. P. T. Dean, who knows Ruby, said the night club operator evidently walked into the building from the north auto ramp, the ramp opposite one that was to have been used by the armored car.

Dean said Ruby apparently "concealed himself as much as he could as a reporter."

Police officers may well have seen and recognized him—but they probably had seen him a dozen times earlier outside the door of the homicide bureau.

Police Chief J. E. Curry refused late Sunday to discuss security aspects of the Oswald shooting.

Curry called a short press conference in which he announced that Oswald was dead of a bullet wound and that Ruby had been booked for murder.

Reporters asked the chief whether he thought the Police Department was to blame for the security breakdown that allowed Oswald to be shot.

"I have nothing more to say," the chief said.

Federal Judge Menaced

DALLAS — (UPI) — Police Sunday reported a telephone threat against the life of the federal judge who swore in President Lyndon B. Johnson.

Several other prominent Dallas persons also were threatened.

The threats apparently came from cranks who delight in harassing police and others in time of crisis or tragedy.

One threat was made against the life of Federal Judge Sarah T. Hughes, who swore in Lyndon B. Johnson as President shortly after the assassination of President John F. Kennedy.

AP Wirephoto

THIS WAS THE DRAMATIC MOMENT JACK RUBY RAN FORWARD WITH REVOLVER
An instant later he shot Lee Harvey Oswald, accused assassin of President Kennedy.

(C) The Dallas Times-Herald, 1963

JACK RUBY, RIGHT, RUSHES FORWARD AND FIRES POINT BLANK AT LEE HARVEY OSWALD
The accused assassin of President Kennedy begins to collapse as the bullet hits him in the abdomen.

Ruby's Rush of Oswald Apparently Unseen by Police

SEE STORY PAGE 1

DALLAS—Policemen present at the shooting of Lee Howard Oswald apparently did not see Jack Ruby until the muzzle of the revolver was near Oswald.

Detective B. H. Combest said Oswald slumped down, moaning, partly supported by the handcuffs linking him with the escorting officer. Oswald's eyes were open but he apparently said nothing.

Adding to the national shock of the Oswald slaying was live coverage of the killing by network television cameras which had been set up in the basement area to cover the jail transfer.

Police Sgt. P. T. Dean, who also knows Ruby, heard the shot but could not see the gun because of the crowd. Dean said Ruby told him, "The main reason I did this was out of sentiment (or sympathy) for Jacqueline Kennedy and for the officer who was shot."

That man was Dallas Patrolman J. D. Tippit, who was slain Friday after the presidential assassination when he stopped Oswald for questioning.

Dallas Attorney Tom Howard described Ruby as "a very emotional man." Howard said it is highly possible that Ruby was "out of his mind."

He and other acquaintances said, however, that they have no knowledge that Ruby was ever treated for mental illness.

Howard said he tried to advise Ruby of his legal rights "but I'm not sure he understood what I was saying." Ruby's sister, Mrs. Eva Grant, said Ruby was "very religious" and visited a Jewish Synagogue Friday and Saturday after the President's death.

MUCH WEEPING

He telephoned her six times Friday, she said, and frequently was crying.

"He spent yesterday (Saturday) watching a television playback of the Kennedy years and he cried," she said. "He loved every president; that's the trouble."

Howard said about the same thing: "He was very loyal to his country and he had a deep respect for all of the presidents—Republicans and Democrats."

Friends said that Ruby was probably a Democrat but was never active in politics.

When a local nightclub editor telephoned Ruby Friday to see if his clubs would be closed that night in memory of the President, Ruby said he would close at least three days.

Ruby seemed to enjoy being an "insider" — someone who knew and associated with policemen, public officials and newspapermen.

When he spoke briefly with his sister in jail Sunday night, Ruby told her not to worry, that he was being well treated and that "I've got friends."

Police records show that Ruby was charged with a series of relatively minor offenses between 1949 and 1960.

They include: disturbing the peace, February, 1949; carrying a concealed weapon in 1953 and 1954; violating a state liquor

hall ordinances in 1959 and 1960. The police records show a disposition of the charges in only one case — that of the liquor violation. The charge was dismissed.

Although it is not shown on the Dallas police record, a local attorney told The Denver Post late Sunday he had defended Ruby in a simple assault case several months ago. The charge arose from a scuffle Ruby had with another man in the Adolphus Hotel in Dallas, the attorney said, and the charge was dismissed.

USUAL PROCEDURE

The scheduled transfer of Lee Harvey Oswald from City Jail to County Jail is the usual procedure in felony cases.

Police Chief J. E. Curry had announced Saturday night to the press that the move probably would be made about 10 a.m. Sunday.

Actually the transfer did not start until after 11 a.m. A large crowd had gathered outside the County Jail — just a few yards from the spot where President Kennedy was shot — and Ruby apparently knew both the proposed time and method of the transfer.

Police had taken the precaution of calling for an armored car to carry the prisoner between jails, though Oswald never reached the vehicle.

After the shooting, an ambulance arrived in about five minutes and carried Oswald to Parkland Hospital.

Reporters noted that Oswald, when he arrived on a stretcher, was ashen and apparently unconscious.

Oswald died at 1:07 p.m., about 90 minutes after he was shot and almost exactly 48 hours after the President was pronounced dead.

Although Oswald was defiant and uncommunicative, Dallas police believed they had an air-tight case against him in the President's death.

Dist. Atty. Henry Wade disclosed Sunday night that an Oswald palm print had been found on the rifle used in the slaying and also on a box in the sixth floor room of the Dallas building from which the shots at the presidential motorcade were fired.

Earlier the mail order purchase of the rifle had been pinned on Oswald by handwriting comparisons in the laboratory of the Federal Bureau of Investigation in Washington, D. C.

In Chicago, Milton P. Klein, president of Klein's Sporting Goods, confirmed that his firm sold the rifle.

Klein said a copy of the sales slip showed the rifle was purchased from the mail order firm and shipped to Dallas in March 1963.

The Italian-made, bolt action 6.5 mm rifle, with telescopic sight, was sold for $19.95, Klein said.

Didn't Interview Oswald—FBI

The Federal Bureau of Investigation denied a published report Monday that agents had interviewed Lee Harvey Oswald, 24, prior to Friday's assassination of President John F. Kennedy.

The Dallas Morning News reported Saturday that FBI agents had interviewed Oswald as a suspected subversive since his arrival in Dallas a few weeks ago. According to the newspaper, the bureau had not notified the U.S. Secret Service or other law enforcement agencies of Oswald's presence.

Gordon Shanklin, FBI agent in charge in Dallas, told The Denver Post Monday the FBI had not questioned Oswald before the assassination. He declined to answer other questions about the investigation for the time being.

Dallas Police Chief J. E. Curry told the press Saturday he had no personal knowledge that FBI agents had previously talked with Oswald, and the chief said the bureau traditionally has "cooperated 100 per cent" with Dallas police.

Questions about the matter to local officals of the Secret Service were referred to Washington.

Attempt to Save Oswald A Nightmarish Rerun

DALLAS, Texas — (AP) — No pulse. No blood pressure. Lee Harvey Oswald, the accused killer of President Kennedy, appeared dead on the emergency room operating table at Parkland Hospital.

"We knew we had a slim, a very slim chance to save him," said Dr. Robert McClelland.

It seemed a nightmarish rerun of a desperate race against an ebbing life. Only Friday, two days earlier, it had been the President in a stark emergency room 10 feet down the hall.

Blood. Transfusion. That was first. Five, six quarts flowed into the 24-year-old self-styled [illegible] gunned down by a night club operator Sunday as he was being switched to a new jail.

Four of the team of doctors working so desperately had been on the team that worked in vain on the President. McClelland, Malcolm Perry, M. T. Jenkins, Ronald Jones.

Jack Ruby's bullet, fired at point-blank range, had smashed through the lower left chest, through the lung and diaphram, nicked the spleen, tore through the aorta and hit the liver and kidney.

The doctors opened his chest, then like a relay team, took turns slowly, attempting to match nature, massiging the heart.

CHAPTER THIRTEEN

Media Coverage - Some Good, Some Horrific

Reporters tackle national disasters such as the Kennedy assassination with much the same verve as firefighters rushing to an eight-alarm blaze. The pressure is often immense; sometimes the memories hang around for a long, long time.

You wouldn't want to do it every day.

"It took me a long time to get over the assassination," CBS newsman Bob Schieffer told me. "I was so emotionally spent. Not until 9/11 did I again have that same kind of feeling as I covered a story."

Of all the reportorial skills that come into play when covering a major catastrophe, the abilities to think quickly, act on instinct, and improvise are among the most important.

Bob, then a reporter for the *Star-Telegram*, was handling the rewrite desk telephones on Friday afternoon when a woman called to ask if anyone at the paper could give her a ride to Dallas.

"Lady," Schieffer told her, "you know the president has just been shot, and besides, we're not a taxi service."

"Yes, I heard it on the radio," she replied. "I think the person they've arrested is my son."

Schieffer told Marguerite Oswald to sit tight, he'd be right over. But first he needed appropriate wheels. "I had this little Triumph TR4 sports car then," he said. "I didn't want to drive her over in that."

So he asked the paper's automotive editor, Bill Foster, what kind of car he was reviewing that week. When Foster said he was driving a Cadillac, Schieffer decided that the two of them would chauffeur Mrs. Oswald to Dallas.

Schieffer made sure the *Star-Telegram* received full value for the favor. On the way to Dallas he conducted the first interview with the accused assassin's mother. Then he used her to penetrate the inner offices of the Dallas police department.

"I just walked up to the first uniformed Dallas policeman that I saw," he recalled, "and said, 'I'm the one who brought Oswald's mother over. Is there any place we can put her so these reporters won't talk to her?'"

The officer found a cubby hole in the Burglary and Theft Bureau where Schieffer stashed Marguerite and then surreptitiously passed back and forth into the hallway, gathering up *Star-Telegram* reporters' notes, which he then phoned back to the city desk from his hideaway.

Mrs. Oswald had astounded Schieffer with her conversation on the drive from Fort Worth. "It was a great lesson for me," he explained, "because she said such outrageous things. She was already talking about how the wife would get all the money and people would feel sorry for her. Marguerite was the mother and she would be forgotten.

"I just thought, this poor woman is under such strain and such pressure, she can't mean what's she's saying.

"Some of the stuff I didn't put into the Saturday paper.

"Well, it turned out that she was obsessed with money. It was all she had on her mind.

"Even years later she'd call me at CBS and say, 'Is there any way CBS would pay me for an interview?' Oh, she was awful. She really was a villain."

Sunday afternoon, Schieffer was part of another *Star-Telegram* coup.

Over at the *News*, Jack Beers had just developed the extraordinary photo of Ruby about to shoot Oswald that he took in the City Hall basement. Standing next to him in the dark room was Bob Jarboe, an AP photographer who doubled as a wire photo operator.

Beers seemed transfixed by the image, Jarboe recalls.

"He just sort of fell back against the wall, and told me to make two prints for him." But Jarboe also made two prints for the AP, which sent the stunning photo out over its wires within the hour.

A short while later, Bill Rives, assistant managing editor at the *News*, approached Jarboe with a smug expression. "We've got a picture I bet you'd love to have," Rives smiled.

"You mean this one?" Jarboe replied, holding up a copy of the Beers photo.

"Rives went bananas," Jarboe remembers.

When the Beers picture popped up on the AP machine over at the *Star-Telegram* that Sunday afternoon, managing editor Loren McMullin decided to use the photo to anchor a special Sunday afternoon edition, essentially scooping the *News* with its own picture.

"We were just thrilled to death," said Schieffer, who phoned in copy from Dallas to the newsroom in Fort Worth for the special edition. "We all just worked our asses off. Everybody had no sleep. We were all worn out. But man, when that *Star-Telegram* truck came by, I just grabbed a bundle of those papers and took 'em right down there to Dealey Plaza.

"I don't think journalism is like that anymore."

Eddie Barker, news director at KRLD-TV, gambled big time and came up a winner. Broadcasting from the Dallas Trade Mart on Friday, Eddie got a tip from a doctor at Parkland that Kennedy was dead a few minutes before the official announcement. While the competition over at WFAA-TV was forced to wait for confirmation, Eddie broadcast what he had.

"When I announced this over the air," he told me, "the network panicked. The validity of my source was questioned. However, I knew this man was trustworthy, so I kept repeating that the president was dead."

In a later *Journalism Quarterly* article, Richard K. Van der Karr called Barker's announcement one of the most important events of the weekend. "It will certainly be one of the greatest snap evaluations of a source in the history of broadcast journalism," wrote Van der Karr.

Bert Shipp, assistant news director at WFAA-TV, got the same tip about the same time—from a man all the media trusted, Sheriff Bill Decker. Decker had told Shipp there was no way the president could be alive, that the entire back of his head had been blown off. Shipp told his bosses, vouched for the source, and begged them to broadcast it.

But he was told the news director had provided a recent directive: "No more dead people mentioned without death certificates."

Associated Press reporter Mike Cochran's long weekend started Thursday night in Fort Worth, where he helped host White House staffers, the press corps and assorted federal agents at the Fort Worth press club bar. They partied until three in the morning, when Mike went home.

However, some Secret Service agents and reporters weren't quite ready to stop. Several of them went on to "The Cellar," a late-late place. Disclosure of this revelry got the group in serious trouble after the assassination next day.

Friday morning, Mike was at Carswell Air Force Base to make sure Air Force One lifted off on time, with the president inside. He filed what was called a floating bulletin, a brief advisory to editors that "President Kennedy left Carswell at 10:45 this morning."

Driving back from the military base, Cochran and his wife, Sondra, were caught in a hopeless traffic jam. So they went to breakfast, and she dropped Mike off at the AP office in the *Star-Telegram* building. Minutes later Cochran heard a copy boy screaming, "The president's been shot!" as he ripped the AP bulletin from the wire machine. Mike tried to reach Dallas by telephone, but the lines were jammed. So he teamed up with *Star-Telegram* reporter Jack Tinsley and some other of the paper's staffers and drove away in Tinsley's car, racing for Parkland Hospital.

"We got within two blocks," Mike recalled, "and couldn't get any closer. Tinsley just abandoned his car in the middle of the street, and we ran on up. When we walked in the front door here came a wave of nurses.

"My memory of this is so vivid. Three or four nurses were just sobbing, almost hysterical. You don't often see nurses get that emotional. I said, 'Kennedy's dead.' We learned later that Malcolm Kilduff had just announced it."

Cochran stayed at Parkland long enough to file an update on Gov. Connally's condition, then headed for the AP's Dallas office, where he worked through the night. Sunday morning, he drove home to Fort Worth to shower and change his clothes. He expected to head back for Dallas where he was to relieve fellow reporter Peggy Simpson on the AP's Oswald watch at City Hall.

Instead, Sondra greeted him at the door with news that Oswald had been shot, so Mike hurried back to the Dallas office to man the desk.

"We started getting telephone calls from papers, wanting a story on Jack Beers' 'Pulitzer' photograph," said Cochran. "I hadn't seen it. Then Bob Johnson, the Dallas bureau chief asked, 'Can't we do a story on this thing?' We were just besieged by calls. A couple of hours later people started asking about Bob Jackson's 'Pulitzer' picture.' I wrote a piece about the two without ever having seen them. I really can't remember what I said. Of course, I can't remember a lot about that weekend."

Then came one of the greatest embarrassments of Cochran's long and distinguished career. Though only two years out of college and fairly new to the AP, he was nonetheless assigned to write the overnight story on Oswald. This was a very big deal, one of perhaps five or six major stories the wire service would promote to its member news organizations around the world.

"I cleverly wrote a lead that in effect convicted Lee Harvey Oswald," Cochran explained, "saying he'd probably go down as the most hated person in American history, or something like that. Somehow it got past the Dallas editors, and New York had to file a 'bulletin kill' on my lead.

"A bulletin kill was the most disgraceful thing you could have happen to you. Raping the president's daughter didn't even compare."

•••••••••••••••••••••••••••••

A bevy of reporters, editors, and photographers rose to the occasion during that weekend and afterward, covering the biggest story of their careers. Among the most notable:

The Dallas Morning News: Kent Biffle, Paul Crume, Wick Fowler, Harry McCormick, Jim Ewell, Tom Dillard, Johnny Rutledge, Mary Woodward, Carl Freund, Jack Beers, Clint Grant, Joe Laird, Bill Winfrey, and Louis Harris.

The Dallas Times Herald: Jim Lehrer, Bob Jackson, Jim Featherston, George Carter, Paul Rosenfield, A. C. Greene, Felix McKnight, Bob Fenley, Darwin Payne, and Keith Shelton.

The Fort Worth Star-Telegram: Bob Schieffer, Jack Tinsley, Jerry Flemmons, and Jon "Bunky" McConal.

Associated Press: Mike Cochran

United Press International: Preston McGraw

WFAA Radio: Pierce Allman

KLIF Radio: Gary Delaune

KRLD Radio: Eddie Barker, Wes Wise, Bob Huffaker, and Jim Underwood.

WFAA-TV: Bert Shipp, Tom Alyea, Vic Robertson, and Ron Reiland.

WBAP-TV: Jimmy Darnell, Jim Kerr, and Bob Welch.

ABC News: Murphy Martin.

But not every reporter's work shone.

There were a few widely disseminated stories that later proved to be in error, deliberately or otherwise. Some of this could be attributed to the stress, confusion and turmoil of the weekend. But some was just plain schlock—imaginative reporting.

Seth Kantor, a former *Times Herald* reporter who was covering JFK's Texas visit for the Scripps-Howard newspapers, wrote that "sometime between 1:30 and 2 p.m." on Friday, Jack Ruby stopped and spoke to him inside the main entrance to Parkland Hospital. Pulling on Kantor's clothing, the reporter remembered, Ruby asked, "Should I close my places for the next three nights, do you think?"

A good tale, but probably untrue. Ruby denied ever going to the hospital that day, and the Warren Commission concluded that Kantor was mistaken, that Ruby's whereabouts were well documented, except for about a 20-minute period that afternoon, certainly not enough time for Ruby to have driven his car through the melee toward Parkland and returned to downtown Dallas.

In a story filed after Ruby killed Oswald, Kantor typed a stirring lead:

Dallas, Nov. 25—In disbelief, I watched a friend of mine, Jack Ruby, gun to death the man charged with killing President Kennedy.

Kantor continued: "It happened less than 10 feet from where I was standing in the basement of the Dallas police station. The last time I had seen Oswald's killer, Ruby, was two days earlier. It was at Parkland Memorial Hospital, moments before the news was official that President Kennedy was dead."

Kantor, whose former *Times Herald* pals laughed at his claim that

Ruby had been a friend, later published a conspiracy theory book, *The Ruby Cover-Up*. In it he concocted a tale that "somebody" phoned Ruby Sunday morning and instructed him to kill Oswald. "A call was placed to the unlisted phone number in Ruby's apartment; Ruby was told where to enter the station and that the transfer van was en route. Ruby made sure the snub-nosed gun with its two-inch barrel was loaded. He put it in his trouser pocket. Never in his jacket. It got the jacket out of shape."

Another fakir was Thayer Waldo at the *Star-Telegram*.

In February 1964, Waldo wrote that the government was holding in protective custody a close "eye-witness" who could solidly identify Oswald as Kennedy's assassin. When this "exclusive" ran in the paper's early editions, the Associated Press called me for comment. I told them there was a solid witness, but that as far as I knew he wasn't being held anywhere. This wasn't the first factual leap I'd seen Waldo take. I think I termed it "a bunch of crap." Justice Department spokesman Edwin O. Guthman concurred. There is no truth to the story at all," said Guthman, "and no such witness exists."

"The story," Mike Cochran remembered, "was a front-page banner to start with. After the AP talked to you, it became about two paragraphs on the last page of the paper. Oh, you talk about an embarrassing cover-up! Thayer Waldo was awful. He became a laughingstock."

Richard Dudman in the *St. Louis Post-Dispatch* also had a great story—that Kennedy could not have been shot from behind because Dudman had seen entry bullet holes in the limousine's windshield. Alas, that scoop went up in smoke when authorities allowed reporters to personally examine the hole-free windshield (which was nicked from the inside).

....

While the print media broke most of the important stories—and bungled a few as well—the electronic media also made missteps. CBS, best remembered for Walter Cronkite's emotional announcement of Kennedy's death, ran a dubious story about alleged FBI advance knowledge of JFK's assassination—a tale that did not withstand critical inquiry, but enjoyed wide approval among conspiracy theorists.

William B. Walter, a clerk who had worked out of the FBI's New

Slaying Site Figure Seen

Witnesses Saw Assassin Poke Rifle Out Window

FEB 1 0 1964

Two witnesses, heretofore undisclosed, saw the figure of a man in the sixth-floor assassination window of the Texas Book Depository Building Nov. 22 when President Kennedy was slain, The Times Herald learned Monday.

The witnesses, a teen-age Negro boy and a construction worker, were standing in the street when the fatal shots were fired. They failed, however, to identify Lee Harvey Oswald as the man in the window after viewing him in a police lineup before his murder in the basement of City Hall.

Qualified sources who told The Times Herald about the witnesses also said a Negro janitor who reportedly claimed seeing Oswald fire the fatal shots at President Kennedy was never considered by official agencies to be an eyewitness to the assassination.

No police agency—Secret Service, FBI, city or county—has the janitor in custody or knows of reported intentions by the Warren Commission to subpoena him as a witness in its Washington probe of the assassination, The Times Herald was told.

The Fort Worth Star-Telegram, in a story by Thayer Waldo, reported Monday morning that an informed source said a witness being held in protective custody could identify Oswald as President Kennedy's slayer and would appear before the Warren Commission.

The Fort Worth paper, however, reported that government spokesmen—Texas and federal—quickly

Official Sources Deny Story Of Assassination 'Witness'

FEB 1 0 1964

By HUGH AYNESWORTH

o substantiation could be found day night for a newspaper y claiming that a witness was g held in protective custody could identify Lee Harvey ald as the slayer of President edy.

e Fort Worth Star Telegram an informed source identified witness as a Negro porter employed at the Texas School Book Depository on Nov. 22.

In its first edition, the newspaper claimed a janitor was at the next window to Oswald, watching the Nov. 22 parade, when he heard a shot "loud and close."

was "scared to death," and that he fled the building and surrendered to police, who charged him with vagrancy so they would have a reason to hold him. He reportedly was jailed in Dallas, then transferred elsewhere.

He reportedly will appear before the Warren Commission in Washington to tell his story.

Roy S. Truly, superintendent of the depository, said Sunday night, "The only janitor we have is still working there. I know nothing about all this."

After the newspaper's first edition story, Dallas Police Chief Jesse Curry said he felt there was no such witness.

"I've talked to the FBI and the

Secret Service and they know nothing about it," he added. "I know for sure we didn't arrest anybody like this and Sheriff Bill Decker's office says the same thing.

"I feel sure we would have known something about it if there was a witness like this," Curry said.

"I've talked to them over there (Fort Worth) and they won't tell me their source—only that they believe it's reliable," he added.

Truly said only one person had left the employ of the depository since the assassination. He was a Negro order filler, who told The ... he was ... ut the ... police ... on the ... earing ... e jani- ... he one ... s well ... ob. ... pokes- ... said ... to the ... itness

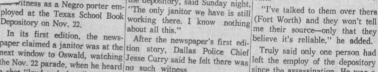

The Fort Worth Star-Telegram, in a story by Thayer Waldo, reported Monday morning that an informed source said a witness being held in protective custody could identify Oswald as President Kennedy's slayer and would appear before the Warren Commission.

The Fort Worth paper, however, reported that government spokesmen—Texas and federal—quickly denied the report and said its source revised his story after it first appeared in print.

Fort Worth Star-Telegram reporter Thayer Waldo (center), *Dallas Morning News* reporter Jim Ewell (left), and Officer Nick McDonald (right), who helped apprehend Oswald at the Texas Theater.

Ugly Rumors--And, One by One, How Report

Hints of Conspiracy Fail to Stand Up

STARK AFTERMATH—Where bullet smashed through windshield of late President's car.

What the Key Figures Say | Belli Doubts

The president's limousine before the assassination and a story saying that the shot was fired from the rear, not the front, as first reported by the *St. Louis Post-Dispatch*.

Orleans office in 1963, told conspiracy monger Mark Lane in 1968 that FBI headquarters sent a Telex to all its domestic offices on Nov. 17, 1963, warning that there might be an assassination in Dallas and alerting its agents to check closely with their informants.

Walter said the memo warned of an attempt on Kennedy's life, and that he was the only one who saw it that night—although four others later saw the teletype, which he said was still in his possession. According to Walter, the memo went to all SACs (Special Agents in Charge) and was headed:

URGENT TO ALL SACS FROM DIRECTOR

Threat to assassinate President Kennedy in Dallas, Texas, November 22–23. Information received by the Bureau has determined that a militant revolutionary group may attempt to assassinate President Kennedy on his proposed trip to Dallas, Texas.

Walter said he contacted several superiors in the bureau and was told never to mention the teletype. Nevertheless, he claimed he kept a copy and locked the original in a bank vault.

At the time, Lane, or somebody close to New Orleans DA Jim Garrison, mentioned Walter to Martin "Moe" Waldron of *The New York Times*. Waldron mentioned it to me and to Jerry Cohen of the *Los Angeles Times* over dinner one night. We all had a laugh over it.

"There is bizarre and there is bizarre," Waldron said, as he explained what Walter was peddling.

"Yeah, I'm sure that here, almost four years later, nobody ever recalled that," Waldron laughed.

We didn't expect to hear of it again, but often those who make up stories, no matter how unbelievable, don't just chuck them. Often it's all that makes them feel important, as though they're *somebody*.

In this case, Lane passed it along to Garrison, who was conducting a high-profile, low-road investigation of the assassination. Garrison also was then battling with NBC News. The DA had threatened to sue the network after an NBC "White Paper" documentary (June 1967) showed his investigation to be a sham, as I had written in a *Newsweek* article the month before.

Anyway, NBC talk show host Johnny Carson invited Garrison to a full hour on Jan. 31, 1968, in which the DA was allowed to malign his detractors and generally solidify his alleged case against businessman Clay Shaw, whom he accused of conspiring to kill the president.

That's when Garrison tossed out the name of William Walter and mentioned his alleged "information."

The FBI quickly investigated, interviewing more than 50 agents and supervisors, checking its messaging in and out, even contacting several offices. Officials decided that Walter, who had left the FBI after being placed on probation, was lying.

Most everybody forgot about William Walter until 1975, when my investigative partner at the *Times Herald*, Bob Dudney, learned Walter was once again making allegations.

Dudney and I interviewed Walter for the *Times Herald*, and he also somehow came to Dan Rather's attention and did an interview with CBS. When I heard his story I didn't believe it. But we had to nail it down. So we took copious notes and then flew Walter to Dallas at the newspaper's expense for a polygraph test. We also called a number of individuals whom Walter claimed knew something of the memo or could vouch for his veracity. We even secured a complete list of FBI Telexes for several days surrounding the alleged date.

Each was in numerical order.

Walter started changing his story—not a lot, but slightly. First, he said he had been an agent, but he wasn't—just a clerk. Another time he gave us a list of those he contacted in the hours immediately following the arrival of the alleged Telex. That list changed as several people denied talking to him. Then he said he didn't have his handwritten copy of the Telex anymore; that he had given it to CBS News, where it apparently had vanished.

Walter seemed confident, energetic, a pleasant fellow. Bill Burnham, the well-qualified polygraph operator we used at the paper on several important sources in the 1970s, said he didn't believe him. Yet professionally, Burnham called the test "inconclusive."

Almost everything Walter told us changed once we contacted any of his witnesses or associates. We fully realized the importance of the story, if true, and also knew how unfair and harmful it would be if untrue. So, *Times Herald* editors—with Dudney and me in complete agreement—concluded it should not be printed.

Dan Rather and the *Times Herald* publisher, Tom Johnson, were friends. Tom thought he should warn Rather away from the story, believing that we had spent more time investigating it than had CBS. Johnson wanted to give Rather knowledgeable input.

They talked, and Rather called back a couple of times as a follow-up. Both Dudney and I told him what we knew and that we felt there was nothing to Walter's story.

We expected CBS to kill the piece. Instead, they ran it aggressively. We responded the next day with an extensive front-page story, outlining the holes and misstatements in Walter's story.

In 1978 when the House Subcommittee on Assassinations interviewed Walter, they concluded he manufactured the story. Walter still was having trouble finding anyone to corroborate his version of events. He told the committee his former wife, Sharon Covert, who had also worked for the FBI in New Orleans, might be able to back him up. She advised the committee that she could not support any of his allegations and that Walter had never mentioned the situation to her during their marriage.

Still later, when the JFK Assassinations Records Review Board was in session in 1996, Marina Oswald—by then herself a conspiracy theorist—wrote its chairman John Tunheim asking what the board was doing about releasing "the full particulars and original of the teletype received by Mr. Walter."

She had read about it in a recent book, Marina said, adding: "I now believe that my former husband met with the Dallas FBI on Nov. 16, 1963, and provided informant information on which this teletype was based."

A story like Walter's, legitimized by a respected media outfit, can live on forever, no matter how slim its proof or believability.

•••••••••••••••••••••••••••••

One of the more absurd tales—one we could legitimately consider "far out"—was concocted later by former *Star-Telegram* reporter Jim Marrs in a book called *Alien Agenda*. Marrs, one of the best-known conspiracy theorists, became semi-famous when filmmaker Oliver Stone bought his book, *Crossfire* (along with Jim Garrison's *On the Trail of the Assassins*) to make his movie, *JFK*.

In his 1997 book, Marrs ponders whether or not the JFK slaying

Inquiry fails to verify JFK warning message

By BOB DUDNEY and
HUGH AYNESWORTH
Staff Writers

A former FBI employe has claimed the agency issued a teletype warning of a potential assassination plot five days before President Kennedy's death, but he has persistently refused to produce a copy of the alleged teletype he says he possesses.

FBI's comments, Page 20-A

The alleged teletype message was outlined to The Times Herald more than three weeks ago but an intensive investigation has provided no evidence to substantiate the account.

Also, the FBI, prompted by questions from The Times Herald several days ago, has conducted its own investigation of the allegations and Tuesday issued an official response saying no evidence could be developed

to support the existence of such a teletype.

William S. Walter, a night security clerk at the New Orleans FBI office in 1963, asserted in an interview Sept. 7 that the alleged teletype originated in FBI headquarters at Washington, D.C., and was received by him personally in the New Orleans field office Nov. 17, 1963.

This report was made public Tuesday by CBS News and several other news-gathering organizations.

However, The Times Herald's efforts to verify the story — which included more than 60 interviews and a polygraph examination of Walter in Dallas — failed to provide any corroboration of any such teletype message.

Walter has claimed to The Times
See **EX-EMPLOYE** on Page 21

With Walter NL
DALLAS AP — Former FBI agent William Walter says he saw a teletyped message in

in Dallas Nov. 22, 1963. In an interview with CBS News Tuesday, Walter said he saw a teletype message Nov. 17, 1963 advising all agents to seek information from informants regarding a possible assassination attempt.

Walter said

The newspaper said Walter has repeatedly failed to produce a copy of the alleged teletype message ''he says he possesses.''

Walter said

Our report of the Walter allegations and an AP wire the same day notes CBS' coverage of the story. News wire stories, like this one, were printed on paper that had the same texture as construction paper, but was softer and thinner.

occurred because Kennedy knew all about alien visitation to Earth and someone didn't want him to tell the American people.

Marrs quoted "a former steward aboard Air Force One" as hearing a cryptic remark by JFK, which later in the book became "tantalizing bits of evidence." In a chapter called "JFK, Marilyn and the UFOs," Marrs quotes Bill Holden, whom he describes as "loadmaster" of the president's 707 Air Force One, as asking Kennedy what he thought of aliens having visited Earth. He said Mr. Kennedy paused then said, "I'd like to tell the public about the alien situation, but my hands are tied."

"Spurred on by such tantalizing bits of evidence, some researchers even claimed that Kennedy's assassination was to prevent him from revealing the news of extraterrestrial visitation to the public," Marrs wrote.

I asked Marrs at a university debate later if he really believed what he had described was "tantalizing evidence."

"What should I have done," he replied, "ignored it?"

•••••••••••••••••••••••••••••

It was the egregious behavior of the legendary Bob Considine, however, that was the most the most painful to me personally. Considine, then writing for the *New York Journal-American*, was a true icon of my trade.

I had handled some recent assassination-related freelance assignments for the *Journal-American*. So when Considine came to Dallas to cover the Ruby trial for the paper he contacted me. Over time, we became pretty close. We sat together at the trial, often ate lunch together, and frequently met for drinks with other journalists after everyone's daily story had been filed.

One day during this period I received yet another tip of a purported connection between Ruby and Oswald. It was a long shot, just like all the tips I received in those days. Nevertheless, it was an intriguing story I felt obliged to run down.

The characters included an Oak Cliff car salesman named Warren Reynolds, who was among the witnesses who claimed to have seen Lee Harvey Oswald flee the J.D. Tippit murder scene. On the night of Jan. 23, 1964, while closing up his brother Johnnie's used car lot on East Jefferson, Reynolds was shot one time in the head by an unknown attacker. He survived.

Next day, an anonymous caller told Johnnie Reynolds he should go see "Dago," Darrell Wayne Garner, 24, a local ne'er-do-well familiar to the cops, in connection with the attack on Warren. Johnnie notified the police, who quickly established that Garner had been at the car lot earlier in the day, and left in evident rage when Johnnie Reynolds refused to buy a 1957 Oldsmobile from him because Garner lacked a valid title for the vehicle.

Garner was arrested and released after an alibi witness, Nancy Jane Mooney, 24, said she was out drinking and driving around with Garner until 3:30 in the morning. The woman passed a polygraph test, as did Garner himself, twice.

Then Nancy Mooney, who also went by the name of Betty MacDonald, got into a brawl with her roommate, Patsy Moore, and was arrested and jailed for disturbing the peace.

Mooney-MacDonald, who was well known to suffer severe periods of depression, hanged herself by her toreador slacks in her cell. In the ensuing investigation, Patsy Moore told the police that Mooney-MacDonald was a former stripper who'd worked at various bars in Dallas, including Jack Ruby's Carousel Club.

Mooney-MacDonald in fact had told the police the same thing in an earlier interview.

The conspiracy spin on this tawdry tale was this: Reynolds somehow had seen too much and needed to be silenced. To accomplish that, Jack Ruby found a willing killer, "Dago" Garner, via his former employee, Mooney-MacDonald, whom he then had murdered in jail to cover his tracks.

The problem with this theory was none of these elements stood the test of inquiry. I found out that Mooney-MacDonald really did commit suicide; she'd tried it several times before, and had the scars on her wrists to prove it. Despite the polygraph results, the Dallas police were convinced Dago Garner really did shoot Warren Reynolds, but his motive was anger over the Oldsmobile, not Lee Harvey Oswald.

Finally, neither George Senator nor anyone else connected to the

Opposite: (A) Front page lead story by Bob Considine the day after the assassination. (B) Considine's Mooney-MacDonald story, which became an exhibit in the Warren Commission. (C) Cordial letter from author to Considine.

figure A

figure B

figure C

Carousel Club had any recall of Mooney-MacDonald working there. I also posed the question directly to Ruby, via Phil Burleson, during his trial. The lawyer reported to me that Jack knew nothing of either Mooney-MacDonald or Darrell Garner.

One day when I had missed a morning session of the trial, Considine asked me where I had been. I told him I had been digging on a story I thought might be really valuable, but that it had turned south on me.

At dinner that evening I explained the complicated allegations, but said, "It just isn't there."

"So you don't think there's anything at all to it?" he asked.

"Not unless you make up a lot of it," I answered.

Later in the week, an AP photographer called me, wondering if I could help him find photos of Garner and Warren Reynolds.

"What for?" I asked.

"Oh," he said, "the *Journal-American* in New York wants their pictures for some feature story they're working on."

Sure enough, on Sunday, Feb. 23, Considine published "Violent Dallas: A New Chapter," telling his readers that the major suspect in the Reynolds shooting had been freed from jail on the say-so of one of Jack Ruby's strippers, who then killed herself.

When I asked Considine why he'd printed a story he knew to be false, he shrugged, "Oh, it's just a yarn."

Of course it was, until a journalist of Considine's considerable credibility and clout legitimized it in print. Gen. Walker saw the story, and invited Reynolds to come visit him. Together, Walker and Reynolds decided the shooting had to be connected to Oswald.

The general later telegraphed the Warren Commission, wondering why Reynolds had not been called as a witness. Still later, Jim Garrison would rehash the story as part of the conspiracy carnival he was gearing up in New Orleans. Dago Garner eventually claimed that there really was a conspiracy involved.

Helen Markham at the Tippit murder scene. I'm standing behind her,
taking notes. (Still from WFAA-TV Dallas broadcast, Nov. 23, 1963)

CHAPTER FOURTEEN

Big Money for Big Stories

I think of Rodney Stalls as a pioneer, an original. On his own, the
unemployed engineer developed a conspiracy theory within hours
of JFK's assassination, and presented it to me (his second choice)
along with his "proof" by that night.

However, Mr. Stalls was only the first.

One Saturday morning shortly after the assassination, as I sat at
my front row desk in the newsroom, a tall, painfully thin man who
stank something awful came up to me. It was not at all unusual for
the public to wander around the newsroom in those days. It was
a much simpler time.

"I'm from the Windy City," he said, "and I've got the story for
you. I know how Oswald got the message. They got to me, too."

I placed him in a chair and rolled my own back a distance to get
away from the stench. He leaned down and rubbed his leg, then stood
up painfully and lifted his trouser leg to reveal a horrendous abscess,
red and gray and oozing pus. "That's how my leg got torn up," he said.

It was necessary to think very quickly.

"Stop right there," I said. "I'm just a lowly reporter. I don't feel
capable of handling what you have to share. So let me give you
someone who handles sensitive issues for us. And one other thing,
don't tell him you talked to me first. Because he might get angry."

Then I pointed my visitor toward Bill Rives, one of the nicer
people at the paper, upon whom the rest of us were always playing
practical jokes. Rives, who spoke to the man from Chicago for
two hours that morning, never learned that I had sent him in.

My colleague Larry Grove once jokingly threatened to blackmail me.

Tom Simmons, the other assistant managing editor who shared an office with Rives, once mentioned how they had to burn candles for days to get rid of the smell after the Chicago man left.

Still another early "buff," as the conspiracy theorists became known, was a local attorney, Carroll Jarnagin. His provocative claim was to have overheard Lee Harvey Oswald in deep conversation at the Carousel Club with Jack Ruby a few days before Nov. 22.

Jarnagin, who looked to be about 45, had the tired face of a drinker. He was evasive throughout our conversation, avoided eye contact, and frequently scratched himself. The major problem with his assertion—he even offered me snippets of direct dialog, although these changed over time—was that he had no proof. He did have a girlfriend who substantiated Jarnagin's claim to have visited the Carousel Club one night in early November, but she remembered nothing about the alleged Oswald-Ruby chat.

When the lawyer later took his story to Chief Curry and Henry Wade, they gave him a polygraph test, and he failed miserably.

"He grinned and said, 'Well, some things you remember and others you don't' and walked out. I never heard of him again," said DA Wade.

Yet—and this part of Jarnagin's story amazed me—the Warren Commission dithered over a version of this story for months. Jarnagin's name was never mentioned, but in March 1964, Mark Lane, the author of *Rush to Judgment* (1966), testified that he had a source who had overheard a lengthy plot session in the Carousel Club (more on Lane shortly).

The kooks and opportunists kept coming, their theories and remembrances in every imaginable flavor. Some, like Mr. Stalls or "Stinky" from Chicago, popped up out of nowhere. Others I thought of as my "regulars." This group, which included one woman, wrote, called, or showed up in person as often as weekly, always willing to share some new tidbit, some new twist.

In the early days, their paranoia centered mostly on the Russians, or H.L. Hunt, or Gen. Walker, singly or in combination. Occasionally a buff would bring up the Bay of Pigs and link Kennedy's mishandling of the 1961 Cuban invasion debacle to his 1963 assassination.

J. Edgar Hoover was another early conspiracy favorite. Most of the alleged plots involving the FBI director began with the assumption that JFK planned to replace the old despot if re-elected in 1964. The recurring rumors, stoked by Lonnie Hudkins's unfortunate article that Lee Harvey Oswald was a paid federal informant, lent credence to these stories.

My salary in December 1963 was $9,500 a year, or $500 more than I was earning a month earlier, thanks to being in the right places at the right times in late November. It had not occurred to me that I might exploit my situation for a whole lot more money, not until I got the call from New York.

Two people were on the other end: a Frenchman I'll call Francois, and Doris, an American book agent. "Everyone in Europe agrees with you about the Kennedy assassination," Francois began in heavily accented English. "And I am a well-known literary publisher who wants to get to the bottom of this. You know, our people loved Mr. Kennedy."

I had no clue what part of my thinking had registered so positively with the collective French psyche. As I spoke with Francois and Doris, I thought back to a recent panel discussion in New York where I was quoted by the wire services as saying there were still too many unanswered questions in the case. I figured that was where Francois was coming from, and he admitted later that, yes, that was how he "discovered" me.

His proposal was simple and left me a bit breathless. Francois offered me $75,000 to produce within three months a book of 50,000 to 60,000 words that addressed what he called "problems" with the evidence against Oswald; the "probability" that Oswald had once been a U.S. agent of some sort; and that the Warren Commission would be politically tainted, nothing more than a tool for President Johnson.

"With your reputation and the fact that you were there," Francois said, "this will be a very important book. It will sweep Europe." I told him I'd have to think it over, and that I needed some time. He agreed.

The offer stunned me. To date, besides my regular stringing income from *Newsweek* and my recent $500 raise at the *News*, the only extra money I'd seen was the $25 that the Newspaper Enterprise Association (NEA) paid me to recap the first weekend of the story.

I decided to seek Larry Grove's advice. Larry grinned when I told him about the $75,000.

"You'd better get an agent, and a good one," he said. Then he told me about a deal he once thought he had to write a small book about his World War II adventures in the South Pacific.

"It started at $10,000," he said. "Then the guy called and said he had to make a special distribution deal and therefore could pay me only $8,000. Then he tried to get it even cheaper than that. He kept saying, 'You don't need an agent. It'll cost you most of what you make. Stick with me.'"

In the end, said Larry, "I got to thinking my deal wasn't so good and I'd end up paying him, so I just eased out of it."

As we spoke and Grove considered my situation, he observed that the Frenchman clearly wanted a conspiracy book, and one written by the newsman with the deepest personal knowledge of the assassination probably could be a best seller.

"But don't ruin your reputation for a few fast bucks," he warned me.

That remark made us both laugh. A few fast bucks? How about the near equivalent of both our salaries for almost five years!

Francois called the next day to discuss the book again. The more we spoke the less I liked the idea, and the less I liked Francois. He was very full of himself, very pushy. At last I told him someone was at the door and got off the phone. As he rang off, he told me to expect a call from Doris, the agent. Doris, who had a decided Brooklyn accent, and I spoke several times before I finally said I couldn't do the project because the *News* wouldn't let me.

"But you don't make that kind of money at the newspaper," she argued.

"Yes, but they don't tell me what to write, either," I replied.

And that was that.

When I later told my managing editor, Jack Krueger, about the failed negotiations, he slapped me on the back, said, "Good choice, Hugh!" and a month later raised my pay another $10 a week.

When I recounted the episode to my wife, then pregnant with our first child, she was none too pleased. "Do you realize how much money that was?" she asked, incredulous. I told her the old West Virginia (my home state) line about how you can put lipstick on a sow but that won't make her homecoming queen.

My wife wasn't amused. Never would be.

The famous picture of Oswald with his rifle and pistol.

Garrison vs. Shaw

Accusations Of Conspiracy Fired Like Shotgun Fusillade

[Third of a Series.]

By HUGH AYNESWORTH

NEW ORLEANS—If New Orleans District Attorney Jim Garrison can prove his case, he will become one of this nation's most honored and famous men. But if he has no case at all, what of the wrath he has spread?

The 6-foot-6-inch prosecutor has excited millions with his claims that he has "solved" President John F. Kennedy's assassination. He has vowed that "unless they kill me," nobody can possibly stop him from bringing the guilty parties to justice.

History will record that Garrison either stood up and pointed his finger at hundreds of scoundrels who conspired in the Kennedy assassination and then convicted them—or that he was, as some of his enemies call him, a power-mad paranoid who, in an insane drive for fame, helped ruin the lives of many persons and made his own country look ridiculous.

A strange combination of circumstances enabled Jim Garrison to emerge as the most notorious prosecutor in America today.

[...] commis[...] com[...] report [...] which [...] spiracy [...] of peo[...] out the [...] resting [...] the half [...] specula[...] volumes

Garrison was surprised himself by his [...] to this writer at the

DAVID FERRIE
Broken man at 45.

Soon the Dallas police and sheriff's office, the FBI, the State Dept., the CIA, President Johnson, the Castroites, the right-wing oilmen, the Dallas district attorney and half a hundred others were being accused in print of involvement in the assassination.

So it was into a receptive arena that Jim Garrison stepped in early 1967 when he announced that he was investigating the case, and that he had many suspects and many witnesses.

time: "God, I didn't know how many people believed as I did. Well, tell 'em to hold tight . . . they ain't seen nothin' yet!"

At that period of his investigation, Garrison had half a dozen suspects in his case. David Ferrie, the onetime airline pilot who had been "fingered" by an alcoholic informant as "Oswald's getaway pilot," was the prime one—at least until his mysterious death in February, 1967.

Ferrie, a brilliant but broken man of 45, looked like a cartoon conspirator. He had posed as an Army captain, a doctor, an Air Force officer—and once he had a midget submarine with which, he said, he aimed to "blow up Havana harbor."

Lengthy Inquiry

Ferrie had been hauled in for questioning a few hours after Mr. Kennedy's death in Dallas, and at that time the DA's office turned him over to Federal authorities. The Secret Service and FBI both investigated Ferrie at length and found him innocent of anything connected with the assassination.

These Federal agencies traced the origin of the "tip" about Ferrie to a New Orleans alcoholic named Jack S. Martin. Martin, who had a long police record, admitted tearfully that he had made the whole thing up to get revenge on Ferrie, a homosexual.

Still, Garrison questioned Ferrie at length, then put a 24-hour surveillance on him. Ferrie noticed that his house was under constant watch because the DA's boys had replaced one pane of a garage window directly across the street with a

Jim Garrison on
New Orleans television.

CHAPTER FIFTEEN

Bribery, Coercion and Opportunists
in the "Big Easy"

In my view, were it not for the pervasive influence of a handful
of individuals, there would be no plague of conspiracy theories
surrounding the Kennedy assassination.

The first of these regrettable characters was Jack Ruby, who by
stealing the executioner's role, created generations of doubters, and
not unreasonably so. It was an audacious, desperate act that would
seem to make sense only if Jack Ruby had a very powerful, rational
motive for killing Lee Harvey Oswald.

The truth is that he did not; the hard evidence in the case
supports no other conclusion.

Based on indisputable facts, I believe that Ruby acted
spontaneously in the basement at City Hall. The opportunity
to kill Lee Harvey Oswald suddenly presented itself, and Ruby
acted accordingly. He could just as well have been driving home
from the Western Union office at that moment.

The second key character was Mark Lane, for whose predations
I must shoulder some blame.

Had I not foolishly given Lane a packet of then-secret witness
statements in December of 1963, believing him when he said his
single motive was to act as devil's advocate for Oswald ("I want to
represent this boy," Lane told me. "I don't think he did it."), I wonder
if people such as Lane, and later Jim Garrison and Oliver Stone,
would be viewed today as brave souls who fought to bring the light
of "truth" to the assassination story.

Lane, an attorney and one-term New York Democratic state
assemblyman from the JFK wing of the party, in early December

wrote a lengthy piece in *The National Guardian* laying out a litany of reasons that made him conclude Oswald could not have killed Kennedy. The story was published well before Lane ever visited Dallas, spoke to any witnesses or investigators or contacted me. It was riddled with inaccuracies and unsupported suppositions.

When he first called me in December, I told him I was very busy, but agreed to meet with him at my apartment the next evening.

"Do you know anybody who knows Jack Ruby well?" he asked. I said that I knew Ruby well enough to intensely dislike him. "Really?" Lane replied, his interest plainly apparent.

"Well, there's no doubt that he and Oswald were involved," he said, "but we don't know exactly how."

Then he mentioned he had an appointment scheduled for the next day with a Dallas business figure who had seen Oswald and Ruby plotting together, just a few weeks before the assassination. "I talked with him on the phone and he sounds like the real thing," Lane offered.

"How many people have you interviewed so far?" I asked.

"Well, you may be the first," he said. "Then this other source, this lawyer with an impeccable memory. Maybe I'll get to him tomorrow. But I will share it with you if you will help me."

"Who's footing the bill for your investigation?"

"I am, completely," he assured me. "I am certainly not in it for the money. This will cost me plenty, but I think it's very important."

Lane came by the apartment again the next evening. He said his good source, the one who could put Ruby and Oswald together in the Carousel Club, had bowed out, for the time being.

"He's had some threats," said Lane, "and he needs some time to think it over. We're going to talk again tomorrow."

At this point, I had not yet met Carroll Jarnagin. But I'd heard about him from Johnny King, who had said Jarnagin was "a nice-enough guy, but a bad lush" and that he thought I should talk to him eventually, if only to discount the story.

"He's told us other stories," King laughed. "One about LBJ that we would have loved to believed, another about John Tower. The guy gets around—especially in his own mind."

At this early stage in the story, I was still running down what at first often looked like great leads that connected Oswald with others in the shootings. It was too soon to dismiss possibilities. And under the general rule that even a blind pig can sometimes find an acorn, I was deeply curious to learn the identity of Lane's source, hardly guessing who he would turn out to be.

Lane tried to impress me with how much he knew about the assassination, which wasn't much at all. I'd recall this conversation three years later when I first sat down with Jim Garrison. The New Orleans DA didn't know much either.

Lane would mention this source or that eyewitness, and I would contradict him. "No, he didn't say that." Or, "She wasn't in a position to hear that."

"But how do you know?" he kept asking.

Because, I explained, in some cases I conducted the first interview with the individual in question, or knew something about them that called their word into question. A lot of them changed their stories as time passed, too.

"A few days after somebody got to them," Lane added, conspiratorially.

There also was another reason I was sure of my facts.

"I know what they said to the cops, too, within hours of the shootings," I said. "They might have 'refined' the facts later, but I know what they originally said."

"What makes you so sure?" Lane asked.

Like a dummy, eager to prove my point to this opportunist, I went into the next room, grabbed a stack of papers, came back and tossed them on the coffee table.

"There are the eyewitness accounts," I said, "made the afternoon of November 22nd."

"Where did you get these?" Lane was amazed.

I could not divulge my source, I said. But the reports were real and legitimate.

Lane began to read; we didn't speak for a long time.

"The only reason I'm showing you these," I finally broke the silence, "is that you made many, many misinterpretations in your article. If you are truly interested in giving Oswald a fair shake from a historical standpoint, I think you need to know what the investigation shows so far."

"Oh, yes," Lane agreed.

He glanced at his watch and asked, "Could I use your telephone? I was supposed to call Oswald's mother about now. I'm meeting with her tomorrow and don't want to miss her, or call too late."

"Are you representing her?" I asked, thinking back over my recent, testy confrontations with Marguerite.

"Not yet. But I intend to."

"Then be my guest," I said, pointing out the telephone resting on a table in the adjoining room.

We lived in a small, one-bedroom apartment at the time, so I couldn't help hearing Lane's conversation even if I tried, which I didn't. Three or four times he said to her, "I really don't think it will make much difference."

When he finished, I softly eased into the subject. "I couldn't help but hearing Mark, what was all that 'doesn't matter' stuff about?"

"Oh, she is quite an opinionated woman," he said. "She thinks Lee was a paid informant of the FBI and she asked how much difference that would make. I told her it probably doesn't matter either way."

He changed the subject.

"You know, you are an important contributor to the truth in this case," Lane said, exuding sincerity.

"Will you help me find the truth? I have to go back to New York in a day or so, and I was wondering if I could borrow these statements for a few days. I want to contact these people to see what, if any, pressure has been brought on them, and if they have something different to say now."

All these years later, I could still kick myself for this next sentence: "Of course. I'm not writing anything more about the witnesses, at least not for now."

I didn't even take the partial precaution of making Lane go photocopy the pages. In part, that was not so simply done in 1963 as it is today; public photocopy machines were not common. Plus, I had made good notes on all the most important witnesses.

Lane, despite his promises, did not return the witness reports to me immediately. But I was busy with other parts of the assassination story, and saw no reason to distrust the earnest young lawyer from New York. I did call his office a few times. He was never in.

Then I began seeing wire service stories from Europe, reporting the fund-raising activities of so-called "Who Killed Kennedy?" committees across the continent. The dispatches said that British philosopher Bertrand Russell was involved with the committees, and reported that Mark Lane was their executive director. I also read about Lane appearing at a press conference, waving a fistful of documents in the air, proclaiming that the papers proved that witnesses in Dallas contradicted the authorities.

I had made a horrific mistake.

A few days later came a telephone call from Bertrand Russell himself in London. "First," the old man said in an authoritative British accent, "I want to congratulate you on stealing all those statements from the Dallas police. I don't profess to understand how you did it, but you have done the world a great service."

Famous as he was, I confess to little detailed knowledge of Russell's thought processes. I knew nothing of his politics and I had no idea why he was calling me. I wasn't even positive, at first, that Bertrand Russell was really on the phone. Were it not for that aristocratic accent, I would have suspected some jokester at the paper. But nobody I knew could sustain such an accent for long.

I told Russell that I had not stolen anything from any investigative agency, and I didn't know where anyone would get that idea, surely not from me.

"Oh, Mr. Lane informed me you would say just that," he replied with a chuckle.

Russell said he had some questions for me "about some of the stories you have written." I advised him to submit his queries in writing and I'd be please to answer them as best I could. This did not please him. He seemed accustomed to people doing as he instructed them. The conversation soon ended.

Yet he did write me three times over the ensuing months, exploring all possibilities of official chicanery, falsification and the like. The only subject I wouldn't touch is one I still don't touch today. I do not know exactly how to explain Kennedy's and Connally's wounds. The Warren Commission might be correct or might be totally wrong about its much-maligned "Single Bullet Theory," the allegation that one shot careened through the president's back and throat and then into Gov. Connally.

But I do know that I heard three distinct shots that afternoon; so did several others whom I interviewed shortly thereafter.

On Feb. 7, Lane finally responded to my demands that he return the files. He also offered me a job as his investigator, assuring me in a letter that "our communications and contacts would be priviledged [sic.] and I need not divulge them to anybody."

I never answered his letter and thought I was through with him at

MARK LANE
ATTORNEY AT LAW
654 MADISON AVE.
NEW YORK 21, N. Y.

TEMPLETON 8-1300

February 7, 1964

Mr. Hugh Aynesworth
4916 Belmont   apt 202
Dallas,
Texas

Dear Hugh:

I enclose the documents that you were good enough to lend to me.

I will be on the west coast later today and then on a fast ten day
swing through the country speaking before groups of lawyers and
others about the case. I may be able to get to Dallas just for a
few hours to pick up Mrs. Oswald who will be coming to New York for
a speaking engagement on the 18th of February. Since I am anxious
to speak with you I will let you know in advance of my trip if I can
make it to Dallas.

I would like to employ you as an investigator for the case. This
work might be done during evenings and on week ends and need not
interfere with your other employment. I, of course, will not under
any circumstances, reveal that you are so employed. Since you would
be working for the purpose of assembling facts for me in a legal case
which I wish to present our communications and contacts would be
priviledged and I need not divulge them to anyone. I hope that you
can give some thought to this matter before we speak next so that we
can finalize our arrangements then.

My very best to your wife.

Sincerely,

Mark Lane

Encls
Special Delivery, Air Mail, Registered Mail

Letter from conspiracy theorist Mark Lane
returning materials I provided.
Opposite: British philosopher Bertrand
Russell, who became enamored with Mark
Lane's theories, requested definitive answers.

Mark Lane
Rush to
Judgment

A critique of the
Warren Commission's
inquiry into the
murders of
President John F. Kennedy,
Officer J. D. Tippit and
Lee Harvey Oswald.
Introduction by
Hugh Trevor-Roper

For more than two and a half years, Mark
Lane, well-known attorney has been investi-
gating the unexplained aspects of President John
F. Kennedy's assassination. Mr. Lane writes: "I

'who killed Kennedy?' Committee
the British

9 October, 1964.

Mr. Hugh Aynesworth,
The Dallas Morning News,
Communications Center,
Dallas 22,
Texas 75222,
U.S.A.

Dear Mr. Aynesworth,

I have had an opportunity now to consider further your letter to me and it has caused me to reflect on many of the points you raise. If you are able to help me by providing information of a specific kind, I should be most grateful.

1. Can you tell me the names and addresses of the five people who saw a man kill Officer Tippit? Your letter states that five people "actually saw a man kill the officer", and if you are able to help me by giving me their names and addresses, I should be very grateful. I emphasise that I do not enquire about people who saw a man flee from the scene, but people who actually saw a man kill the officer.

2. Can you tell me precisely what you heard Mrs. Markham say about the killer of the officer to the police when she described the killer? Did you point out to the police any discrepancy between her story to you and to them? Was there any discrepancy between her story to you and to them?

3. What was Mrs. Markham's description of the killer which was made to you? I have in mind the statement of Mrs. Markham that the killer was "short, stocky and bushy haired".

4. Please send me your story in the Dallas Morning News presenting Mrs. Markham's original description.

I assure you that I have not taken your letter lightly and

Yours sincerely,

Bertrand Russell

Bertrand Russell

DISTRICT ATTORNEY
PARISH OF ORLEANS
STATE OF LOUISIANA
2700 TULANE AVENUE
NEW ORLEANS 70119

JIM GARRISON
DISTRICT ATTORNEY

March 18, 1970

Mr. Hugh Aynesworth
Newsweek Magazine
1010 Milam Street
Houston, Texas

Dear Mr. Aynesworth:

In view of the meeting of the District Attorney's in Houston,
I am convinced that you, and others like you who are trying
to suppress the truth about the assasination from the public
through false reporting, will go to great lengths to discredit
my office, the investigation and me personally.

Therefore, in advance of these devious acts, I am reminding
you that there are laws to deal with you and others like you.
This would also apply to those District Attorney's who see
fit to assist you in telling lies about me.

It is further reasonable to assume that an utterly ridiculous
story about my conduct in the New Orleans Athletic Club will
be discussed at the local bars during this period. It is shameful how people who dislike me for doing so much good for my
country would resort to such malicious tactics.

Anything derogatory said about me is untrue.

Very truly yours,

Jim Garrison

lcs

Above: District Attorney Jim Garrison's letter to me.
Opposite: Reply to author from Congressman Gerald Ford,
who became the 38th president of the United States.

GERALD R. FORD
FIFTH DISTRICT, MICHIGAN

MICHIGAN OFFICE:
425 CHERRY STREET SE.
GRAND RAPIDS

Congress of the United States
Office of the Minority Leader
House of Representatives
Washington, D.C.

June 29, 1965

Mr. Hugh Aynesworth
The Dallas Morning News
Communications Center
Dallas, Texas 75222

Dear Mr. Aynesworth:

Your letter of June 16th has been received. I regret the
tardiness of my reply but the legislative schedule has pre-
cluded me from replying more promptly.

You have asked some very important questions but I do not
believe it appropriate for me as one member of the Warren
Commission to answer either your "first" or "second" inter-
rogatory.

Your "third" question of course involves a matter beyond the
jurisdiction of the Warren Commission inasmuch as the Commission completed its work and was officially discharged upon
the submission of the report to the President. I have no
knowledge of the allegation that the Secret Service now has
a "tag" on Marina's telephone.

I appreciate your kind comments concerning "Portrait of the
Assassin" and I look forward to reading your book.

When you are in Washington or I am in Dallas I will be glad
to chat with you.

Warmest personal regards.

Sincerely,

Gerald R. Ford, M.C.

GRF:l

that point. But less than a month later, Lane testified before the Warren Commission about his secret source: Carroll Jarnagin.

Lane told the commission that he considered his informant "a reliable and responsible" person who had been present at an assassination plot meeting at the Carousel Club attended by Ruby, Weissman, and Officer J.D. Tippit! The alleged session occurred a few days before the assassination.

The lawyer told the commission that he would try to convince his informant to testify. Of course that never happened. The commission pleaded with him and finally paid Lane's airfare from Europe to testify. Still he would not divulge his source.

Perhaps Lane knew of Jarnagin's attempt to sell his ever-changing story or had been told that he had miserably failed a polygraph given by the district attorney's office. For whatever reason, Lane resisted.

Chief Justice Warren didn't like it.

"We have been pursuing you...with letters and entreaties to give us that information so that we might verify what you have said—if it is a fact or disproving it if it is not a fact," Warren said.

The surprise to me was not that Lane would not back up his tale; he had made many, many assertions that were untrue to this point. I was more amazed at the commission's poor background investigation. Several people in Dallas were well aware of Jarnagin's tale, and that he later admitted making it all up.

Henry Wade and Chief Curry testified before the commission, at length. No one thought to ask them about Jarnagin, even though Wade had personally arranged for Jarnagin's polygraph and later told me "it went off the charts—far off the charts."

This is the sort of evidence Lane typically produced in support of his various conspiracy theories of the JFK case and, later, the assassination of Rev. Martin Luther King, Jr., which he has argued was the work of off-duty FBI agents under J. Edgar Hoover's personal control.

To dismiss Lane's imaginative scenarios as rubbish, as I did at first, is to completely miss the point.

Lane found that he could make almost any assertion about the assassination—even under oath—with impunity. He almost single-handedly invented the lucrative JFK conspiracy industry.

No wonder he and Marguerite got along so well.

His book, *Rush to Judgment*, was a mishmash of unproven and unlikely allegations and off-the-wall speculations. Fifteen publishing houses turned it down, because they were too far behind Lane on the manufactured-controversy learning curve.

Only Holt, Rinehart and Winston guessed the true potential for profits in *Rush*. They issued the book as a $5.95 hardback in 1966 and sold 30,000 copies in just two weeks. It was a publishing home run, and it showed the way for legions of other buffs to get rich and famous.

In addition to Ruby and Lane, the third leg of the conspiracy stool was Jim Garrison, the unhinged New Orleans district attorney who by virtue of his office lent reassuring, mainstream legitimacy to the wildest theories—governmental sanction for just about any crackpot claim.

As *Rush* rocketed to the top of the bestseller lists in the autumn of 1966, Garrison happened to meet Louisiana senator Russell Long on an airplane trip from Washington to New Orleans.

Long, who always believed there had been a conspiracy behind the 1935 assassination of his father, Huey Long, the famous "Kingfish," harbored doubts about the Kennedy case too, and urged Garrison to look into the matter.

In late 1966, the district attorney began checking out volumes of the much-maligned Warren Commission report from his local library.

Fast forward to mid-January 1967. Jack Ruby had just died of cancer. I was just starting my new job at *Newsweek* in Houston, when I received a call from Garrison. He invited me over to discuss the Kennedy assassination.

"I keep running into your name." he said. "I think you have information that could help me in an ongoing investigation— and I'm very sure I have information you would consider more than just interesting."

Jim Garrison (originally Earling Carothers Garrison) at the time enjoyed a favorable press. A few months earlier Jim Phelan had published an admiring profile of the hulking one-time FBI agent in *The Saturday Evening Post*.

Garrison told me he was investigating the Kennedy assassination, and thought I could "fill in some holes" for him. Sensing this might be the start of a great story, I agreed to what would become a long series of encounters with Garrison.

It was one of the strangest days of my life. Jim Garrison, tall and unkempt, a little crazy around the eyes, had a booming voice and animated manner—precisely the opposite of the sober character Kevin Costner portrayed in Oliver Stone's movie *JFK*. He dominated conversations with a sort of zig-zag discourse that was both nutty and disturbing for the fact that a high-level elected official could believe the nonsense Garrison professed to believe.

He greeted me at his home in January 1967, a month after he secretly started his crusade. We began by looking over some photos of Dealey Plaza together. "Now, Hugh," Garrison would say in that deep voice, pointing at a picture, "who are those people in this photo?"

I would identify the ones I recognized and share what I knew of their roles and actions on the day of the assassination. Each time, Garrison growled, "You don't understand, Hugh. Let me tell you how this really came down!" I argued with him a few times, then realized I was going to get thrown out on the street if I kept it up. If I wanted access to Garrison, I just needed to sit there and listen.

From time to time we were interrupted by telephone calls. Garrison would take them in the adjoining room, where I clearly heard him bellowing strange phrases like "tiger fifteen" or "lion three," then angrily hanging up.

"Jim," I finally asked. "I couldn't help

NEW ORLEANS STATES-ITEM	
Number Found in Notebooks	P.O. 1 9 1 0 6
Translate P. O. Exchange to Number; Translate P. O. Box Numbers to Letters	1 3 A C E D B
Translate Number 13 to WHitehall Exchange; Unscramble Numbers	WH A B C D E / 1 6 9 0 1
Substract Standard Masking Number	- 1 3 0 0
Ruby's Number	WH 1 - 5 6 0 1

SIMPLE GUIDE TO OSWALD'S REPORTED DECODING SYSTEM

Simple Enciphering System Used To Encode Oswald Notebook--DA

By HOKE MAY

The telephone number code which Dist. Atty. Jim Garrison son says Oswald first used once says he has discovered in Lee Harvey Oswald's notebook is of gym standard decoding sy

threat; to outsiders it is ridiculous drival)) Chances are he'll have unwound another difficult code used by Lee Harvey Oswald, Jack Ruby and Swen Saddad (the second assassin?). First you take all the money "earned" by Mark Lane in his relentless quest for the truth, divide it by the mentally unbalanced people who have written Garrison this year (including the one who wanted to find her husband; he immediately became the second assassn for a time), subtractthe number of strippers on Bourbon Street, divide by the number of people threatened or bribed to give false evidence in the case and you'll have a code. Simple as that. It will probably be the secret C.I. A. number in Dallas, XXXXX Oswald's street saddress in Minsk, Russia, orthe number of letters in the psuedonem used by Garrison when he investigated in Las Vegas last March.

Article on another "Garrison code" and my musings on the "actual" meaning of the code, typed at the time of the investigation but not used in a story.

233

but hear. What was all that about—the animals?"

"Ah, that's an old Navy code," he replied expansively, obviously very pleased with himself. "The Feebies will never break it."

At the time, I knew of no reason why the "Feebies"—the FBI—would be interested in Garrison's home telephone conversations, or wouldn't know how to break an old Navy code if they were. On the evidence of that afternoon, the New Orleans district attorney was a more likely object of interest at the state mental hospital.

"Hugh," he said at last, "you're lucky you're in town today. We've just verified this guy and believe me, it's dynamite."

Explaining no further for the moment, Garrison then called one of his assistant DAs, an ex-boxer named Andrew "Moo Moo" Sciambra, who arrived a short while later with Garrison's newly-discovered star witness in tow. He was a slight little guy from Houston, a piano player, who proceeded to relate how he knew that Ruby and Oswald were longtime gay lovers.

He went into great detail, naming names of clubs he said he had played at when Ruby and Oswald dropped by—clubs in Dallas, even in Houston. He even described one occasion where he said the owners of one club in Houston had booted the two out because they had been "groping each other all evening long."

Garrison beamed. "You might be the most important witness we've run across yet," he told his new witness. "And you are certain they were with each other on several occasions?" The little man shook his head in assent, obviously pleased that Garrison believed him.

"What do you think of that, Hugh?" Garrison asked when his witness was finished. "Isn't this it?"

I mumbled something and stared closely at the man, certain that I'd seen him somewhere before. Then it came to me: I knew who he was! And I remember where I had first seen him.

He had come forward within three days of the assassination, telling exactly the same story to the Dallas police. When they didn't believe him and he failed a quickly arranged polygraph, the angry DPD detectives told him he was going to jail.

The last I'd seen of the piano man, he was crying. And scrambling out the police station door.

"What are you going to do with this guy, Jim?" I asked, more bewildered than I had been with the kooky phone code. "When are you going to announce this?"

"Due time," he answered smugly. "We're putting our pieces together."

One of these "pieces" turned out to be Rodney Stalls, the wacky engineer who showed up on my doorstep shortly after the assassination. UPI reporter H.G. "Doc" Quigg told me that Stalls approached him with what sounded like the same paper bundle of "proof" in a hallway of the Criminal Courts building in New Orleans. "He said he had an appointment with Garrison later that day," Quigg said.

We both laughed.

Neither Stalls nor the Houston piano player lasted long in Jim's good graces. As his theories changed—as they did with each moon—his "main witnesses" changed also.

Another of Garrison's witnesses was a former mental patient from the West Coast, a rangy character who affected a red toga and sandals and called himself Julius Caesar. Mr. Caesar claimed to have been present at a hotel in Alexandria, La., where Oswald met with Clay Shaw, the pitiable New Orleans businessman whom Garrison would falsely prosecute for conspiracy to assassinate Kennedy, plus Jack Ruby, whom Caesar said arrived with a package of money for the other two.

For a brief time Julius Caesar was the district attorney's guest in New Orleans. When the inevitable holes developed in his story, Garrison put his witness out on the street. In my one conversation with him, conducted on the courthouse steps, Caesar made the even bolder claim to have directly participated in the assassination himself.

Then came Cedric Von Rollston, who said he met Oswald in a New York bowling alley and had come to adore "this cherubic, beautiful young man." He hastened to tell Garrison that his relationship with Oswald was not sexual, but swore that one of the Russian "diplomats" who was often with Oswald was homosexual and took Oswald away from him.

Cedric, who traveled to New Orleans with a wife who looked more like a man that he did, intrigued Garrison for a few days with tales of Russian intrigue, illicit sex, and secret assignments that he claimed Oswald was involved in. But then he, too, was banished from the Giant's "inner sanctum."

Von Rollston phoned me a few times, wanting to tell me what Garrison had done to him. One day he said, "You know, if my father was alive, he wouldn't have had the balls to treat me like this."

His father, he said, was Paul Robeson, the famous opera singer and very much a black man. Von Rollston was white.

There was also Annie Patterson, an American woman who was a prisoner in a Mexican jail. She told Garrison if he helped her get freed, she would tell him all she knew about a plot she overheard in Laredo, Texas—a plot to kill JFK and one that had LBJ offering a bag of money to an assassin.

She told Garrison she saw Johnson meet with Oswald in a dim cabaret bar and hand him the money. Later when I found her and called her—at the jail—she said that Clay Shaw had been there too. When I found that there had never been a bar in Laredo that came close to her description, and that Shaw and Johnson had been at public events the day she allegedly witnessed the meeting (pinpointed by her arrest the following day), I no longer accepted Annie Patterson's collect calls.

<hr />

The case that Jim Garrison finally took to court against Clay Shaw originated with a sometime journalist who called himself Jack Martin. He was in fact a convicted felon who had changed his name from Edward Stewart Suggs.

Suggs-Martin belonged to a splinter religious group that boasted a total membership of three in Louisiana: Suggs-Martin, a commercial pilot named David Ferrie, and one other individual. Ferrie was an ordained bishop of the church. For no better reason than he coveted Ferrie's position for himself, Suggs-Martin turned Ferrie in as a suspect in the Kennedy assassination.

Ferrie, who was utterly hairless and wore a bright red wig with matching eyebrows, might have made an interesting defendant had he not suddenly expired from a cerebral aneurysm in late February 1967. He had been fired by a major airline a few years earlier for sneaking a young boy in the cockpit on a flight. While there was little doubt he was a pedophile, there was never any serious connection between him and the assassination.

'Guerrilla Team' Killed Kennedy, Garrison Claims

NEW ORLEANS (AP)—District Attorney Jim Garrison said Tuesday that guerrilla fighters shooting in a crossfire from three points assassinated President John F. Kennedy.

His eight-month investigation also shows, Garrison said, that the Central Intelligence Agency is concealing the whereabouts of the assassins.

Garrison said the killers — anti-Castro adventurers — were helped by an unmarried fellow conspirator who caused a disturbance in Dealey Plaza.

"W ho appointed Ramsey Clark, who has done his best to torpedo the investigation of the case? Who controls the CIA? Who controls the FBI? Who controls the Archives where this evidence is locked up for so long that it is unlikely that there is anybody in this room who will be alive when it is released? This is really your property and the property of the people of this country. Who has the arrogance and the brass to prevent the people from seeing that evidence? Who indeed?

"The one man who has profited most from the assassination — your friendly President, Lyndon Johnson!" — *Jim Garrison*

Ferrie's death brought the DA back to a rotund, oddball New Orleans attorney named Dean Andrews, who claimed after the assassination that he had represented Lee Harvey Oswald in a couple of minor legal matters. Andrews further alleged he had been contacted to represent Oswald again, just a few hours before Jack Ruby fired his shot.

Andrews' story was that a man called Clay Bertrand had phoned him and asked him to get to Dallas that Saturday afternoon to become Oswald's lawyer. Only problem was, that afternoon Andrews had been in serious condition in Hotel Dieu Hospital, under heavy sedation in a room with no telephone. Even the alleged caller changed with Andrews' telling of the story. Sometimes it was Marguerite Oswald who called, other times he said it was Bertrand.

The fact Andrews claimed to have represented Oswald before intrigued Garrison.

Andrews fully recanted his entire story, but that did not seem to faze Jim Garrison one bit. Garrison got even, indicted Andrews for perjury. A jury convicted him.

As the late Bill Gurvich, once Garrison's chief investigator, would

The Vietnam conflict was escalating throughout the aftermath of the Kennedy assassination.

FERRIE NOT TIED TO JFK SLAYING

Secret Service, FBI Inquiries Recounted

By DON BACON
(The Times-Picayune National Service)
WASHINGTON — The Secret Service and the Federal Bureau of Investigation in separate inquiries in 1963 turned up no evidence linking David W. Ferrie with the assassination of President John F. Kennedy.

Because of these negative investigative reports, the Warren Commission gave only passing notice to Ferrie. "I'll be frank with you," commented a commission member Thursday, "I don't even remember anyone named Ferrie."

Officially, the FBI and individual members of the War-

SAW OSWALD WITH SHAW, SAYS WITNESS

MARKETS FINAL SPORTS

NEW ORLEANS STATES-ITEM
RECORDING TODAY'S STORY OF PROGRESS
RED FLASH

VOL. 92—NO. 211   TUESDAY, FEBRUARY 11, 1969   PRICE 10c

Didn't Hear Shaw, Oswald Agree To Kill Kennedy, Russo Admits

'Ferrie Only 1 of Trio to Declare Self'

237

recount to me, the DA called a staff meeting in December 1966 to announce that he was going to find "this homosexual Clay Bertrand fellow." Gurvich specifically recalled his amazement when Garrison said he knew the man's real name was Clay, "because they never change their first name. I learned that in intelligence."

So the group consulted its collective knowledge of homosexuals who lived in the French Quarter, and someone mentioned Clay Shaw. On the strength of that alone, Shaw was questioned a few days before my first meeting with Garrison.

Shaw denied ever meeting Oswald or knowing anything about the Kennedy assassination. After Ferrie died and Andrews refused to tell Garrison it had been Clay Shaw who had previously hired him, "The Jolly Green Giant," as Garrison was called, was momentarily stymied.

Then, as often happens when folks make up the rules of the game as they go, Garrison suddenly "found" another "witness"—exactly at the same time several of his more professional assistants were trying to talk him out of the investigation.

It came in the mail—a letter from a part-time insurance salesman/student in Baton Rouge. Perry Raymond Russo explained that he had known the strange bird, Ferrie (who by that time had been publicized as Garrison's No. 1 suspect), and would be glad to talk to Garrison.

Sciambra was quickly dispatched to Baton Rouge to talk to Russo. Russo laid out a fantastic tale of meetings and parties where Ferrie had entertained Cuban freedom fighters, a man who looked like Oswald, and others that whetted Garrison's appetite.

Russo was quickly ensconced in a New Orleans hotel, given several polygraph tests (which he failed) and fed sodium pentothal (so-called truth serum). Then during a bizarre hypnotic session, for the very first time he described a participant in one of Ferrie's "plot sessions" as Clay Shaw. The fact that the hypnotist first described Shaw and urged Russo to include him in his tale did not become apparent for months.

"It was so apparent that Perry was making it all up," said Gurvich. "We tried to talk Jim out of continuing this stuff when Ferrie died. We told him, 'You will look good. Everybody knows Ferrie was your No. 1 suspect. You can just say you solved it and walk away.' He wasn't buying that. He was already pumped up with the adoration of the conspiracy people and all. He was getting calls from all over the country, from Europe, even from Japan and Australia. He couldn't buy a meal in New Orleans. Or pay for a cab ride. He was exciting the whole town—and boy, was he caught up in it."

Gurvich had expressed his doubt to Garrison on several occasions—as the DA sent him to several places to follow people, dig in trash cans behind people's houses, even photograph a Las Vegas nightclub act that Garrison thought might have a tie-in with Jack Ruby and his friends. "Can't you tell me what evidence we've got?" Gurvich would ask. He got the usual reply: "We know who the assassins are and they can't get away. They know we will pursue them everywhere."

Garrison told one of his assistants about this time that he distrusted Gurvich. Assistant District Attorney Alvin Oser told me a few years later—after he had become a district judge—that Gurvich had argued "a bit too forcibly" about shutting down the investigation after Ferrie's death.

"While he didn't think Bill was completely on board, he didn't want to lose him," Oser said, "so he let him make the big announcement on March 1."

Even after the failed polygraphs, which troubled several others in the DA's office, Garrison seemed solidly committed to Russo as his star witness. Less than a week after Garrison first heard Russo's name, Garrison assigned Gurvich to make the startling announcement of Clay Shaw's arrest. Russo's embryonic allegations were all he had—and most of them were later denied by Russo himself.

Later there would be charges that Garrison's crew offered bribes and coerced friends of Ferrie, that they tried to induce a cat burglar to plant evidence in Shaw's home, that Garrison threatened perjury for those who didn't tell what he wanted to hear before the grand jury—even that Garrison had molested a 13-year-old at the local athletic club. In the latter case, I interviewed an uncle of the molested youth and a police officer and found the story believable. When *Newsweek* refused to use it (several media outlets had already been threatened with massive libel suits by Garrison) I gave it to nationally syndicated columnist Jack Anderson, who printed the story Feb. 23, 1970.

I later obtained transcripts of Garrison's grand jury testimony—some 35-40 witnesses—and he did, indeed, threaten several witnesses if they didn't conform to whatever theory he held at the time.

Gurvich became so alarmed with Garrison's actions that when he found that Bobby Kennedy was scheduled to appear in Louisiana in mid-1967, he flew at his own expense to New York to meet with JFK's

mes-Picayune

ational Gateway Since 1837

Y MORNING, MARCH 1, 1969 · Second-Class Postage Paid at New Orleans, La. · SINGLE COPY 10 CENTS

SHAW FOUND NOT GUILTY OF PLOTTING TO KILL JFK

Jury Takes Less Than One Hour Before Reaching Verdict

An all male jury took less than an hour early Saturday to find Clay L. Shaw not guilty of conspiring to murder President John F. Kennedy.

The jury returned at approximately 1:14 a.m. When the verdict was read a loud burst of applause and cheering broke out in the crowded Criminal District Courtroom.

Shaw shook hands with the jury members as they were paraded out of the courtroom and Judge Edward

Los Angeles Times

EQUAL RIGHTS — LIBERTY UNDER THE LAW — TRUE INDUSTRIAL FREEDOM

HARRISON GRAY OTIS, 1881-1917   HARRY CHANDLER, 1917-1944
NORMAN CHANDLER, 1944-1960

OTIS CHANDLER
Publisher

NICK B. WILLIAMS   ROBERT D. NELSON
Executive Vice President & Editor   *Executive Vice President & General Manager*
FRANK HAVEN   JAMES BELLOWS   JAMES BASSETT
Managing Editor   *Associate Editor*   *Director, Editorial Page*

8–Part II   TUESDAY MORNING, MARCH 4, 1969   2★

The Times' official position on issues is expressed only in the two columns below. Other material on this and the next page is the opinion of the individual writer or cartoonist and does not necessarily reflect that of The Times unless otherwise indicated.

Judicial Farce in New Orleans

ISSUE: A jury has exonerated Clay Shaw of the conspiracy charge against him. But what should be the fate of his prosecutor?

It took a New Orleans jury less than an hour to put an end to the two-year ordeal of Clay Shaw and give a proper legal burial to the absurd and malicious case which Dist. Atty. Jim Garrison had concocted against him. Justice was thus done, if only belatedly and after the processes of justice had been outrageously abused.

But the inexcusable persecution which went before, and which continues now with charges of "perjury" against Shaw, cannot simply be forgotten.

The American Bar Assn. has said it will recommend that the Louisiana Bar Assn. consider disciplinary action against Garrison. Surely this is the very least that could be asked or expected. That a jury unanimously found Shaw innocent of the charge against him in no way reduces Garrison's culpability in the matter.

From the beginning he had sought to show that the Warren Commission report on the assassination of President Kennedy was a deliberate attempt to cover up what the district attorney maintained was a conspiracy to commit murder. To attack the credibility of the report and support his own sensational allegation, Garrison had to prove a conspiracy. Shaw was his vehicle—and his victim—in that effort.

The conspiracy case collapsed under its own fantastic pretensions and, ultimately, admissions of perjury. As weird a collection of witnesses as ever decorated a courtroom was brought in by the prosecution, only to destroy themselves by their own testimony. It was not a question of Garrison failing to prove his case against Shaw. It was a question of Garrison having no case at all.

It has been said by some who know Garrison that he is sincere in his belief of a conspiracy. Perhaps this is true. But what is also apparent is that this belief became an obsession, one in which the means were taken to justify the end. The victimization of Clay Shaw was nothing more than a convenient tool by which Garrison hoped to make his point.

The really frightening thing about all this is that Shaw could have been any man.

His involvement in the case, after all, was based on the most tenuous of evidential supposition, along with a great deal of imagination by the prosecution. In this tragic Kafkaesque nightmare, fate and Jim Garrison might have singled out any citizen. Could one less rich and less well placed socially have survived—emotionally and financially—as Shaw did?

If there is one fact proven beyond all dispute in the Shaw case it is that Jim Garrison is unfit to hold public office. Decency, to say nothing of a sense of common humility, requires that he resign. Since that is probably expecting too much, the voters of Orleans Parish should expel him from office in the election later this year.

Garrison's continued occupancy of his position is an affront to American justice, one on a par with the indictment and prosecution of Clay Shaw.

brother to warn him not to come.

"He said if Bobby Kennedy set foot in his jurisdiction, he'd arrest his ass and see if that didn't force the government to 'come clean,'" Gurvich told me soon afterward.

Somebody tipped Garrison of Gurvich's trip and before Gurvich could return to New Orleans, Garrison quickly fired him, charged him with "removal of a moveable"—the investigation file, I guess—and locked him out of his office. From that point on, Gurvich proved invaluable to the Shaw defense. He was never taken to trial.

•••••••••••••••••••••••••••

While some might question the caliber of Garrison's witnesses, nobody in New Orleans in 1967 and 1968 doubted his skill in turning them up.

I tried to stay close enough to the DA to watch the evolving drama—and wrote nothing critical for several weeks, a bit tongue-in-cheek perhaps, but not seriously anti-Garrison.

Then shortly after the Shaw preliminary hearing, I learned that two of Garrison's closest associates had approached a friend of David Ferrie in a strange "investigative" effort. Essentially, they told Alvin

Beauboeuf, a service station attendant, that if he would "help them out," Garrison would pay him and get him a job with an airline.

Beauboeuf's lawyer recorded the conversation.

That prompted me to write a story for the May 15, 1967, *Newsweek* that caused consternation in New Orleans—a story that for the first time explained how the Garrison case was being manufactured, often at the expense of innocents and the poor or vulnerable (homosexuals, blacks, or Cuban exiles, for example).

My story, headed "The JFK Conspiracy," mentioned the promise of $3,000 and the job, if Beauboeuf—one of several young boys who hung around with Ferrie—would "fill in the facts."

Two New Orleans cops, assigned to Garrison, Lynn Loisel and Louis Ivon, had been interviewing Beauboeuf, assuming that because he knew Ferrie, he had some sort of evidence Garrison could use. At this point, Ferrie had been dead several days, but they hoped to tie in Clay Shaw in some manner.

About 10 p.m. on March 9 of that year, the two cops arrived at Beauboeuf's home in Arabi, La., and asked him to identify a snapshot they had of him and Ferrie together—something Beauboeuf had ID'd at least three times previously. They told him Garrison thought he knew all about the assassination. As before, the 21-year-old newlywed denied knowing anything about it.

"You know Al, my boss has got unlimited money and we know you know something so we're in a position to do something for you, perhaps pay you $5,000, $10,000, $15,000 and a guaranteed job with an airline," Loisel began. "Al, we want you to fill in the missing links in the story."

Beauboeuf said he got excited when Loisel mentioned a job with an airline. He said he would talk to his wife and call Loisel back the next day.

Instead he called his lawyer, Hugh Exnicious, who asked Beauboeuf to come to his office. Exnicious said he suspected an attempt to buy false information and with Beauboeuf's agreement, he telephoned Loisel and asked him to visit his office, west of downtown New Orleans in Jefferson Parish.

Loisel showed up later that afternoon and as they waited, Exnicious placed a tape recorder near his desk behind a curtain.

Loisel explained that Ivon could not make it, that things were very busy at the DA's office, then he got down to business.

recommends rehabilitation and the Secretary of the Army accepts its finding, the American Legion plans to have the body taken to Montana and reburied with all military honors in the national cemetery at the site of Custer's Last Stand. There, at long last, Maj. Marcus Reno would join forces with the fabled men of the old Seventh Cavalry.

NEW HAMPSHIRE:

Northern Hospitality

Sojourner George C. Wallace flew north once again last week, this time to New England, and after bouncing off his chartered Convair at Concord, N.H., the Presidential hopeful said he was still undecided whether to try his luck in the state's primary. For the moment, the assistant governor of Alabama insisted he had brought his campaign team to New Hampshire mainly "to put our ear to the ground." As it turned out, the little ex-governor got an earful.

Screaming, hissing, stomping and cursing, hecklers at Dartmouth College stirred up one of the nastiest protests that Wallace has yet encountered on his northern forays—more bitter by far than the demonstration he met a week earlier in Syracuse (NEWSWEEK, May 8), and more unruly, said Dartmouth observers, than any disorder on that usually staid campus in the last generation.

Virtual pandemonium broke out in Dartmouth College auditorium as soon as Wallace—the invited guest of The Daily Dartmouth editors—took his place behind the podium. Sarcastic banners waved wildly ("George, can you walk on water too?"), and students—led by members of the Afro-American Society—set up an incessant rumbling chant: "Wallace is a racist . . . Wallace is a racist." Wallace tried to speak during the lulls. But nearly everything he said drew gibes.

Hustled Off: The demonstration reached a near-riotous peak when roughly a score of sign-bearing protesters marched menacingly down the aisle toward the stage—heralded by ~~~~~~~~~ yelling ~~~~~~~~~~~~~~~~~~~~~~~~ ing to ~~~~~~~~~~~~~~~~~~~~~~~~ was i~~~~~~~~~~~~~~~~~~~~~~~ while V~~~~~~~~~~~~~~~~~~~~~~ by his o~~~~~~~~~~~~~~~~~~~~

Later ~~~~~~~~~~~~~~~~~~~~~ surroun~~~~~~~~~~~~~~~~~~~ dented ~~~~~~~~~~~~~~~~~~~~ inside, i~~~~~~~~~~~~~~~~~~~ clear a p~~~~~~~~~~~~~~~~~~ milling t~~~~~~~~~~~~~~~~~~

Dartm~~~~~~~~~~~~~~~~~~~ have be~~~~~~~~~~~~~~~~~ Thaddeu~~~~~~~~~~~~~~~~ apologies~~~~~~~~~~~~~~~~~ Dartmou~~~~~~~~~~~~~~~~ mark. "A~~~~~~~~~~~~~~~~~ said, "can get you killed."

District Attorney Garrison: Who were the real plotters in New Orleans?

THE JFK 'CONSPIRACY'

What lies behind New Orleans District Attorney Jim Garrison's increasingly notorious investigation of a "plot" to kill John F. Kennedy? To find out, NEWSWEEK sent a veteran reporter, who covered the assassination and its aftermath, to New Orleans for five weeks. His account follows.

by Hugh Aynesworth

Jim Garrison is right. There has been a conspiracy in New Orleans—but it is a plot of Garrison's own making. It is a scheme to concoct a fantastic "solution" to the death of John F. Kennedy, and to make it stick; in this cause, the district attorney and his staff have been indirect parties to the death of one man and have humiliated, harassed and financially gutted several others.

Indeed, Garrison's tactics have been even more questionable than his case. I ~~~~~~~~~~~~~~~~~~~~~apping ~~~~~~~~~~~~~~~~~~~~~~willing ~~~~~~~~~~~~~~~~~~~~an air-~~~~~~~~~~~~~~~~~~~~cts" of ~~~~~~~~~~~~~~~~~~~~ath of ~~~~~~~~~~~~~~~~~~~n the ~~~~~~~~~~~~~~~~~brib-~~~~~~~~~~~~~~~~~rded, ~~~~~~~~~~~~~~~~o the ~~~~~~~~~~~~~~~~~him ~~~~~~~~~~~~~~~~hours ~~~~~~~~~~~~~~~~vain ~~~~~~~~~~~~~~~ssas-~~~~~~~~~~~~~~been ~~~~~~~~~~~~~~~.A.'s ~~~~~~~~~~~~by Garrison himself. Others—Cuban exiles, convicts, drug addicts, homosexuals,

bums—have been hounded in more subtle ways. For most of Garrison's victims are extremely vulnerable men. Some are already paying for their vulnerability. Chief among them is Clay L. Shaw, the New Orleans businessman-socialite, who now faces trial on a charge of conspiring to kill the President.

How did it all begin?

Garrison first became earnestly interested in the Kennedy assassination when he and Louisiana Sen. Russell Long rode side by side on an airplane bound for New York. Long said he had never actually believed the Warren commission report, that he still had doubts. Garrison later told me that he immediately decided that if such an important man thought there was something odd about the case, it was time to start digging.

Cleanup: Garrison is known in New Orleans as a smart operator, a bit unorthodox, but nobody's fool. He made his name by cleaning up his old haunt—the French Quarter—and putting a temporary halt to B-girl practices and lewd dancing in its gaudy strip joints. Later, he amazed the whole city by accusing eight criminal judges of taking too many days off and of winking at Mafia activity. But although the judges sued him for libel, Garrison's right to criticize the judiciary was finally upheld by the U.S. Supreme Court. Thus, when he first announced his "conspiracy" case, most New Orleanians believed that "Big Jim must have something."

What Garrison had to start with was a colorfully pathetic "suspect" named David Ferrie. A onetime airline pilot, Ferrie had been questioned shortly after the

The 'Plot' to Kill JFK PAGE 36

The speculation, accusation and innuendo sparked by New Orleans District Attorney Jim Garrison to prove a "conspiracy" in the Kennedy assassination has included intimidation of witnesses and—according to evidence turned up by Newsweek's **Hugh Aynesworth** (left) —actual bribery by Garrison investigators. Aynesworth reported the assassination of the President, the murder of Lee Harvey Oswald and the Jack Ruby trial. Now, after five weeks in New Orleans, he examines the "plot" to kill John F. Kennedy.

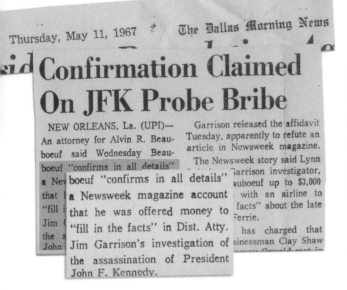

Thursday, May 11, 1967 — The Dallas Morning News

Confirmation Claimed On JFK Probe Bribe

NEW ORLEANS, La. (UPI)— An attorney for Alvin R. Beauboeuf said Wednesday Beauboeuf "confirms in all details" a Newsweek magazine account that he was offered money to "fill in the facts" in Dist. Atty. Jim Garrison's investigation of the assassination of President John F. Kennedy.

Garrison released the affidavit Tuesday, apparently to refute an article in Newsweek magazine.

The Newsweek story said Lynn ... Garrison investigator, ... auboeuf up to $3,000 with an airline to ... facts" about the late ...errie.

... has charged that ...sinessman Clay Shaw ...

"Now let me bring you up to what Al and I were talking about last night. I told him we had liberal expense money and I said the boss is in a position to put him in a job, you know, possibly of his choosing, of Al's choosing. And there would be...we would make a hero out of him instead of a villain, you understand. Everything would be to your satisfaction. There's no...I mean we can...we can change the story around, you know, enough to positively beyond the shadow of a doubt, you know...eliminate him, you know, into any type of conspiracy or what have you."

Exnicious said he just nodded as Loisel continued:

"The only thing we want is the truth, you know, no deviations on his part, you know. We want to present the truth. We want the facts and the facts of the assassination. That's what we want. And for this, the release, you know, the thing will be typed up in such a way that Al, you know, will be free and clear."

Exnicious: "Now in other words what you want him to do, he will come up and give you such evidence that you will be able to couch him in terms of being a hero?"

"That's correct," Loisel assured.

Exnicious: "And you'll also...you have an unlimited expense account, you said, and you're willing to help him along?"

"I would venture to say, well I'm, you know, fairly certain we could put $3,000 on him just like that, you know. I'm sure we would help him financially and I'm sure real quick we could get him a job," Loisel added.

They discussed the previous night's offer of an airline job.

"Al said he'd like a job with an airline and I feel like the job can be had," Loisel assured.

He mentioned an air freight company and said "with just one phone call he [Beauboeuf] could write his own ticket, you know."

Exnicious wanted to make sure Garrison was making the offers, and Loisel confirmed it twice. Then the lawyer asked how his client could "help" Garrison.

"Well, first off, Loisel began, "I feel…well, we feel that Al is as close to Dave as anybody could have been. All right, now we know this is a rough…I'm drawing you a rough sketch. We have a man who has come forth recently, told us he was sitting in a room with Ferrie, Shaw, two Cubans, and Oswald."

Loisel said the meeting was at Ferrie's house, and the discussion was how to kill JFK in a crossfire.

"I believe it was Clay Shaw and Ferrie or maybe it was Clay Shaw and Oswald, having a little heated argument. Clay Shaw wanted some of his methods used or thoughts, you know, used but anyhow, that's what we have in mind, along that line."

Loisel said he knew Beauboeuf was not present at that meeting, but added, "Well, Al is in…Al being close to Ferrie, has to know the whole thing from beginning to end. He has to know it."

Lawyer Exnicious asked the DA's investigator how Beauboeuf could avoid being charged if he had concealed such knowledge for years.

"You understand now that poor Dave is gone," said Loisel. "Al has voluntarily come forward and told of his knowledge. I mean there's 99,000 ways we could skin that cat, you know. I mean, it's something you know…that's his patriotic duty."

Beauboeuf denied knowing anything about the alleged meeting and Loisel departed. But that wasn't the end of the story.

The *Newsweek* story prompted denials and an investigation by the New Orleans Police Department and the Orleans Parish Grand Jury.

Garrison saw my story as just another nasty impediment to his "search for truth."

In a hurried call to me, he said, "no such tape exists and you know it. I hope *Newsweek* has good lawyers and you may have a surprise when you come back to town." Before I could comment, he hung up.

As I was interviewing and putting together the story, the DA's office got wind that I was on it. I assume that when Exnicious went to the Jefferson Parish DA and tried to get DA Frank Langridge to indict Loisel for public bribery, the word traveled fast. Anyway, on April 11, Loisel and Ivon returned to the Beauboeuf home about 11 p.m. and the exchange quickly got mean.

"You know Al, you play dirty politics, you get hurt," said Loisel, according to Beauboeuf. He said the cop added, "Al, I don't want to get into any sh__ and before I do, I'll put a hot load of lead up your ass."

On April 12, Beauboeuf was summoned to Garrison's office,

where he was pressured to sign a statement saying he didn't consider the taped conversation a bribe. He said he signed it because the DA's investigators promised to leave him alone and not distribute an embarrassing picture of him and Ferrie.

Within days of the *Newsweek* story, Garrison filed a complaint to the state bar ethics and grievance committee, complaining that lawyer Burton Klein, who had since become Beauboeuf's lawyer, was "leading a counterattack against an increasingly successful investigation by the district attorney's office." The bar association ignored the complaint.

The New Orleans Police Department, at its absolute most ineffective stance, "investigated" and found the "interview" had not been a bribe, just damn good investigating.

In the New Orleans *Times-Picayune* on June 15 that summer reporter Robert Ussery wrote "PAIR CLEARED IN BRIBE PROBE: Police Find No Violation in Beauboeuf Case." He quoted Deputy Police Superintendent Presly J. Trosclair Jr., who said Loisel and Ivon "have not violated any rules of the code of conduct of the New Orleans Police Department."

Asked if the two cops were, in fact, innocent, Trosclair reminded attending reporters that the officers had admitted offering money and a job with an airline to Beauboeuf. He said it was common practice for local, state, and federal officials to reward informants financially and added, "We do not interpret it as a violation."

Trosclair said he had listened to the tape recording.

Meanwhile, at the time and for the rest of his life, Garrison denied there was a tape.

In his book called *On the Trail of the Assassins*, Garrison wrote:

"Aynesworth, who seemed a gentle and fair enough man when he interviewed me for several hours in my home, never did get around to revealing whose life our office had shortened. As for the $3,000 bribe, by the time I came across Aynesworth's revelation, the witness our office had supposedly offered it to, Alvin Babeouf (sic.) had admitted to us that it never happened. Aynesworth, of course, never explained what he did with the 'evidence' allegedly in his possession. And the so-called bribery tape recording had not, in fact, ever existed."

Exactly two years after Shaw was arrested, a New Orleans jury—despite being buttressed by scores of stories by the New Orleans newspapers trumpeting Garrison's myriad theories and a populace that seemed to want desperately to believe in their flamboyant DA—found

Clay Shaw innocent. Not just innocent, but on a single ballot, unanimously, in less than an hour.

•••••••••••••••••••••••••••••••

The most bizarre witness in this parade of crazies was without a doubt Charles Spiesel, a New York accountant. I haven't seen his like in my 55-year journalism career.

And, but for an extremely lucky break, he might have come across as sane.

A few days prior to trial, I obtained a copy of Garrison's witness list. I seem to recall there were more than 15 names on it. All but two of them were either familiar local crazies or fantasizers I had encountered earlier in Texas. The remaining two were from out of state. One was a professor of some sort in California, and the second was Spiesel. Sal Panzeca, one of Shaw's lawyers, had acquired a similar, almost identical list.

I knew that to convict Shaw, Garrison must come up with not only a conspiracy meeting (he had Russo, but Russo was already flirting with the defense team, giving them information and weaseling out of much of his strong preliminary hearing testimony), but also something much stronger. While most of those on his witness list were throw-aways—opportunists whose stories had already been disproved—I suggested to chief defense lawyer F. Irvin Dymond that they needed to prepare for the unexpected.

Dymond, one of Louisiana's best, agreed, but after conferring with Edward Wegmann, Shaw's longtime friend and civil lawyer who handled the financing, he was told that Shaw was nearly broke. They already had spent a lot of money—veering this way and that preparing for Garrison's changing theater of the absurd.

(Garrison once described his investigation as "Like through the looking glass. Alice in Wonderland. White is black and black is white.")

Still I persisted and finally introduced the attorneys to a Dallas private investigator I knew to be excellent and willing to work for very little. In the end, they relented and sent the PI off to check out Mr. Spiesel.

A few days later the investigator arrived back from New York with his documentation after midnight, just hours before the defense was to cross examine Spiesel. They spent much of the night going over the material.

What the defense learned would ignite a bombshell under Mr. Spiesel, who on direct examination had seemed a very impressive witness for Garrison.

He had testified, strongly and distinctly, how he was present when Clay Shaw, Lee Harvey Oswald, David Ferrie and others had met in a French Quarter apartment and plotted how Kennedy would be shot in Dallas.

Martin Waldron, the *New York Times* reporter covering the trial, not a Garrison groupie, threw up his hands and left the courtroom.

"No way this kook is telling the truth, but that's the ballgame," he said.

Next morning, defense attorney Dymond asked Spiesel about a $16 million lawsuit he'd filed. The witness explained that he'd sued the New York police, a detective agency, and a psychiatrist for hypnotizing him and ultimately ruining his business and sex life.

"Why $16 million?" Dymond asked.

"One million dollars for every year of the conspiracy," Spiesel replied.

"And are you the same Charles Spiesel who fingerprints his daughter when she comes to visit?"

"I certainly am," said Spiesel.

"Why?"

"They always disguise themselves."

Slowly, deferentially, Dymond elicited a tale of a pitiful, demented human being. One had to feel sorry for the New York paranoiac. He said he had been hypnotized 50 or 60 times and while he knew detectives had followed him in New Orleans, he didn't think they had succeeded in hypnotizing him this time.

James Kirkwood, one of the originators of *A Chorus Line*, who was covering the trial for *Playboy*, turned to me and said, "At least he's not bleeding. He doesn't know anything is wrong. He just keeps smiling."

"I would have stopped a long time before I did," said Dymond sympathetically later, "but for us, for Clay Shaw, this was it. We had to show that jury just how deranged the whole Garrison case was."

The courtroom was alive, whispering, and giggling as Dymond continued. The DA's staff tried to act as though the disintegrating witness was of no concern to them, but in reality—and two jurors told me this later—that was the end of Garrison's case.

Judge Edward Haggerty agreed with Dymond's suggestion that

since the witness so convincingly described the apartment where the alleged conspiracy meeting had been held, perhaps he could show jurors where it was.

Next morning, jurors and the media tramped all over the French Quarter, as Spiesel tried to pinpoint that important meeting. Suffice it to say he hasn't found it yet.

Commenting on Spiesel's direct testimony (for the prosecution), which had been almost spellbinding in both content and delivery, James Kirkwood wrote in *American Grotesque*:

"If James Alcock could have pressed a button and sent Spiesel careening out of the witness chair and back to New York at that very moment, no further questions asked, he would have been a most damaging witness."

Garrison, for his part, described his shock at Spiesel's testimony in his book, *On the Trail of the Assassins*:

"I realized that the clandestine operation of the opposition was so cynical, so sophisticated, and, at the same time, so subtle, that destroying an old-fashioned state jury trial was very much like shooting fish in a barrel with a shotgun. The chief defense counsel uncannily seemed to know just what questions to ask Spiesel."

Obviously this, to Garrison, was just another rung in the ladder of conspiracy—against him and his version of "truth." It probably never occurred to him to check out his own star witness, even if the witness was relating a terribly important story, if true. Dymond later ventured, "He didn't want to know. Every witness he had was a flake, a liar, or an opportunist. No sense in confirming what they already suspected. They just didn't think we knew."

"For one very long moment, while I am sure my face revealed no concern, I was swept by a feeling of nausea," continued the DA in his 1988 book (which captured Oliver

I interviewed Judge Edward A. Haggerty, Jr. (left), who presided over the Clay Shaw trial.

243

Stone's interest and led to his movie *JFK*).

That sensitive moment, appealing as it might appear, was about as truthful as Spiesel's tale of the conspiracy meeting. Garrison was not even in the courtroom when Spiesel was cross-examined. I recall his leaving earlier, leaving James Alcock, his top assistant, to handle Spiesel. A local newspaper commented on his absence and asked him why he wasn't present. He was "preparing further for Perry Russo's testimony," he said, which followed Spiesel's.

Though he won acquittal, Clay Shaw ended up broke. He later filed suit against Garrison for malicious prosecution, but died of cancer before he had a chance to present his case in court.

If the net effect of Jim Garrison's lamentable foray into the Kennedy assassination case had been confined to the complete ruin of an innocent man, then Garrison's circus would have been just another bizarre historical footnote in a city accustomed to such wacky doings.

After the jury ruled and Garrison cronies like Mark Lane and comedian Mort Sahl had drifted out of New Orleans, reporters began exposing some of the more lurid adventures of the Shaw debacle. Garrison later was charged with taking bribes from the mob-regulated entertainment industry, but beat the rap by claiming to jurors, "the only reason I am on trial here is because I solved the Kennedy assassination."

Most of the conspiracy theorists retreated for several years. Some even charged that Garrison had been participating in a cover-up to assist the government.

But then Mark Lane stepped up to bat once again. By his own estimate, Lane personally visited at least 100 members of Congress in 1975 and 1976, lobbying them to form a House Subcommittee on Assassinations. The first of his converts were members of the Black Caucus, whom Lane sold on his scheme with the idea of reinvestigating not only the Kennedy killing, but also that of Rev. Martin Luther King, Jr.

The resulting JFK House subcommittee would eventually

Many Fear Oswald Had Help

By George Gallup
Director, American Institute of Public Opinion
12-6 PRINCETON, N. J.

Gallup Poll

The need for such a commission as President Johnson has now set up to investigate the assassination of John F. Kennedy is revealed by widespread fears that Lee Harvey Oswald did not act on his own.

A Gallup Poll just completed shows a majority of the American public holding the view that some group or element—or other individual—was also involved in the assassination. Another 19 per cent express uncertainty. Only about a third of those persons interviewed think the assassination was the act of a single person alone.

President Johnson recently named a top-level seven-man commission, headed by Chief Justice Earl Warren, to try to bring to light all the facts surrounding the tragic death of President Kennedy.

In interviews that began on Tuesday following Mr. Kennedy's death—and the subsequent murder of the accused assassin, Lee Harvey Oswald, by Jack Ruby, a ——— club owner—the ——— asked this questi ——— across the natio ———

"Do you think ——— who shot Kenn ——— his own, or was a ——— element also res ———

The results: ———
Assassin acted ———
on his own ———
Some group or e ———
also responsi ———
Uncertain ———

While the in ——— to the Presid ——— may have led some persons to believe that an extremist

group was behind the assassination, the survey results show that very few people at present single out any specific group.

Only about one person in a hundred thinks Russia, Cuba, or "the Communists" may have been involved in the assassination. Almost no one mentions the "extreme right."

Whatever the beliefs and fears of Americans at this time, one thing is clear—the whole nation is awaiting any answers that the newly-formed commission will be able to provide regarding the tragic events of recent days.

a major conspiracy to persons who think the assassin was hired by another person to carry out his ends.

The results:
Assassin acted
  on his own 29%
Some group or element
  also responsible 52
Uncertain 19

Since the first Gallup poll in December 1963, the American public has never been convinced that Oswald acted alone in the assassination of President Kennedy.

endorse the theory that along with the three bullets Lee Harvey Oswald fired, a fourth shot came from the so-called grassy knoll, thus officially embracing one of the hoariest conspiracy theories.

Although the acoustical analysis upon which the fourth-shot scenario is based was fatally flawed—and was refuted in subsequent investigations—the theory stuck. Additional studies of that phenomenon are underway as I write this, which may or may not indicate whether or not there was, indeed, a fourth shot.

So, the House subcommittee relit the flame and into its lucrative light flitted an inspired man—known for his imagination if not his accuracy—Oliver Stone.

Stone's saga *JFK* not only fattened his wallet by millions, but it catapulted what had been a dying breed of anti-government fanatics toward new prominence and importance. More important, it convinced a whole new generation that hardly anything officially stated about the assassination or its aftermath had been truthful.

There was no room under Stone's tent for anybody who questioned the questioning.

Harry Connick, the man who defeated Garrison for Orleans Parish district attorney in 1973 and who just retired last year, told me how Stone and his star Kevin Costner asked him to lunch as they prepared to film part of *JFK* in New Orleans.

"He asked me what I thought of Garrison and his investigation," said Connick. "I told him it was the biggest bunch of crap ever to be allowed in a courthouse. And you know what he replied? He said, 'Well we're going to make it anyway.'"

I have been asked why Stone never even asked me a question while filming *JFK*.

"That's not exactly true," I told a reporter from *Entertainment Tonight*. "Actually he sent a question through an intermediary. He asked me, 'Do you have a press badge from that day that we could borrow?'"

"No kidding," a wire service reporter asked me, "what did you think of the movie?"

"Well, he got a couple things right on the money," I replied with a serious countenance, "the date and the place."

Stone, commented columnist George Will, is "one of those activists who have been so busy trying to make history they have not learned any."

"In his three-hour lie," Will added, "Stone falsifies so much he may be an intellectual psychopath."

At this moment, the father of Scott McClellan, President Bush's press secretary, has a hot new book, claiming Lyndon B. Johnson was behind the JFK murder. A former New Orleans woman claims she was Oswald's lover and was told of the plan. A convict in an Illinois prison says no, no, it was he who shot JFK, at the behest of the Mafia. A half dozen others are just as bizarre, including one book that claims the government falsified the Zapruder film to cover up "the real story."

It never stops—and thanks to Jack Ruby, Mark Lane, and Jim Garrison (plus his late-arriving admirer Oliver Stone), it probably never will.

•••••••••••••••••••••••••••••••

A final word: I have been soundly criticized for my belief that Oswald acted alone and that Ruby was in no way connected with him. I'm considered a bad guy by some of those who have profiteered by manufacturing "facts" and "scenarios" in the never-ceasing cottage industry that has sprouted up via the assassination, because over the years I have tried to point out the legitimacy or lack thereof concerning many of the scores of conspiracy theories. When there seemed no way to counteract what I had seen, been a part of or written about, these detractors called me a government agent (CIA to some, FBI to others), a liar, or other choice denigrations.

I am often asked why I do not believe there was a conspiracy in the assassination. After all, most Americans do, according to several legitimate polls in recent years. I usually say that I do not know if there was or there wasn't.

All I know is, there is absolutely no evidence of it.

I'm still a reporter. Still looking for possible evidence 40 years later. If it exists.

President John F. Kennedy's
Assassination

A special report on the events of November 22, 1963

T HE DEATH OF PRESIDENT John F. Kennedy still casts a shadow across the traditional optimism of America after a quarter of a century.

Many Americans remember the moment they learned of the shooting of the president. For some, the fallen leader was transformed into a martyr and a myth. For others, the circumstances of his slaying turned into an obsession.

For nearly everyone, this tragic event, which seemed to tell us more about ourselves than we wanted to know, became a symbol of national loss that each of us defines in our own way.

This special report on that day and its aftermath was prepared under the direction of Hugh Aynesworth, now a reporter for The Washington Times, who was an eyewitness to more of the events surrounding this dark moment than anyone else.

I was there as the sound of shots split the air

By Hugh Aynesworth
THE WASHINGTON TIMES

DALLAS

T he first shot, maybe because it was so unexpected, sounded to me like the backfire of a Dallas police motorcycle.

Standing on Elm Street, at the corner of Houston Street, I glanced slightly to my left to identify the noise and almost immediately, a second and, shortly afterward, a third rang out.

In those scant seconds, what had begun as an exciting, almost festive afternoon suddenly churned toward fear, disbelief and chaos, finally to a rumbling stomach and a heavy heart.

I recall explicitly my reactions for a brief period, but some of the twists and turns for the next few minutes don't come back so easily 25 years later — not even with the help of my notes (written hastily on two envelopes) and the sharing of remembrances with others close by.

I'll never forget the large black woman holding a small child, wearing a dress almost the color of the pink suit worn by Jackie Kennedy.

The president's limousine drifted slowly by as it made the hard left at the Texas School Book Depository building, and a woman with her shouted, "Hey, look, she's got your dress on!" and the woman waved wildly, almost dropping the youngster as she bristled with pride.

Seconds later, possibly even before the third shot hit, people started moving. One tall man in a Western hat raised his hands, booming out, "Hey, hey," as if his assertiveness could stop whatever was happening.

People started yelling, grabbing at each other, even falling into each other. Cops, both uniformed and in plain clothes, darted this way and that. A man close to me holding a small boy gently laid him down and covered him with his body.

Out of the corner of my eye I saw the lady in the pink dress thrust her child toward her friend, clutch her stomach and retch on the sidewalk.

Several people pointed toward the depository building, at the disappearing motorcade, at the policeman driving his motorcycle up on the grass to our right.

"The president's been hit," one man cried out. "Oh my God, the president's been hit."

"I think Lyndon Johnson was hit too," added another.

Within five minutes I was interviewing as many people as I could stop. Some were crying, others surprisingly composed.

Later that day, I would learn and

see SEE, page E12

■ People started yelling, grabbing at each other, even falling into each other.

For 25 years, Dallas bore brunt of a nation's anger

By Hugh Aynesworth
THE WASHINGTON TIMES

DALLAS

T wenty-five years ago today this city was the site of one of America's worst tragedies. And though most of the wounds have healed, scars are still visible — mute evidence of what occurred on a bright autumn Friday afternoon in a simpler era.

You need no reminder: John F. Kennedy, a bright, young president from whom many expected much, was shot down like a dog while waving and thanking those who had come out to welcome him.

■ See related stories on P.5 and E9-E12.

Within hours, Lee Harvey Oswald, a poorly educated, secretive former Marine who had once renounced his U.S. citizenship to live in the Soviet Union, was captured in a suburban theater — a suspect in both the slaying of Mr. Kennedy and a subsequent fatal shooting of Dallas Patrolman J.D. Tippit.

At Dallas' Love Field, where just before noon Mr. Kennedy and his entourage had landed to routing cheers, Lyndon B. Johnson quickly was sworn in as chief executive on board the presidential airplane — before hurrying back to Washington to nullify the government.

Nobody knew for sure if the attack here was but one of others to come from some foreign power.

Aides to Mr. Kennedy, his widow, Jacqueline — still dressed in her bloodied pink suit — and those Washington press "regulars" who covered Mr. Kennedy flew back to Washington in a virtual state of shock. Mr. Kennedy's body was rushed to Bethesda Naval Hospital for autopsy.

Meanwhile, in Dallas another kind of shock was setting in.

The city had been castigated four weeks earlier because a handful of rabid, right-wing activists jeered at U.S. Ambassador to the United Nations Adlai E. Stevenson, spat on him and hit him in the head with placards after the diplomat delivered a speech.

So nasty had it been that some had warned Mr. Kennedy not to include Dallas in his two-day Texas swing — which was designed to mend a factional fight within the Texas Democratic Party.

An embarrassed Mayor Earle Cabell had challenged the city to rebuke

see DALLAS, page E11

Photo by Arthur Rickerby © 1988 Time Inc.
President and Mrs. John F. Kennedy arrive at Love Field, Dallas.

THE DALLAS TIMES HERALD
FINAL EDITION

Books for Everyone
On Your Gift List!
CHRISTMAS
BOOK SECTION
Coming Sunday

PRESIDENT DEAD

Connally Also Hit By Sniper

INDEX